Terror and War

Twenty Essays on Theory and Lived Experience

Kieran Jackel

Publisher: Inspiring Publishers,
P.O. Box 159, Calwell, ACT Australia 2905
Email: publishaspg@gmail.com
http://www.inspiringpublishers.com

A catalogue record for this book is available from the National Library of Australia

National Library of Australia The Prepublication Data Service

Author: Kieran Jackel
Title: Terror and War
Genre: Non-fiction
ISBN: 978-1-925346-35-0

Preface

During my military career I have seen first-hand the devastating impact of military conflict and terrorism. This occurred when deployed on expeditionary military operations centred on counter-terrorism actions against Al-Qaeda, the Taliban and most recently the Islamic State. I have been privileged to command Australian soldiers, been told what I'm doing wrong by those same soldiers, served with and developed host nation defence forces and combined with coalition militaries to counter the threat of terrorism.

During this incredibly immersive period, I witnessed the very best and very worst of humanity, however, I managed to identify similarities when it came to the effectiveness of the 'teams' involved. Why do individuals willingly join the military and knowingly offer their life as the ultimate sacrifice if needed? What compels an individual to transition from passionate bystander to active, and at times, suicide terrorist? How does the impact of the group and group identity spawn effectiveness? These questions have shaped my thinking throughout these essays and when I reviewed them as a collection of works thematic similarities occur in several areas.

I have for a number of years had a deep interest in motivational constructs, which is identifiable as the first thematic thread throughout the essays. Most recently my thinking on these concepts has centred on an individual's involvement in and commitment to conflict. These innate human drivers are seen as primordial factors that influence engagement in violence. The essays explore the concepts of human belongingness, esteem, and group identity all of which act as levers that stimulate action and can trigger violent outcomes. This is as equally relevant to the individual as it is to a democratic state or a stateless terrorist organisation. Understanding the inter-connectivity of these relationships provides powerful insight that can be leveraged to support disengagement from terrorism and at times should temper the desire to engage in state-based conflict.

How this is achieved presents as a second thematic thread, that being the impact of information superiority and messaging. In military lexicon this is covered under a multitude of terms, however, I refer to it simply as Information Operations. The power to leverage the message and maintain information superiority has equal utility to a terrorist organisation as it does a state entity pursuing national interests. The use of Information Operations can both stoke commitment to a cause and, if leveraged correctly, becomes a powerful lever to support disengagement. This includes the radicalised individual and terrorist but when employed correctly can deliver a coercive or neutralising effect to a military force. The outputs from a multitude of formal and informal Information Operations are clearly present and pervasive across the globe today.

The essays within Terror and War were, for the most part, completed during two Masters Degrees throughout 2017 to 2019. The first focused on strategy and defence and the second analysed the theoretical makeup of terrorism, including radicalisation and counter-terrorism. Compiling them as a collection to form a publication was never the intent, it has evolved based on trusted counsel and after witnessing hypothesised arguments come to fruition.

Essay one discusses the rise of right-wing terrorism and the frictions within society around rational moderate thinking as opposed to the polarisation currently corroding society. It hypothesises that the global counter-terrorism actions following 9/11 have in effect contributed to the fractured state of many societies as seen in 2021. This is a painful statement for someone who has committed a large part of their adult life to support what was seen as a just cause.

Essay four makes an assessment on the retrograde actions the Islamic State may enact to recuperate and regenerate following the successful counter campaigns waged from 2014-2019. I wrote this in 2019 when deployed to Baghdad and planning Security Sector Reform initiatives for the Iraqi Ministry of Defence and Iraqi Military. The signs of change were apparent then, and it is assessed they continue today aligned to the hypothesised future trends.

Essay fifteen, written in 2017, discusses the misalignment of Australia's strategic economic and military policies and the vulnerabilities therein. I hypothesised that economic coercion could be employed against Australia due to the interconnectivity of the DIME paradigm. The economic sanctions imposed against Australia in 2020 and 2021 has rendered this less hypothesis and more fact.

And finally, globally, we continue to struggle with the issue of radicalisation and how it leads to terrorism. I do not consider myself a strong writer; my language and the grades of essays vary. However, thoughts sitting silent in a computer are of no help. If, in some small way, the contents support any member of the profession of arms, those studying terrorism or those who develop or support the implementation of national policy, then it will have been worth the effort.

These thoughts are published for the limbless, those of foggy mind who crave clarity of thought, the insurgent of pure unshakable intent, the current and future widows and the belligerents of both natures who may seek an alternate line of thinking and, ideally, dialogue.

In the fight against terror, the best and only outcome is stalemate. In war, there are only spoils and sorrow.

Contents

Part 2 - War

Part 1 - Terror

Counter-Terrorism

A critical assessment on the war on terror that has been prosecuted since 9/11 *(Written late 2019)*

Introduction

Historical precedence can be used to demonstrate how acts of human violence may be so significant they become catalysts for societal change. An example of such an action which continues to affect global stability and cohesion were the terrorist attacks against the United States of America that occurred on the 11th of September 2001 (9/11). Far from being random and opportunistic acts, these terrorist events were calculated and deliberate seeking to deliver a tactical strike that would trigger enduring strategic outcomes. From an asymmetric warfare perspective, these actions can only really be viewed as ingenious and stunningly successful. As was soon to be appreciated, these terrorist actions represented the realisation of a shift in Salafi-Jihadist terrorist strategy toward a concept of *far enemy* targeting.[1] From a threat perspective, Al-Qaeda's leadership, notably Osama Bin Laden, viewed the United States collectively. The civilian populace, through their tacit support of government action, including military action within the Middle East, made the population as a whole complicit, and hence, targetable.[2]

The actions of 9/11 were designed to target America's hubristically self-perceived pillars of strength, being its dominance of global markets and positioning as the time's sole global military superpower. The strikes were intended to initiate a series of cascading effects which, today,

---

1 Fishman, *The Master Plan: ISIS, Al-Qaeda, and the Jihadi Strategy for Final Victory.* 12-13.

2 Bruce Hoffman, *Inside Terrorism* (New York: Columbia University Press, 2006). 69: Seumas Miller, "Terrorism and Collective Responsibility," in *Terrorism and Counter-Terrorism: Ethics and Liberal Democracy*, ed. Seumas Miller (Hokoken: John Wiley and Sons, Inc, 2008), 61-62.

continue to support Bin Laden's strategic intent. First, it imbued a sense of fear in the target population. Grandiosity aside, the United States was vulnerable. The realisation of this had a psychosomatic and humbling effect on the culture of the United States at large. In its essence, this is the primary output required from any terrorist action as the population is now a participant in the belligerents' strategy and becomes the critical influencer that spurs follow on action; notably government action.[3] For the population of the United States and western countries more broadly, this sense of fear appears to have no temporal boundary and remains a pervading presence.[4]

A second-order effect that Bin Laden's *far enemy* strategy sought was to elicit an expeditionary military response from the United States, resulting in an increase of foreign forces in Muslim countries.[5] This concept of 'Provocation' is a proven strategic objective of terrorist action.[6] For Bin Laden, the ensuing war on terror played directly into his 'clash of civilisations' narrative on which the *far enemy* strategy hinged.[7] The enduring effects of 9/11 are less tangible. However, almost two decades later, these effects continue to manifest themselves throughout society, including enduring global instability being driven in part by increasingly divisive thought throughout the world. The purpose of this paper, however, is not to analyse the effectiveness of Al-Qaeda's actions of 9/11, as it has become painfully clear the tactical actions achieved the strategic intent. The focus of this paper will be to assess the effectiveness of the war on terror that has been prosecuted since that day.

Context

To determine the effectiveness or otherwise, the 'war on terror' must first be articulated. Given 9/11 was an action initiated by a stateless

3 Gus Martin, *Essentials of Terrorism*, 3rd ed. (London: SAGE Publications Ltd, 2014). 8.
4 Anne Aly, "Countering Violent Extremism Social Harmony, Community Resilience and the Potential Counter-Narratives in the Australian Context," in *Counter-Radicalisation: Critical Perspectives*, ed. Baker-Beall (London: Routledge, 2014), 72.
5 A Merari, "Terrorism as a Strategy of Insurgency," in *The History of Terrorism: From Antiquity to Al Qaeda*, ed. G Chaliand and A Blin (Berkeley: University of California Press, 2007), 14.
6 A K Cronin, "Chapter One: The Strategies of Terrorism," *The Adelphi Papers* 47, no. 394 (2007): 12.
7 Hoffman, *Inside Terrorism*. 92-93

organisation that sought to generate fear and influence government action, it aligns to one contextual definition of a terrorist act being:

> 'A premeditated and unlawful act in which groups or agents of some principal engage in a threatened or actual use of force or violence against human or property targets. These groups or agents engage in this behaviour intending the purposeful intimidation of governments or people to affect policy or behaviour with an underlying political objective'.[8]

The 'war on terror' should more accurately be defined as a co-ordinated global counter-terrorism activity. The difficulty in determining effectiveness hinges on two fundamental issues. Firstly, what are the metrics used to define effectiveness and, secondly, what constitutes a counter-terrorism activity?

Driven in part by popular culture, many would view a counter-terrorist action as largely the purview of security forces when they become involved in a direct security response to a terrorist event under way.[9] This, however, is incorrect and only represents a single component within what should be a holistic and multi-layered counter-terrorism framework. To guide the discussion, an analogy will be used. Counter-terrorism actions can potentially be viewed as the therapeutic options available that address an unhealthy symptom within society, that symptom being the ability and desire to execute a terrorist act. Although an effective security response is critical, it only really *cures* the problem after the fact. A given terrorist event, however, could potentially be avoided if the intelligence apparatus of a given region had identified a planned terrorist activity allowing pre-emptive disruption actions to occur. Clearly then, some organisations and institutions play an *inoculation* role to alleviate the unhealthy symptoms. Better still, what if individuals were impervious to the concepts of violent extremism and radicalisation? Or societies were more cohesive and hence void of the constituent components required for radicalisation to occur, such as personal or group grievance?[10]

---

8 Martin, *Essentials of Terrorism*. 8.
9 Commonwealth of Australia, "Australia's Counter-Terrorism Strategy: Strengthening Our Resilience" (Canberra, 2015).
10 Clark McCauley and Sophia Moskalenko, *Friction: How Radicalization Happens to Them and US* (New York: Oxford University Press, 2011). 19-29.

Alternatively, what if the broader target audience of a terrorist attack possessed higher levels of resilience negating the intended psychological effects of an act? This concept of enhanced societal resilience is increasingly seen as a critical pillar in any counter-terrorism strategy.[11] If viewed through this therapeutic analogy, there are also a suite of *preventative* actions that contribute to the management of the symptoms surrounding terrorism.

The point being, to address the effectiveness of counter-terrorism, one must understand that at any given point in time an individual may sit at differing points along a transition spectrum as is depicted in Figure 1.[12] Then, dependant on their positioning along this spectrum, different levers can be applied to generate the desired counter or neutralising effect. Without understanding this, it is not plausible to define effectiveness.

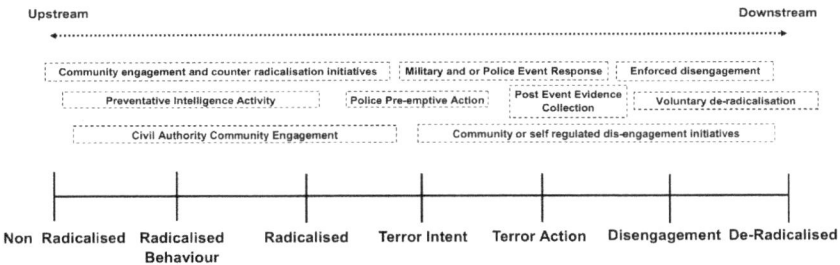

Upstream .... Downstream

| Community engagement and counter radicalisation initiatives | Military and or Police Event Response | Enforced disengagement |

| Preventative Intelligence Activity | Police Pre-emptive Action | Post Event Evidence Collection | Voluntary de-radicalisation |

| Civil Authority Community Engagement | Community or self regulated dis-engagement initiatives |

Non Radicalised   Radicalised   Radicalised   Terror Intent   Terror Action   Disengagement   De-Radicalised
                   Behaviour

Figure 1
Individual Transition Spectrum and Counter Levers

Therefore, defining the effectiveness of counter-terrorism remains problematic as the metrics of success are not easily quantifiable. To bind this discussion, however, two metrics of success have been identified. Firstly, since the commencement of the war on terror following 9/11 are people less likely to engage in terrorist actions? And secondly, is society more cohesive?

This argument hypothesises that not only have western governments and their associated security apparatus been ineffective but equally so,

---

11 Aly, "Countering Violent Extremism Social Harmony, Community Resilience and the Potential Counter-Narratives in the Australian Context." 76.

12 Figure 1: Individual Transition Spectrum and Counter Levers developed by the author.

western societies intelligentsia and academic communities that should drive theory to inform action, has been similarly poor. A sobering reality when the scab is lifted and damage inspected. As the world approaches 2020 society seems more divisive with regards to almost all issues open for debate, including religious and political issues. Disturbingly, the appetite to engage in terrorism is not abating, and as will be shown, has increased. The symptoms of terrorism are persistent throughout society. This ongoing presence of terrorism is not only Salafi-Jihadist aligned terrorism, but also increasingly right-wing terrorism which is enjoying a popular resurgence of sorts. As the 2019 New Zealand terrorist events demonstrate, the concepts of right-wing terrorism have well and truly manifested in action which places additional strain on the cohesiveness of societies.[13]

It will be argued, that western counter-terrorism responses over almost two decades have not only failed to impede the rise of Salafi-Jihadist terrorism, but the response has also failed to anticipate the potentiality for a rise in terrorism that may be right-aligned. To date, the global counter-terrorism strategy has been singular in focus, whereas, in contemporary society, counter-terrorism needs have become increasingly complex and multipolar. It has fast morphed into a wicked problem requiring a diverse response that considers an increasing number of stakeholders and objectives.

Green Machine

Following 9/11, western governments developed a variety of counter-terrorism strategies that sought to address the reality that Salafi-Jihadist aligned terrorism can achieve domestic reach. The United Kingdom had the CONTEST strategy which operated along four lines of operation being prevent, pursue, protect and prepare.[14] This strategy recognised the overlap between domestic security forces, the military, community and also intelligence services. Australia has had a variety of counter-terrorism strategies since 9/11 including the 2010 Counter-Terrorism White Paper, which like the CONTEST strategy, centred on four key

---

13 Lizzie Dearden, "Islamophobic Incidents Rocket by 600% in UK during Week after New Zealand Terror Attack," *Independent*, 2019.

14 Edgar Tembo, *US-UK Counter-Terrorism after 9/11: A Qualitative Approach* (New York: Routledge, 2014). 38-42

elements being Analysis, Protection, Response and Resilience.[15] Within this strategy, it was recognised that the Australian Defence Force (ADF) played a role both in a domestic context associated with *Response* and also internationally through a *Protection* role by contributing to 'international counter-terrorism efforts for the foreseeable future'.[16] Ironically, western militaries also saw the logic in targeting a far enemy.

The most recent version of Australia's Counter-Terrorism Strategy continues to see the Australian government willingly commit the ADF to international efforts to 'Shape the Global Environment'.[17] These contributions mostly present as efforts to destroy or degrade terrorist capabilities on foreign soil, or to facilitate an increase in foreign military skills that would enable indigenous forces to manage terrorist events independently.[18] These are broadly known as building partner capacity operations.[19] Almost immediately after the attacks of 9/11 the widely held belief among western governments was that to defend against domestic terrorist threats, a countries military needed to be employed in an expeditionary manner to degrade and defeat terrorist threats in the country of origin.[20] This shift to a pre-emptive posture which sought to degrade a threat before it could fully materialise remains central in western military counter-terrorism thinking.[21]

Armed with this contemporary thinking, which represented a shift in decades-old thinking on the United States behalf on how to defend itself, an increasingly willing coalition began executing a global war on terror that sought to defend civilisation itself.[22] First came the 2001 push into Afghanistan to degrade both the Taliban and Al-Qaeda to reduce the threat of mega-terrorist operations.[23] Then came the 2003 thrust into Iraq due to the ill-fated Weapons of Mass Destruction narrative

---

15 Commonwealth of Australia, "Counter-Terrorism White Paper: Securing Australia - Protecting Our Community" (Canberra, 2010). Iii.
16 Australia, "Counter-Terrorism White Paper: Securing Australia - Protecting Our Community." 47.
17 Australia, "Australia's Counter-Terrorism Strategy: Strengthening Our Resilience." vi-vii.
18 Commonwealth of Australia, "Annual Report 2017-2018" (Canberra, 2018). 4.
19 Australia, "Australia's Counter-Terrorism Strategy: Strengthening Our Resilience." vi-vii.
20 Thomas E Ricks, *Fiasco, The American Military Adventure in Iraq*, 2006. 30.
21 Ricks, *Fiasco*. 38-39.
22 Richard Falk, *The Great Terror War* (Gloucestershire: Arris Books, 2003). 4.
23 Falk, *The Great Terror War*. 12-18

and tenuous links with Al-Qaeda.[24] What needs to be appreciated at this time is that not only had the United States and many nations engaged in military operations that shifted from traditional concepts of state defence, they were executing these with expeditionary forces, in multiple areas of operations and with ambiguous objectives. To compound these issues the operating environment was complex both with regards to the physical environment including deserts, three-dimensional urban areas and mountainous regions, but perhaps more so the human environment which consisted of a highly complex web of competing politico and religious factions. These social factors, of course, varied depending on the area of operations with the differences between Iraq and Afghanistan poorly understood. It is little wonder that almost two decades later, the results are dubious at best.

The early counter-terrorism intervention into Afghanistan and Iraq could rightly be termed a military misadventure. The ineffectiveness of these early actions could be likened to conducting brain surgery with a pickaxe. For those that may repulse at this metaphor, the task at hand and the forces available to execute the operational strategy need to be considered. Conventional land forces are structured to win the land battle through the application of lethal effects.[25] The entire culture, organisational make-up, training continuum and equipment of such a force is designed to deliver lethal effects against, in theory, a state adversary. They are not, as a result of deliberate and considered strategic reasoning, well trained, practised and structured to enact constabulary like roles, below the threshold of conventional war.[26] It is a consideration, but one that is poorly practised and subsequently poorly executed when required. However, these were the very roles that conventional military forces were exposed to both within Afghanistan, then disturbingly within Iraq, where military planners had failed to consider post-victory requirements.[27] There was no plan

---

24 Peter W. Galbraith, *The End of Iraq: How American Incompetence Created a War Without End* (London: Simon and Schuster, 2006). 74-80.

25 Commonwealth of Australia, *Land Warfare Doctrine: Employment of Infantry* (Canberra: Australian Government Publishing Services, 2008). 1-2.

26 Australian Army, *Land Warfare Doctrine 1: The Fundamentals of Land Power*, Unclass (Canberra: Commonwealth of Australia, 2014), https://www.army.gov.au/sites/g/files/net1846/f/lwd_1_the_fundamentals_of_land_power_full.pdf. 23.

27 Galbraith, *The End of Iraq: How American Incompetence Created a War Without End*. 90-91.

for 'catastrophic success' within Iraq, no Phase IV considerations, which in western military parlance are known as *Stability Operations*. These are the lesser, unwanted, yet arguably more complex cousin of Phase III actions, *Dominate*. Any military planner would shudder at the thought of Phase IV planning lacking in an expeditionary military operation.[28]

A toss of the coin

The attempts to counter terrorism at the point of origin became murky fast. Within Iraq, conventional military forces found themselves engaged in not only constabulary like roles, but also acting as pseudo immigration and customs officers.[29] This is not, rightly, the remit of a US Infantry Division, the United Kingdom's Commandos or the Australian Infantry who are trained to win the fight to protect national interests.[30] Across the road in Afghanistan, metaphorically speaking, a war amongst the people which predicated a need to 'win the hearts and minds and acquiescence of the population' had become the cornerstone of military operations permeating all levels of military thinking.[31] Somehow, the western offshore experiment to counter a global terrorist threat which sought to target the far enemy was shifting. Worse still, counter-terrorism activities seemed to be drifting into the realm of nation-building because, during Phase VI, military forces must *Enable the Civil Authority*.[32] To be blunt, a warrior culture is poorly aligned to the inherent requirements of the operational phases post-combat.

There are two predictable consequences of this drift. First, newly established governments are perceived as puppet regimes and hence lack the support needed from the populace to stabilise a country. And secondly, foreign military forces are seen less as potential liberators and more so as occupying forces.[33] This has a dramatic effect on the host

---

28 Ricks, *Fiasco*. 150-152; Gustav A. Otto, "The End of Operational Phases At Last," *Interagency Journal* 8, no. 3 (2017): 79.
29 Ricks, *Fiasco*. 151.
30 Army, *Land Warfare Doctrine 1: The Fundamentals of Land Power*. 23
31 David Kilcullen, *Counter Insurgency* (Carlton North: Scribe Publications, 2010). 29; Rupert Smith, *The Utility of Force: The Art of War in the Modern World* (IBook: Penguin, 2008). 307-
32 Otto, "The End of Operational Phases At Last." 79.
33 Galbraith, *The End of Iraq: How American Incompetence Created a War Without End*.120-123.

population's perspective, altering the dynamics of the human terrain. Based on this shift, individuals who previously may have had no affiliation or desire to support Al-Qaeda or the Taliban, are now willing to engage in activities to resist occupying forces or degrade interim or newly established government security forces. Consequently, both parties become targetable and the preconditions required to create an insurgency have now been met.

Insurgencies, terrorism and insurrections are poorly understood with the terms often being incorrectly interchanged. To be precise, an insurgency is:

> 'an organised protracted politico-military struggle designed to weaken the control and legitimacy of an established government, occupying power, or other political authority while increasing insurgent control'.[34]

Insurgents will employ the concepts of asymmetric warfare, which include acts of terrorism.[35] In this respect, *terrorism* is a tactic employed to support the objectives of evolving domestic insurgencies. Consequently, many of the terror attacks against occupying forces within both Iraq and Afghanistan were a symptom of independent domestic insurgencies, not components of a co-ordinated global terrorist campaign. Having been drawn into two separate (and to this day enduring) insurgencies under the pretext of a global counter-terrorism effort, western militaries scrambled to implement actions to negate the risk to forces and generate a positive effect. In doing this, however, catastrophic failures were made which continue to hamper the effectiveness of the war on terror.

Within Iraq, a litany of mistakes were made including the dissolution of the Iraqi Army, the National Police Force, the Ministry of Interior and the implementation of an institutionalised de-Baathification process.[36] These actions are more accurately defined as grand strategic failures based on an inadequate appreciation of the human terrain. In short, the United States Military and her willing deputies had effectively removed all mechanisms of governance, including the

---

34 United States Army, *Counterinsurgency* (Government, 2006). 1-2
35 Kilcullen, *Counter-Insurgency*. 187.
36 Ricks, *Fiasco*. 158-166.

multiple layers of security required for even a peacetime Iraq. They broke the country.

In Afghanistan, the hunt for Bin Laden continued. To defeat the insurgency within Afghanistan, the thinking shifted towards a line of operation that sought to degrade terrorist funding lines. There is logic in this thinking with clear linkages between organised crime and the flow of associated funding to terrorism.[37] The crime-terror continuum in Afghanistan was linked to a narcotic nexus due to the production of opium. Operations, therefore, manifested in two actions. First was a questionable eradication campaign that, in theory, would compensate the producers of opium poppies. The reality was compensation was limited, leaving farmers at risk due to outstanding debts.[38] The other line of action focused on targeting the leadership that controlled the flow of narcotics funding.[39] Perhaps not as profound as within Iraq, but western military intervention within Afghanistan still had a direct impact of the governance and flow of money within the regional provinces. This, in turn, acted as an incentivising factor that saw a percentage of poppy farmers, now viewed as criminals, align with the Taliban.[40]

CURSIT

The western attempts to counter-terrorism at the source of risk, which was on foreign soil, have failed. The strategists and advisors of the time got it wrong, and hence military counter-terrorism actions were doomed. Kilcullen, a leading theorist during early interventions and now armed with the knowledge of hindsight, admits as much:

> It was the experience of being out in Afghanistan, where I've worked on and off since 2005, and realising that much of the violence there is created by economic, tribal and contracting-

---

37 Tamara Makarenko, "The Crime-Terror Continuum: Tracing the Interplay between Transnational Organised Crime and Terrorism," *Global Crime* 6, no. 1 (2004): 129–45.

38 Phillip A Berry, "From London to Lashkar Gah: British Counter Narcotics Policies in Afghanistan (2001-2003)," *The International History Review* 40, no. 4 (2018): 713–31.

39 Christopher J Coyne, Abigail R Blanco, and Scott Burns, "The War on Drugs in Afghanistan: Another Failed Experiment with Interdiction," *The Independent Review* 21, no. 1 (2016): 95–119.

40 Coyne, Blanco, and Burns, "The War on Drugs in Afghanistan: Another Failed Experiment with Interdiction." 107.

driven patterns of conflict, and very little of it is directly connected to Islamist extremism, the Taliban, Al-Qaeda, and so on.[41]

Remembering that these initial interventions into Afghanistan and Iraq focused on two primary terrorist organisations, being the Taliban and Al-Qaeda, the current situation relating to the defeat of terrorism in these countries is confronting. First to Al-Qaeda. Once merely a unitary organisation, it has now morphed into a global ideology that has spawned any number of internationally aligned franchises.[42] Ayman al Zawahiri, the once deputy to Osama Bin Laden and current leader since 2011, remains at large and on the 18th anniversary of the 9/11 attacks continues to push the terrorist organisation's ideology, including the operational objective of targeting the *far enemy*.[43]

Al-Qaeda remains a legitimate and global terrorist threat. However, based mainly on the instability generated within Iraq, the conditions were established that allowed challengers to Al-Qaeda to emerge.[44] The Islamic State, or ISIS, represents a post Al-Qaeda brand of Salafi-Jihadist terrorist organisation that not only seeks to target the west, but also leverages deep divides between Sunni and Shia Muslims.[45] Perhaps worse still, and thanks largely to the demonstrable success of Al-Qaeda's previous communication strategies, ISIS has managed to export its ideology to a global market.[46] This generated large recruitment pools both internally to the Middle East but also to sizeable external population bases. Consequently, this extreme version of Salafi-Jihadist terrorism (so extreme Al-Qaeda disavowed ISIS from their brand) has managed to establish satellite branches throughout South-East Asia,

---

41 Thomas E Ricks, "Kilcullen Speaks: On COIN Going out of Style, His Recent Book, Syria and More," *Foreign Policy*, 2014, https://foreignpolicy.com/2014/02/12/kilcullen-speaks-on-coin-going-out-of-style-his-recent-book-syria-and-more/.

42 Bruce Hoffman, "The Changing Face of Al Qaeda and the Global War on Terrorism," in *Terrorism Studies: A Reader*, ed. John Horgan and Kurt Braddock (New York: Routledge, 2012), 393-394.

43 CBS, "On 9/11, Al-Qaeda Leader Calls for Attacks on U.S. and Slams Jihad 'backtrackers,'" *CBS News*, 2019, https://www.cbsnews.com/news/september-11-attacks-anniversary-al-qaeda-leader-ayman-al-zawahri-calls-for-attacks-on-us-today-2019-09-11/.

44 Fawaz A Gerges, *ISIS: A History* (Princeton: Princeton University Press, 2016). 10-12.

45 Gerges, *ISIS: A History*. 24.

46 Abdel Bari Atwan, "Masters of the Digital Universe," in *Islamic State: The Digital Caliphate* (Oakland: Saqi Books, 2015), 15–32.

Africa and indeed Afghanistan.[47] One only needs to look at Marawi in the Philippines, which has been referred to as 'the Mosul of South-East Asia' to appreciate the security implications of this self-franchising phenomenon that ISIS has managed to cultivate.[48]

The effectiveness of improved governance within Afghanistan is questionable, it remains a fractured society with only Syria ranking lower on the global peace index in 2017.[49] The military, despite western capacity-building efforts, is dubious at best being referred to as 'unsustainable' by the Special Inspector General for Afghanistan Reconstruction in 2017.[50] Although negotiations may have stalled, one of the immediate targets following 9/11, the Taliban, is actively involved in peace negotiations.[51] They are, perverse as it may seem, now recognised as a viable source of government, assuming, of course, they actively suppress terrorist groups within Afghanistan.[52] Perhaps more worrisome is that ISIS, through its ISIS-Khorasan affiliate, is active within Afghanistan, adding yet another layer of complexity to societal cohesion.[53] Absurdly, current attempts to defeat terrorism within Afghanistan mirror failed attempts of earlier interventions, including oddly, counter-narcotic operations.[54]

The result, unfortunately, of the western intervention to counter the threat of global terrorism has had the unintended consequences of fracturing the governance of at least two countries. As a result, a more insidious and globally diverse terrorist organisation emerged.

---

47 "Pro-ISIS Groups in Mindanao and Their Links to Indonesia and Malaysia," 2016. 1; Claire Parker, "The Islamic State Is far from Defeated. Here's What You Need to Know about Its Affiliate in Afghanistan," *The Washington Post*, August 19, 2019. ; Aymenn Jawad Al-Tamimi, "The Dawn of the Islamic State of Iraq and Ash-Sham," *Current Trends in Islamist Ideology* 16 (2014): 5–15.

48 Greg Fealy, "Philippines," in *Counterterrorism Yearbook 2018*, ed. Isaac Kfir, Sofia Patel, and Micha Batt (Canberra: Australian Strategic Policy Institute, 2018), 31–36.

49 Leah Farrall, "Afghanistan," in *Counterterrorism Yearbook 2018*, ed. Isaac Kfir, Sofia Patel, and Micha Batt (Barton: Australian Strategic Policy Institute, 2018), 51–58.

50 Farrall, "Afghanistan." 52.

51 Johnny Walsh, "A Deal With the Taliban Is Only the First Step Toward Peace," *Foreign Affairs*, 2019, ttps://www.foreignaffairs.com/articles/afghanistan/2019-09-05/deal-taliban-only-first-step-toward-peace.

52 Walsh, "A Deal With the Taliban Is Only the First Step Toward Peace."

53 Farrall, "Afghanistan." 52-53.

54 W Hennigan, "The U.S. Sent Its Most Advanced Fighter Jets to Blow Up Cheap Opium Labs. Now It's Canceling the Program," *Time*, 2019, https://time.com/5534783/iron-tempest-afghanistan-opium/.

Perhaps organisation is not the entirely correct term. The reality is the pervasiveness of the underpinning ideology of ISIS-inspired Salafi-Jihadist terrorism is the real risk; this is what has taken hold within disenfranchised communities globally.[55] ISIS has a global reach. Their ideology enables freedom of action void of the constraints that may have existed under traditional terrorist hierarchies or command structures.[56] To address the two-key metrics of success hypothesised in this argument, it would be fair, on qualitative reasoning, to suggest that since 9/11 not only are people more likely to engage in terrorist actions but society at large is less cohesive and increasingly fractured. Therefore the war on terror enacted since 9/11 remains a vain endeavour, at least with regard to expeditionary military intervention.

The Western Snake

As mentioned previously, Bin Laden's strategic objectives from 9/11 were intended to elicit a series of responses. The decision for western militaries to deploy expeditionary forces to the Middle East was a predictable second-order response through the concept of provocation.[57] Under this concept of provocation, the counteraction from government forces and any associated collateral damaged can be leveraged by terrorist organisations to generate an asymmetric advantage via a supporting Information Operation campaign.[58] The intended outcome of any Information Operation is for a given commander to exploit the initiative through the use of a series of information related capabilities.[59] Operational imagery is an example of an information related capability that, when leveraged effectively, can have a direct impact on foreign audiences.[60] The intent is to shift perspective, elicit an emotional

55 Gerges, *ISIS: A History*. 23
56 George Michael, "Leaderless Resistance: The New Face of Terrorism," *Defence Studies* 12, no. 2 (2012): 263.
57 Martha Crenshaw, "The Causes of Terrorism," in *Terrorism Studies: A Reader*, ed. John Horgan and Kurt Braddock (New York: Taylor and Francis, 1981), 105.
58 No Author, "FM 3-13 Information Operations: Doctrine, Tactics, Techniques, and Procedures" (Fort Leavenworth: Department of the Army (US), 2003). 6-7
59 Author, "FM 3-13 Information Operations: Doctrine, Tactics, Techniques, and Procedures." 11
60 No Author, "Operation Series: Information Activities," *Australian Defence Doctrine Publication 3.13*, 2013, http://www.defence.gov.au/FOI/Docs/Disclosures/330_1314_Document.pdf. 1-11.

response, impact objective reasoning and ideally, influence behaviour in favour of the originator's objectives.[61]

The Al-Qaeda leadership did not need to wait long as western militaries would soon deliver a series of strategic blunders that would support their informational objectives. The actions within Abu Ghraib prison in 2003 are well documented and clearly, the operational imagery surrounding the 'sadistic, blatant and wanton criminal abuses' of the period were widely promulgated.[62] Not only were the actions repulsive by any sense of human decency, but the methods of dehumanisation enacted by members of the western military against those of the Muslim faith demonstrated a profound lack of cultural regard. When processed by the viewer, or more specifically, the intended recipient within the communication process, the acts can only be decoded as repulsive and abhorrent.[63] It is riling, and an affront to religious decency. This, coupled with images of detainees in orange jumpsuits at Guantanamo Bay and the associated collateral damage within Iraq, gifted the Al-Qaeda leadership the narrative they sought. The outcome of provocation had been achieved; however, it is the third-order effects associated with this that continue to render the war on terror since 9/11 ineffective.

A key line of thinking regarding radicalisation theory centres on the issues of group grievance and how an individual's sense of shared identity contributes to the transition toward terrorist.[64] In short, many theories hypothesise that there is a strong emotional pull toward radicalisation based on a perception of injustice.[65] This sense of injustice can occur when an individual has a strong connection with a like group and therefore has a vested interest in the welfare of this shared group.[66] The initial western intervention into both Iraq and Afghanistan in the early 2000s has become an own goal that directly supported Al-Qaeda's global

---

61 Author, "FM 3-13 Information Operations: Doctrine, Tactics, Techniques, and Procedures." 25-26.

62 Seymour M Hersh, "Torture at Abu Ghraib," *The New Yorker* May (2004), https://www.newyorker.com/magazine/2004/05/10/torture-at-abu-ghraib.

63 P Seib and D Janbek, "Terrorists' Online Strategies," in *Global Terrorism and the New Media* (New York: Routledge, 2011), 45.

64 Fathali M Moghaddam, "The Staircase to Terrorism," in *Psychology of Terrorism*, ed. Bruce Bognar et al. (New York: Oxford University Press, 2007), 69–80.

65 John Horgan, *The Psychology of Terrorism*, Revised ed (New York: Routledge, 2014). 79.

66 McCauley and Moskalenko, *Friction: How Radicalisation Happens to Them and US*. 16-29.

ambitions. Military actions, coupled with an intentional informational campaign based on group grievance, has acted as a catalyst to awaken a dormant pool of interested parties.[67] The Al-Qaeda ideology and the desire to support their associated objectives had gone (and remains) global. Worryingly, this can be linked to deliberate strategic planning on behalf of Al-Qaeda and is known as *The Eye-Opening Stage 2003-2006.*[68]

Arousal

The effectiveness of this mobilisation process manifested in a series of significant global terrorism events which occurred throughout the early 2000s. Many are well documented including the Madrid train bombs of 2004, the London transport bombings of 2005 and the siege of Mumbai in 2008.[69] Although there are many more, these three in particular highlight several pertinent points. Firstly, all were enacted by Islamist aligned extremist organisations. Second, all targeted westerners or western interests. And finally, all were of a scale that required a high degree of planning, suggesting therefore that a level of organisational leadership existed in directing and preparing the events.[70] Their direct links to Al-Qaeda are questionable, but none the less, the leadership of Al-Qaeda had emboldened ideologically aligned terrorist organisations to act. As such, large scale deliberate and co-ordinated terrorist attacks remained the *modus operandi* during the first decade of this century.

Domestically, security and intelligence organisations were becoming increasingly adept at identifying established terrorist cells. Advances in Technical Intelligence (TECHINT) allowed those terrorists that sought to engage in, or utilised, the internet as a tool for reconnaissance or planning to be identified.[71] Amendments to telecommunications legislation allowed increased levels of electronic communication interception, which in conjunction with traditional sources of Human

---

67 Fishman, *The Master Plan: ISIS, Al-Qaeda, and the Jihadi Strategy for Final Victory.* 14.
68 Fishman, *The Master Plan: ISIS, Al-Qaeda, and the Jihadi Strategy for Final Victory.* 31-84
69 "Terrorism Timeline," *Since 9/11,* accessed September 19, 2019, https://since911.com/explore-911/terrorism-timeline#jump_time_item_391.
70 "Terrorism Timeline."
71 Julian Richards, "Intelligence and Counterterrorism," in *Routledge Handbook of Terrorism and Counterterrorism,* ed. Andrew Silke (New York: Routledge, 2019), 396.

Intelligence (HUMINT) would enable pre-emptive action to occur.[72] This shift toward a 'pre-crime' mentality within western domestic security organisations is directly attributable to the effectiveness of the terrorist attacks following 9/11.[73] As such, pre-emptive disruption activities became operationalised within the domestic policing architecture.

This shift, however, came with several risks and a unique series of unintended consequence. First, preventative police counter-terrorism actions are often driven by intelligence sources and less so the traditional policing remit of evidentiary operations.[74] The delineation between what is intelligence and what is evidence became increasingly blurred. This led to additional complications because unlike evidence, intelligence is not a fact but rather an assessment based on available information.[75] Based on a perceived need to protect the community, intelligence-driven pre-emptive actions have on occasion resulted in the arrest of innocent parties.[76] Often these individuals, such as Mohamed Haneef in Australia or Maher Arar in Canada were, as it turns out, not affiliated with terrorist organisations other than being representative of the perceived risk demographic.[77] This naturally exacerbated the perception of religiously aligned injustice and group grievance; the consequence of this was that extremist Islamist ideology had entered a positive development spiral.

This shifted how terrorist attacks, inspired by Salafi-Jihadist ideology, were to be executed. Based in large part by the disruption of terrorist organisational structures, the concept of leaderless resistance or lone wolf

---

72 Cat Barker, Helen Portillo-Castro, and Monica Biddington, "Telecommunications and Other Legislation Amendment (Assistance and Access) Bill 2018," *Bills Digest* 49, no. December (2018) 6.

73 Jude McCulloch and Sharon Pickering, "Counter-Terrorism: The Law and Policing of Pre-Emption," in *Counter-Terrorism and Beyond: The Culture of Law and Justice After 9/11*, ed. Nicola McGarrity, Andrew Lynch, and George Williams (New York: Routledge, 2010), 13–29.

74 McCulloch and Pickering, "Counter-Terrorism: The Law and Policing of Pre-Emption." 14

75 Kent Roach, "The Eroding Distinction between Intelligence and Evidence in Terrorism Investigations," in *Counter-Terrorism and Beyond: The Culture of Law and Justice After 9/11* (London: Routledge, 2010), 48–68.

76 Roach, "The Eroding Distinction between Intelligence and Evidence in Terrorism Investigations." 57-64.

77 Roach, "The Eroding Distinction between Intelligence and Evidence in Terrorism Investigations." 57-64.

actions emerged.[78] Under these concepts, individuals act independently simply through the inspiration drawn from ideological rhetoric.[79] The result was an emergence of low tech independent and opportunistic terrorist attacks. These varied from small scale yet effective bombing actions such as the Boston Marathon in 2013, stabbings and decapitation attempts such as that enacted against Lee Rigby in the United Kingdom in 2013, through to the increasingly common yet viable vehicular terrorism such as that committed against the Christmas markets in Berlin in 2016.[80]

This rise in independent ideological inspired domestic terrorism coincided with the rise and actions of the Islamic State from 2012. It seems apparent that in conjunction with the degradation of formalised networks, those individuals that could not travel to Iraq or Syria to support Abu Bakr Al Baghdadi's vision chose instead to execute individual domestic terror acts.[81] The outcome, however, was the same; terror still permeated western society. More worrisome was the fact that identifying potential terrorists and executing pre-emptive disruption operations had become increasingly difficult due to the absence of formalised hierarchal terrorist structures.[82] Therefore, linking back to the hypothesis of this argument, it would appear that not only are more people likely to engage in terrorist acts, but society at large has become less cohesive due to shifts in legislation and the by-products of domestic policing operations. Defining the war on terror enacted since 9/11 as effective would be a dubious proposition at best.

Roll to the right

This paper has already highlighted the role personal and group grievance plays in the radicalisation process.[83] It is crucial to appreciate that this

---

78 Hoffman, *Inside Terrorism*. 271-272.; Chris Dishman, "The Leaderless Nexus: When Crime and Terror Converge," in *Terrorism Studies: A Reader*, ed. John Horgan and Kurt Braddock (New York: Routledge, 2012), 331–44.

79 Hoffman, *Inside Terrorism*. 271-272.; Dishman, "The Leaderless Nexus: When Crime and Terror Converge."

80 "Terrorism Timeline."

81 Anthony Bergin et al., "Gen Y Jihadists: Preventing Radicalisation in Australia" (Canberra, 2015). 31

82 Catherine Appleton, "Lone Wolf Terrorism in Norway," *The International Journal of Human Rights* 18, no. 2 (2014): 135.

83 McCauley and Moskalenko, *Friction: How Radicalisation Happens to Them and US*. 16-33.

grievance can develop only by a perception of injustice, meaning it can emerge simply by one's outlook on world events.[84] There is a logic thread here which suggests that this aspect of the radicalisation process is independent of any given terrorist ideology and is instead, amorphous.

The concept of multiculturalism has long been touted as a panacea for societies that may experience tension due to the complications of highly diverse societies. This issue and its potential failings are being linked to contemporary debate relating to the resurgence in nationalist politics which is occurring throughout Europe (and western societies more broadly).[85] The increasing visibility of Islam within what were the traditional Judeo-Christian societies of Europe is having an indelible impact on the demographic norms that once existed.[86] This migration is being driven by several factors, such as the enduring exponential growth of the world's population.[87] However, it must also be recognised that such migration is also being driven by conflict due to increases in Salafi-Jihadist violence throughout the Middle East and Northern Africa.[88] These, of course, are an output of military counter-terrorism activity within both Iraq and Afghanistan. This migratory effect could, therefore, be seen as an indirect result of western intervention based on Al-Qaeda's provocation strategy. Regardless, the shift has occurred and opportunities for perceived injustices present.

Andres Behring Breivik's transition from radicalised individual to terrorist culminated on the 22nd of July 2011 with the killing of 77 individuals; the majority of whom were young members of the ruling Labour party within Norway. This organisation is left aligned and supportive of multiculturalism.[89] Like Bin Laden's perspective on American civilians, Breivik viewed the young Labour supporters as targetable only by association. The method and targets of his terrorist actions delivered a jarring realisation to the world that almost a decade

---

84 McCauley and Moskalenko, *Friction: How Radicalisation Happens to Them and US*. 17.

85 Felice Blake, "Global Mass Violence: Examining Racial and Gendered Violence in the Twilight of Multiculturalism," *Ethnic and Racial Studies* 40, no. 14 (2017): 2620.

86 Virginie Andre, "Merah and Breivik: A Reflection of the European Identity Crisis," *Islam and Christian-Muslim Relations* 26, no. 2 (2015): 183–204.

87 David Kilcullen, *Out of the Mountains: The Coming Age of the Urban Guerrilla.* (Melbourne: Scribe Publications, 2013). 35-

88 Padraig O'Malley, "Migration and Conflict," *New England Journal of Public Policy* 30, no. 2 (2018): 1–15.

89 Andre, "Merah and Breivik: A Reflection of the European Identity Crisis." 187.

on from 9/11 terrorism was poorly understood and even utopic pockets of the world were not immune. Breivik did not target Muslims; instead, he targeted the group he saw as supporting the demise of Judeo-Christian norms. His actions fit the definition of terrorism used throughout this discussion; he engaged in a premeditated violent act to target a specific group with the purposeful intent of intimidating the government to affect policy. Publicly, Breivik's terrorist acts were denounced; however, the fact remains that European governments are increasingly challenged politically by opposing right-wing groups, and the introduction of restrictive immigration policies is an increasing norm.[90]

This issue of *reciprocating* terrorism appears to have remained dormant until individuals felt obliged to act based on right-wing ideology and the perception of Muslim aligned injustice.[91] This was the case for Breivik who held grave concerns about the growing 'Islamisation of Europe' declaring:

> Before 2020, Muslims should convert to Christianity, adopt Christian names, abandon non-European languages, and get rid of foreign customs, or prepare for expulsion and death. The Armed Forces in every European country need to seize political control by *coup d'etats*, declare martial law, suspend the constitution, execute all traitors, expel all Muslims and permanently ban Islam.[92]

Breivik's actions have, in part, inspired other right-wing terrorists to act including Brenton Tarrant, the perpetrator of the 2019 New Zealand Mosque attacks. In Tarrant's manifesto, he claimed to have found inspiration from Breivik's actions as he felt Breivik was an individual who took a stand against 'ethnic and cultural genocide'.[93] Breivik's manifesto has also been linked to the US Coast Guard member Christopher Hannson who was arrested in a pre-emptive counter-terrorist activity mid planning for an active shooter terrorist attack.[94]

---

90 Andre, "Merah and Breivik: A Reflection of the European Identity Crisis." 188.
91 *Reciprocating Terrorism* is a term coined by the author.
92 Andre, "Merah and Breivik: A Reflection of the European Identity Crisis." 187.
93 Adam Taylor, "New Zealand Suspect Allegedly Claimed 'Brief Contact' with Norwegian Mass Murderer Anders Breivik," *The Washington Post*, 2019, https://www.washingtonpost.com/world/2019/03/15/new-zealand-suspect-allegedly-claimed-brief-contact-with-norwegian-mass-murderer-anders-breivik/.
94 J Berger, "The Dangerous Spread of Extremist Manifestos: By Sharing the Writings of Terrorists, Media Outlets Can Amplifier Their Impact," *The Atlantic*, 2019, https://www.theatlantic.com/ideas/archive/2019/02/christopher-hasson-was-inspired-breivik-manifesto/583567/.

Additionally, Breivik is seen as a revolutionary hero in any number of White Nationalist or alt-right forums within the United States.[95]

The conclusion that can be drawn from this increase in right-wing terrorism is that there is a degree of interconnectivity that exists between Salafi-Jihadist terrorism and far-right terrorism.[96] This connectivity and the subsequent advent of reciprocating terrorism was not anticipated when the war on terror commenced in 2001. Returning to the hypothesis of this argument; it is apparent that as a result of the war on terror not only has terrorism not been defeated, but more people are supportive of various ideologies and are willing to align to and engage in terrorism. Society then is far less cohesive.

New Battlegrounds

It would appear that society is now at war for the opinions of members within multicultural societies. A quest for moderate thinking and normalcy likely represents the new battleground. The ability to stem the exodus of rational centrist thinking to opposing extremist viewpoints will be an informational war but will be central during the next phase of the war on terror. Figure two highlights what could be referred to as a 'NORMAL-STABLE Societal Stability Continuum'.[97]

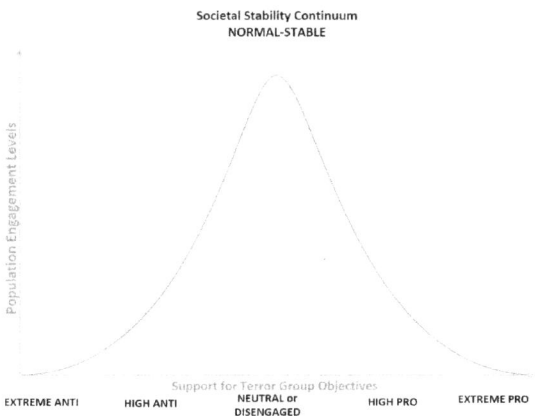

Figure 2: Societal Stability Continuum NORMAL-STABLE

95 Berger, "The Dangerous Spread of Extremist Manifestos: By Sharing the Writings of Terrorists, Media Outlets Can Amplifier Their Impact."
96 Andre, "Merah and Breivik: A Reflection of the European Identity Crisis." 184.
97 Societal Stability Continuums developed by author.

Extremist views exist; however, they are the minority, with the population of a given society mostly neutral or disengaged to the concepts of terrorism. The requirement of a given ideology is irrelevant for these examples and could apply equally to Salafi-Jihadist terrorism as they could to environmental terrorism. The fact remains that for each form of terrorism, there will be an opposing group that will vary in their level of *reciprocating* commitment.

Figure 3, however, is likely representative of what is occurring throughout Europe and western societies. Here the Societal Stability Continuum is 'UNSTABLE-FAILING' resulting in an increase of opposing extremist views and a subsequent reduction in numbers of the population that would identify as neutral or disengaged.

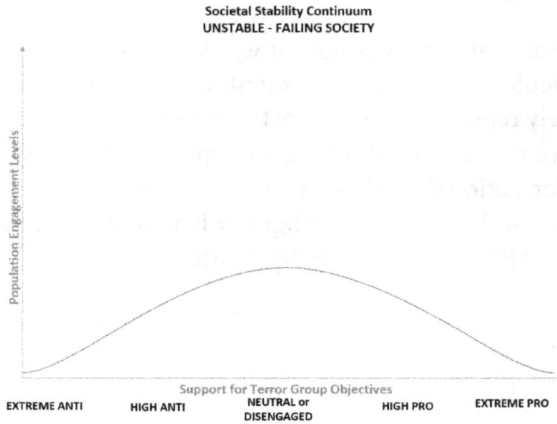

Figure 3: Societal Stability Continuum is UNSTABLE-FAILING

Figure 4, however, could be what concerns governments and decision-makers globally and pending the effectiveness of the informational war on terror may be what occurs across multiple societies.

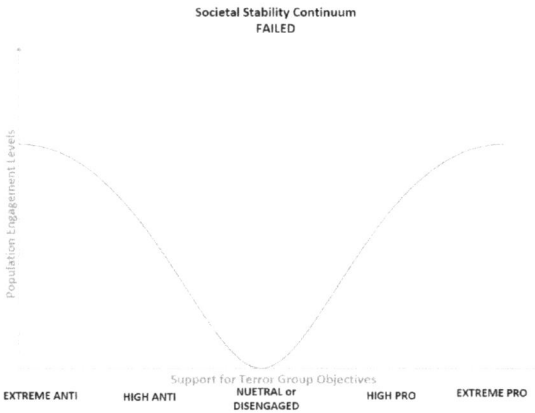

Figure 4: Societal Stability Continuum FAILED SOCIETY

In this scenario, the population as a collective is highly supportive of one form or the other of terrorist action. Here the Societal Stability Continuum represents a 'FAILED SOCIETY' and maybe what confronted those engaged at the height of fighting against ISIS both with regards to Sunni-Shia conflict and the Western commitment to defeating ISIS. There was no neutral middle ground; ISIS was either seen as an abomination of human norms or the crusaders for the Caliphate.

Conclusion

The war on terror, as initially envisioned, has become an unsightly weeping wound. The original strategic objectives, if they existed, continue to drift. Al-Qaeda remains a viable terrorist organisation; its ideology extant. Its offspring, the Islamic State, remains a destabilising influence within the Levant but also globally. The Taliban continue to mock security forces within Afghanistan and pending any usurping action from the ISIS-Khorasan look set to form a government of sorts and likely have members join Afghanistan's security architecture. The rise of Salafi-Jihadist organisations and the subsequent attack on western values has stimulated an increase in right-wing terror acts. Terror and terrorists, as defined, are far from defeated; it is difficult to see how the effectiveness of the war on terror could be seen as anything other than a failure.

The intervention of western militaries did not defeat the Taliban or Al-Qaeda and in doing stimulated previously dormant pools of hatred that now exist both with regard to how the West is viewed but also how Muslim communities are viewed. This, in turn, is harming the cohesiveness of many societies; notably, western societies were extremist right-wing terrorists have become active. Below the surface of terrorism moves an undercurrent of nationalism that can be seen in Europe, the United States, the United Kingdom and Australia. Although not necessarily extremism, one must question how such thinking within society has emerged and why various groups are now emboldened to act for 'their cause'.

The ability for the Taliban and Al-Qaeda to survive, despite concerted security efforts has in essence, highlighted how a terror campaign can be effective in achieving a political objective. The ineffectiveness of security actions against Salafi-Jihadist terrorism may be a potential contributor to increases in violent political action such as the demonstrations occurring in Hong Kong.[98] These actions seen through one prism is an insurgency employing terrorism. With that proposition in mind, society can only be seen as less cohesive with terrorism becoming an increasingly palatable option for individuals or interest groups to employ to seek a favourable political outcome. The western military intervention prosecuted following the 9/11 terror attacks has failed to achieve the original operational and strategic objectives. Perhaps worse still, the military actions have contributed to a destabilising effect on global cohesion which is stimulating the growth and membership of competing terrorist organisations. Violent terror acts, will unfortunately remain a pervading presence throughout the world for the foreseeable future.

---

98 "The Hong Kong Protests Explained in 100 and 500 Words.," *BBC News*, 2019, https://www.bbc.com/news/world-asia-china-49317695.

A History of Terrorism

'Why Do Terrorists Stop? Analysing Why ETA Members Abandon or Continue with Terrorism' a review of Rogelio Alonso works.[99] *(Written 2018)*

This account of why individuals remain engaged with a given terrorist organisation is a timely and relevant article for scholars or practitioners in the field of counter-terrorism or counter-radicalisation. It is an articulate article in which the author, through an effective analysis of the Spanish Terrorist group *Euskadi Ta Askatasuna* (ETA), seeks to identify critical factors that may trigger individual disengagement from a given terrorist organisation. This individual disengagement may then in turn contribute to the demise of that terrorist organisation. Additionally, the article has a focus on continuance which highlights how counter-terrorist actions may actually contribute to increased levels of engagement. Rogelio Alonso wrote the article whilst lecturing within the School of Politics at the *Universidad Rey Juan Carlos* in Madrid. Although a professional institution, it is not highly ranked on the global list of recognised universities and was only ranked at 29th in Spain at the time of writing. The article is, however, a peer-reviewed publication being originally distributed by the respected publication 'Studies in Conflict and Terrorism' in 2011 and more recently hosted by Routledge within the Taylor and Francis Group.[100] The lessons therein remain as relevant today as they were when written.

Alonso seems skilled in his ability to convey the historical context surrounding the ETA situation in Spain, without the article becoming

---

99 Rogelio Alonso, "Why Do Terrorists Stop? Analysing Why ETA Members Abandon or Continue with Terrorism," *Studies in Conflict and Terrorism* 34, no. 9 (2011): 696–716.

100 Universidad Rey Juan Carlos was ranked 26th in the European University Research in 2010: http://www.researchranking.org/index.php?orgtype=EDUCATION&c=5&country=ES&year=2010&action=ranking.

a cumbersome historical monologue. Importantly the article and key themes would be equally consumable by those associated with the study of countering terrorism as much as those who haven't studied the field in depth. His introduction is clear highlighting key components associated with terrorism, however at times fails to expand or capitalise on the concepts he introduces. As an example, he situates the reader in the first paragraph to the 'type' of Terrorist organisation that ETA can be defined as, being a leftist nationalist inspired movement.[101] He, therefore, identifies the link to Rapoport's four-wave theorem, rightly categorising ETA as residing in the third wave, without the article becoming bogged down in describing this theory.[102] It is noteworthy however that this reference to the 'third wave' is lacking an academic reference on which to guide the inquisitive reader toward a text that would allow the reader to develop a deeper understanding on Rapoport's concepts. Also, when laying the foundation for the article, he stipulates that it was Franco's dictatorship and the repression of the Basque people as an ethnic minority that aided mobilisation and recruitment for ETA. A reference to Fromkin's writings and the concept of proportionality regarding security forces response, would not only add academic weight to his arguments, it would again aid the inquisitive reader.[103] All said, however, the introduction clearly positions the reader to the direction and flow of the article with three focal areas for discussion identified being disbandment, social reinsertion measures and the utility of violence. These were to be discussed in context relating to the strategic, organisational and psychological aspects of terrorism and would further frame his argument.[104] This positioning of the reader is assessed as a key strength of the article.

Although the article highlights that the repression imposed by the Franco regime was a key contributor to the formation of ETA, it fails to fully convey the fractures that existed within Spanish society at that

---

101 Alonso, "Why Do Terrorists Stop? Analysing Why ETA Members Abandon or Continue with Terrorism." 696.

102 David Rapoport, "The Four Waves of Modern Terror: International Dimensions and Consequences," in *An International History of Terrorism: Western and Non-Western Experiences*, ed. Jussi Hanimaki and Bernhard Blumenau (New York: Routledge, 2013), 281–310.

103 David Fromkin, "The Strategy of Terrorism," *Foreign Affairs* 53, no. 4 (1975): 683–98.

104 Alonso, "Why Do Terrorists Stop? Analyzing Why ETA Members Abandon or Continue with Terrorism." 698.

time and prior to the process of democratisation.[105] This is critical to the argument as providing the reader with an understanding on the levels of individual identity associated with self-representing as 'Basque' would enhance the readers understanding on why concepts for disbandment were ultimately successful. Alonso highlights that during the democratisation process concerted efforts were made to increase the professionalisation of the Spanish security architecture, including the National Court systems who began introducing pardons in 1982.[106] However, the article fails to articulate why this was so successful with regard to disengagement. There are key components at this stage that relate to his introduction and framing that would be beneficial to link to, specifically the strategic and psychological aspects of engagement or otherwise.

ETA had consistently struggled with internal conflicts relating to organisational strategy, the application of violence and operational objectives, with these issues proven to be contributors that influence individual disengagement from a given terrorist organisation.[107] Consequently, and as highlighted by Alonso, the counter-terrorism initiatives employed during the democratisation period (post-Franco) sought to exploit these frictions. This would be achieved via strategic efforts to blunt ETA's messaging and recruitment initiatives centred on the premise of a Basque nationalist argument.[108] The National strategy in fact endorsed many of ETA's ideal end-state objectives, most notably the recognition of a Basque parliament and autonomy.[109] This did result in a decrease in violence, with a large percentage of those that would have identified as members of ETA questioning why terrorist actions continued given that many of the original objectives had been achieved.[110] It is here when the article fails to fully exploit the psychological aspect

105 Edward Moxon-Brown, *Spain and the ETA: The Bid for Basque Autonomy* (London: Centre of Security and Conflict Studies, 1987). 1-11

106 Alonso, "Why Do Terrorists Stop? Analysing Why ETA Members Abandon or Continue with Terrorism." 698.

107 Paul Gill, Noemie Bouhana, and John Morrison, "Individual Disengagement from Terrorist Groups," in *Terrorism and Political Violence*, ed. Caroline Kenndey-Pipe, Gordon Clubb, and Simon Mabon (London: SAGE Publications Ltd, 2015), 247-248.

108 Alonso, "Why Do Terrorists Stop? Analysing Why ETA Members Abandon or Continue with Terrorism." 696.

109 Randall D Law, *Terrorism a History*, 2nd ed. (Cambridge: Polity Press, 2016). 240-243

110 Alonso, "Why Do Terrorists Stop? Analysing Why ETA Members Abandon or Continue with Terrorism." 700-701.

of engagement or disbandment that was alluded to in the introduction, which is assessed as a key weakness of the article.

These strategic level counter initiatives were deliberate attempts on behalf of the Spanish government to further fracture individual affiliation with ETA whilst simultaneously enhancing a sense of belonging to Spanish society at large. The importance of this inherent human need for affiliation, belonging and social identity is an important component relating to organisational (including militant) effectiveness.[111] During the early 1980s violent actions, including murder, was effectively ETA policy toward those individuals within ETA who considered reintegration into mainstream society.[112] In reality this individual thought relating to reintegration was only being considered based on the strategic counter-manoeuvres being implemented by the Spanish government.[113]

In this case, the counter-terrorism strategies employed leveraged the decreasing levels of affiliation that existed internally to ETA, whilst simultaneously highlighting the benefits of 'inclusivity' within society.[114] It was a successful strategy, yet not fully appreciated or conveyed by Alonso. Appreciating and articulating the importance of this psychological need for group acceptance, and then the risk to organisational cohesion if individuals perceive rejection or become disillusioned would have acted as a powerful adjunct to his arguments.[115] In this aspect there is an imbalance in his article as it focused too heavily on the organisational aspects and less on the psychological components and is a clear opportunity for development. In short ETA's leadership was reinforcing the government's strategies as the violent actions against their own membership aided the organisational decay.

---

111 Boas Shamir et al., "Leadership and Social Identification in Military Units: Direct and Indirect Relationships," *Journal of Applied Social Psychology* 20, no. 3 (2000): 612–40; Rolf Van Dick and Rudolf Kerschreiter, "The Social Identity Approach to Effective Leadership: An Overview and Some Ideas on Cross-Cultural Generalisability," *Front. Bus. Res. China* 10, no. 3 (2016): 363–84.

112 Alonso, "Why Do Terrorists Stop? Analyzing Why ETA Members Abandon or Continue with Terrorism." 701

113 Gill, Bouhana, and Morrison, "Individual Disengagement from Terrorist Groups."

114 Alonso, "Why Do Terrorists Stop? Analysing Why ETA Members Abandon or Continue with Terrorism." 697-700.

115 Matthew J. Slater, Andrew L. Evans, and Martin J. Turner, "Implementing a Social Identity Approach for Effective Change Management," *Journal of Change Management* 16, no. 1 (2016): 18–37.

Alonso highlights that this internal decay was complemented by a decrease in popular support for ETA, largely due to their insistence on the continued application of violence and therefore associated collateral damage. This was recognised internally by elements of the ETA leadership who felt that the de-legitimisation of violence by the Basque population had effectively put an end to armed struggle.[116] Social support is a proven component driving individuals to or from engagement with a terror organisation and Alonso is right to identify this was a key driver to disengagement.[117] Why this occurred is not so clear within the article, was it simply poor target choice, cumulative fatigue relating to violence, the loss of a unified objective (had it already been achieved?), or simply via a more effective counter-narrative campaign being waged by the Spanish Government? This aspect again is worthy of thought and does not evidently present in the article

It would seem logical that an article titled 'Why Do Terrorists Stop? Analysing Why ETA Members Abandon or Continue with Terrorism' would flow seamlessly from abandonment issues to continuance aspects, however, this is the greatest shortfall of the article. The introduction and set up of the article flows through the areas of which the author specifies will be discussed, as are highlighted above. The conclusions and reasons for continuance seem disconnected and ultimately unnecessary. In fact, the key premise relating to continuance with ETA relates to issues associated with government negotiations, albeit relevant, reads like a separate paper and is disconnected from the introduction. In this component, Alonso suggests that the Spanish governments continued efforts to engage with ETA for the peaceful cessation of actions did, in fact, engender greater levels of animosity toward the Spanish government from ETA.[118] Alonso also points to two enduring aspects that continue to inhibit the individual disengagement from ETA (hence ensure its existence at some form) with that being the strength of Basque Nationalist identity and a sub-culture of violence.[119] Both these areas

---

116 Alonso, "Why Do Terrorists Stop? Analysing Why ETA Members Abandon or Continue with Terrorism." 704
117 Gill, Bouhana, and Morrison, "Individual Disengagement from Terrorist Groups." 253.
118 Alonso, "Why Do Terrorists Stop? Analysing Why ETA Members Abandon or Continue with Terrorism." 708
119 Alonso, "Why Do Terrorists Stop? Analysing Why ETA Members Abandon or Continue with Terrorism." 710-711.

seem to lack maturity of thought and again seem disconnected to the main argument.

On reading the introduction to *'Why Do Terrorists Stop? Analysing Why ETA Members Abandon or Continue with Terrorism'* by Rogelio Alonso, the article shows promise of being a 'how to guide' on how to facilitate individual disengagement from terrorist organisations. There is a clear framework highlighted, with the terrorist group *Euskadi Ta Askatasuna* acting as the lens to affirm Alonso's hypotheses. The article initially flows through the three aspects of disbandment, social reinsertion, and evolution on the utility of violence, however, fails to fully exploit the psychological aspects that may ultimately lead to this disengagement. The concepts are there; however, it is harder to grasp holistically in comparison to other writings on individual disengagement, notably from Gill, Bouhana and Morrison.[120] What should be called Part 2, not conclusions, seems out of place, unnecessary and ultimately detracts from the initial components of the article. Criticism aside, the article provides worthy and valid considerations with regards to individual disengagement or continuance with terrorist organisations whilst simultaneously providing sufficient stimuli for additional research.

---

120 Gill, Bouhana, and Morrison, "Individual Disengagement from Terrorist Groups."

'Critically discuss and assess the emergence, evolution and destiny of Euskadi Ta Askatasuna with reference to precedent, theory and theorists' *(Written 2018)*

Introduction

Historical analysis is a proven tool to seek guidance with regard to countering contemporary issues faced by society. Terrorism is not a new phenomenon with the requirement to counter the actions of the terrorist having received increasing attention from governments and society at large due to the increasing profile of contemporary attacks.[121] This analytical report will centre on the Basque Homeland and Freedom organisation, specifically the *Euskadi ta Askatasun* (ETA), being formally recognised in 1997 as a terrorist group.[122] This organisation has been selected as the lessons that can be identified leading to the organisation's emergence, the responses from a government (and associated security apparatus), impacts on the broader populace and finally ETA's subsequent evolution holds valuable precedent with regards to countering contemporary terrorist organisations. Interestingly ETA straddles two of Rapaport's recognised 'waves' of terrorism, initially forming during the second wave associated with anti-colonial struggle and then being firmly anchored in the third wave, centred on leftist ideology.[123]

---

121 Bruce Hoffman, *Inside Terrorism* (New York: Columbia University Press, 2006).69

122 US Department of State, "Foreign Terrorist Organisations," accessed 29 April 18, https://www.state.gov/j/ct/rls/other/des/123085.htm.

123 David Rapoport, "The Four Waves of Modern Terror: International Dimensions and Consequences," in *An International History of Terrorism: Western and Non-Western Experiences*, ed. Jussi Hanimaki and Bernhard Blumenau (New York: Routledge, 2013), 281–310.

Understanding how an organisation may shift strategy and tactics based on these waves is of critical importance to governments and contemporary counter strategies. The neutralisation of ETA as an active terrorist organisation has today largely been successful with a historic surrender of arms in 2017 indicating that close to 50 years of violence had come to an end.[124] This report will focus not only on the organisation's emergence and evolution but also on what aspects led to its demise. Put simply it was not only government counter actions that led to the organisation's demise; ETA failed in large part due to inept strategic leadership and an inability to adapt to the shifting political landscape.

Before proceeding further however it is important that a 'terrorist' organisation be defined as this is central to this analytical report. Without clear definition, reflections and precedents drawn from ETA could be ambiguous based on one's perception of their actions. For this discussion, terrorism will be defined as:

> 'A premeditated and unlawful act in which groups or agents of some principal engage in a threatened or actual use of force or violence against human or property targets. These groups or agents engage in this behaviour intending the purposeful intimidation of governments or people to affect policy or behaviour with an underlying political objective.'[125]

This definition has primarily been chosen as ETA's terror actions were firmly founded on affecting policy and achieving a political objective.

Catalytic impact of identity

Euskadi ta Askatusuna was formally founded in 1959 (evolving from EKIN meaning to act) by a collection of students buoyed by contemporary counter-revolutionary writings and inspired by the original publication associated with the Basque Nationalist Party, written in 1895.[126] This paper highlighted the importance of a national identity

---

124 Jonathan Powell, "ETA's Weapons Surrender Brings to an End 50 Years of Killing," *Financial Times*, 2017.

125 Gus Martin, *Essentials of Terrorism*, 3rd ed. (London: SAGE Publications Ltd, 2014). 8.

126 Michael Burleigh, *Blood and Rage: A Cultural History of Terrorism* (London: Harper Press, 2008).271-272.

associated with the 'Basque People'.[127] It is this need for identity founded on ethno-nationalist drivers that can be identified as the primary motivational driver leading to future terrorist actions.[128] The Basque people do not consider themselves as Spanish or French and have long been caught up in the politics of these larger countries including as far back as 1659 when a shared border region was identified for the 'Basque People'.[129] The Basque people have their own unique culture, unique sporting traditions and, when coupled with one of the oldest and most distinct dialects in the region, drives a powerful sense of self.[130]

However, this individual Basque identity was increasingly threatened by demographic shifts driven by socio-economic changes attributable to the industrial revolution.[131] This resulted in a rapid population influx to the region by individuals who arrived from provinces and countries external to the recognised Basque area.[132] Uptake of the language suffered due to its complexity and, in time, the cultural identity of the Basque people was diluted and compromised. It was this fact that triggered Sabino Arana's 1895 seminal text *Euzko Alderdi Jelt-zalea* detailing the lost history of the Basque people. By 1895 the Basque's had formalised their identity having a uniquely Basque flag, an anthem and a foundation text that would later drive the terrorists of ETA.[133]

The need to 'belong' is a powerful and inherent human motivational driver assessed as a higher order need.[134] As such, actions that may compromise the salience of this belongingness or cultural identity is likely to trigger a counteraction to retain or regain the sense of identity.[135] The importance of protecting identity is as recognisable in

---

127 John Bew, Martyn Frampton, and Inigo Gurruchaga, *Talking to Terrorists: Making Peace in Northern Ireland and the Basque Country* (London: Hurst and Co., 2009). 169.

128 Randall D Law, *Terrorism a History*, 2nd ed. (Cambridge: Polity Press, 2016). 241

129 Bew, Frampton, and Gurruchaga, *Talking to Terrorists: Making Peace in Northern Ireland and the Basque Country*. 170.

130 Burleigh, *Blood and Rage: A Cultural History of Terrorism*. 268-269

131 Bew, Frampton, and Gurruchaga, *Talking to Terrorists: Making Peace in Northern Ireland and the Basque Country*. 171-172.

132 Burleigh, *Blood and Rage: A Cultural History of Terrorism*. 268-270

133 Bew, Frampton, and Gurruchaga, *Talking to Terrorists: Making Peace in Northern Ireland and the Basque Country*. 172.

134 Kathryn M Bartol et al., *Management: A Pacific Rim Focus* (North Melbourne: McGraw-Hill Book Company Australia Pty Limited, 1995). 418-419.

135 Rolf Van Dick and Rudolf Kerschreiter, "The Social Identity Approach to Effective Leadership: An Overview and Some Ideas on Cross-Cultural Generalisability," *Front. Bus. Res. China* 10, no. 3 (2016): 366.

the ETA context as it is in being a contributing variable to the ongoing conflict between Palestine and Israel.[136] Arana recognised that Basque culture was being threatened in the late 1800s and subsequently his 1895 text sought to strengthen the Basque identity through political and non-violent means. He ultimately formed the political party *Partido Nacionalista Vasco* (PNV). It is important to note that this text and his principles were heavily founded on an importance of religion and an opposition to socialism, as this would clearly influence the later actions of ETA.[137]

The relative success of the PNV ebbed and flowed through the early 1900s being driven underground at times, yet remaining a popular and viable political force until being forced into exile in the mid-1930s.[138] Whilst in exile PNV leadership sought support from the United States in relation to the Basque cause; clearly, under the Franco regime, Basque autonomy was not supported.[139] Franco envisioned a unified Spain and this was to come at the cost of Basque identity through absorption of the region into Spain.[140] The United States far from supporting Basque identity was instrumental in aiding Franco's regime through both economic and military aid.[141]

Although this is a somewhat crude attempt to summarise a millennial long history of the Basque people, it does provide a historical precedent that is of relevance to contemporary counter-terrorism strategies. There are two critical issues that are identifiable and can be attributed to the application of violence by ETA. Firstly, the cultural identity of a people is under-valued and threatened; and if the sense of individual self is linked to this collective, it is likely to trigger protectionary action.[142] Cultural

---

136 Edward H Price, "The Strategy and Tactics of Revolutionary Terrorism," *Comparative Studies in Society and History* 19, no. 1 (1977): 62-63.

137 Bew, Frampton, and Gurruchaga, *Talking to Terrorists: Making Peace in Northern Ireland and the Basque Country.* 172.

138 Bew, Frampton, and Gurruchaga, *Talking to Terrorists: Making Peace in Northern Ireland and the Basque Country.* 172-173.

139 Bew, Frampton, and Gurruchaga, *Talking to Terrorists: Making Peace in Northern Ireland and the Basque Country.* 175-176

140 Jeremey R Spindlove and Clifford E Simonsen, *Terrorism Today: The Past, The Players and The Future*, 6th ed. (New York: Pearson, 2018). 142.

141 Bew, Frampton, and Gurruchaga, *Talking to Terrorists: Making Peace in Northern Ireland and the Basque Country.* 175-176

142 Van Dick and Kerschreiter, "The Social Identity Approach to Effective Leadership: An Overview and Some Ideas on Cross-Cultural Generalizability." 364-366.

recognition and social cohesion remain central to counter-terrorism strategies being integral to Australia's 2015 and 2017 counter-terrorism strategies.[143] The intentional repression of Basque identity by the Franco regime runs counter to this concept and is clearly an attributable trigger for ETA terror actions. The second critical issue is that the attempts to protect the Basque identity had for decades been pursued through largely non-violent political means via engagement with both domestic and international audiences. These actions had failed to achieve Basque autonomy, let alone stem the cultural decay. They felt a lack of empowerment and abandonment from the international community being forced to live under a regime that failed to appreciate their intent for Basque autonomy. Violent action to influence a political objective is clearly then seen as a viable option, arguably for ETA leadership, the only viable option.[144]

Link to the Left and the Political Objective

The historical reflection above provides insight into the thinking of ETA's leadership and their subsequent actions. As indicated, the rise and fall of ETA straddle two widely recognised waves of terrorism or ideological types of terrorism being separatists (often referred to as revolutionary or anti-colonial) and left-wing terrorism.[145] ETA would leverage emotional elements contained within both these ideological terrorist concepts to articulate their political objective and in turn drive recruitment and public support. Establishing an independent Basque state free from Spanish rule was clearly the motivating driver for ETA with their actions being referred to as a 'revolutionary war' against the state.[146] This desire for independence remained consistent throughout ETA's decade's long campaign, and would ultimately be leveraged as a

---

143 No Author, "Australia's Counter-Terrorism Strategy: Strengthening Our Resilience" (Canberra, 2015). 4; No Author, "National Counter-Terrorism Plan" (Canberra, 2017).

144 Martha Crenshaw-Hutchinson, "The Concept of Revolutionary Terrorism," *The Journal of Conflict Resolution* 16, no. 3 (1972): 385.

145 Zeynep Sutalan, "Major Ideologies Motivating Terrorism and Main Characteristics of Terrorism," in *Organizational and Psychological Aspects of Terrorism*, ed. Centre of Excellence Defence Against Terrorism (Ankara: IOS Press, 2008), 13–21.; Rapoport, "The Four Waves of Modern Terror: International Dimensions and Consequences."

146 Jose A Trevino, "Spains Internal Security: The Basque Autonomous Police Force," in *Terrorism in Europe*, ed. Yohan Alexander and Kenneth A Myers (London: Croom Helm, 1982), 142–53.

counter strategy by the ruling Spanish government. In time and as the socio-political climate changed within Spain and the world at large, these separatist ideologies would shift or morph to contain elements of leftist terrorism centred on social revolutionary principles.[147]

The influential theorists of the time inspired by Marxists philosophical concepts led to ETA drawing on concepts contained within Mao Tse-Tung and Che Guevara texts to drive an approach to achieve their political objective.[148] These were often used to leverage support as ETA's objectives have always been communal in nature.[149] ETA, therefore, sought to employ Maoist principles of social mobilisation to support the realisation of their political intent.[150] This need to garner and retain popular support would prove to be an integral component of ETA's strategy and again would be leveraged by the Spanish government as a counter strategy.

Action, reaction and counteraction

ETA's first successful act of terrorism came through assassination in 1968, with previous attempts of terrorism proving largely unsuccessful.[151] Although a somewhat fortuitous act from an ETA perspective, the assassination of a member of the security forces by a leading member of ETA became instrumental in the evolution of ETA.[152] First, it clearly signals the resolve from within ETA's senior leadership (albeit the assassin Txabi Etxebarrieta was only 24 years old) to secure their political objectives through violent driven coercion, a proven pillar of

---

147 Sutalan, "Major Ideologies Motivating Terrorism and Main Characteristics of Terrorism."14-15.

148 Spindlove and Simonsen, *Terrorism Today: The Past, The Players and The Future*. 142-143.

149 James M Lutz and Brenda J Lutz, "The Rise of the New Left and the Failure of Communism: Increasing Terrorism on a Global Scale," in *Terrorism: Origins and Evolution* (Gordonsville: Palgrave Macmillan, 2005), 108.

150 Sebastian Kaempf, "Violence and Victory: Guerrilla Warfare, 'Authentic Self-Affirmation' and the Overthrow of the Colonial State," *Third World Quarterly2* 30, no. 1 (2009): 129–46.

151 Javier Argomanz and Alberto Vidal-Diez, "Examining Deterrence and Backlash Effects in Counter-Terrorism: The Case of ETA," *Terrorism and Political Violence2* 27, no. 1 (2015): 164.

152 Bew, Frampton, and Gurruchaga, *Talking to Terrorists: Making Peace in Northern Ireland and the Basque Country*. 178.

the terrorist resolve.[153] This deliberate shift to engage in violent action had been endorsed as a potential strategy during the 1964 assembly were 'Insurrection in Euskadi' was endorsed by the ETA leadership.[154] Secondly, the response from the Spanish security apparatus would act as a catalyst in garnering popular support ultimately legitimising ETA's objectives. Etxebarrieta, the assassin, and his accomplices fled the scene following the assassination, however, their vehicle was subsequently intercepted. The fate for Etxebarrieta was a predictable roadside execution delivered at the hands of the Guardia Civil.[155] The ETA had their martyr.

ETA capitalised on this action, identifying the opportunity that the ensuing mass demonstrations and commemorative services that occurred throughout northern Spain afforded their political objectives. They subsequently leveraged this public support seeking to drive a public uprising against what was then the Franco regime.[156] This was easy enough to achieve when the Franco regime enforced a state of emergency in the affected provinces, and following other successful terrorist actions throughout 1969, extending this to the whole of Spain. What followed was what can be defined as a 'hard' response from a government with regards to countering terrorists.[157] The subsequent response from the security apparatus resulted in an increased presence of security forces in Basque regions leading to mass arrests of those considered of having links to ETA. This culminated in a 1970 trial, which, ill-conceived by the Franco regime, was largely open to the public resulting in increased levels of public support for ETA once the severity of sentencing (including the death sentence) was delivered to the accused.[158]

This governmental counter-terrorist response during ETA's infancy can be held directly accountable to ETA's increasing popular support and consequent increasing levels of violence during the 1970's. Responding in an overly repressive and militant manner is now widely recognised

---

153 David Whittaker, *The Terrorism Reader* (London: Routledge, 2001). 130.
154 Whittaker, *The Terrorism Reader*. 130.
155 Burleigh, *Blood and Rage: A Cultural History of Terrorism*. 274.
156 Burleigh, *Blood and Rage: A Cultural History of Terrorism*. 274.
157 Anne Aly, *Terrorism and Global Security: Historical and Contemporary Perspectives*. (Melbourne: Palgrave Macmillan, 2011). 172.
158 Bew, Frampton, and Gurruchaga, *Talking to Terrorists: Making Peace in Northern Ireland and the Basque Country*. 178-179.

as a counter-productive response to acts of terrorism and ultimately benefits the terrorist objectives.[159] The Franco response was predictable enough. Unimaginably they merely followed contemporary responses to insurgent and terrorist actions from their neighbour France. Franco was simply following the failed actions of the French to counter the Algerian insurgency.[160]

Franco had failed to appreciate that the terrorist actions being enacted by ETA were being done not to achieve a military victory, but more so to elicit a disproportionate emotional response from the security apparatus; a response that in turn would achieve a third order psychological effect within the population that would engender support for ETA and drive further repulsion of the Franco regime. These repressive actions effectively propagated ETA's separatist strategic narrative; being the Basque people were a repressed people suffering an ideological attack from a military dictatorship.[161] Buoyed by the success of this violent strategy and the ongoing cycle of over-reaction enabling popular support, recruitment and legitimacy, ETA enjoyed success throughout the 1960s through to mid-1970s.[162] It is clear that recognition of the risks associated with a disproportionate response from a government continues to shape contemporary counter-terrorism strategies. Australia's most recent counter-terrorism strategy has a strong focus on social integration and rehabilitation as opposed to simply a security response or the imprisonment of terrorists.[163]

However, even during this relatively successful period the strategic leadership and unity of command within ETA suffered.[164] This was centred largely on a leadership conflict relating to the weight of effort that would be afforded to a militant line of action, versus a political line of action. The resultant was a fractured organisation consisting of

---

159 Jeff Goodwin, "A Theory of Categorical Terrorism," *Special Forces* 84, no. 4 (2004): 2027–46.

160 Mathew Carr, *The Infernal Machine: An Alternative History of Terrorism* (London: Hurst and Co., 2011). 120-126.

161 Rogelio Alonso, "Why Do Terrorists Stop? Analyzing Why ETA Members Abandon or Continue with Terrorism," *Studies in Conflict and Terrorism* 34, no. 9 (2011): 696.

162 Paddy Woodworth, "Why Do They Kill? The Basque Conflict in Spain," *World Policy Journal* 18 (2001): 1–12.

163 Author, "National Counter-Terrorism Plan." 18-19

164 Edward Moxon-Brown, *Spain and the ETA: The Bid for Basque Autonomy* (London: Centre of Security and Conflict Studies, 1987). 5.

ETA-Political Military (ETA-PM) and ETA-Military (ETA-M). Both appreciated the need for a continuance of the 'armed struggle' however the weight to be afforded differed.[165] It is interesting to note ETA's appreciation on the need for both a political and militant approach which further highlights their appreciation on contemporary strategists. It is difficult to not draw parallels with General Giap's *Dau Tranh* strategy employed during the Vietnam War which highlights the importance of a political and military struggle.[166] In time, however, a failure to appreciate key elements of this approach, notably *Dan Van,* or action amongst the people, would contribute to the demise of ETA which can link directly to this conflict relating to ETA-PM and ETA-M.

The power of politics

Following Franco's death in 1975 Spain pursued a political direction focussed on democratic reform, with a multi-party democracy being established.[167] Openly at least, the government sought to implement a shift in counter-terrorist strategy from the hard approaches employed under Franco to a more inclusive and soft approach.[168] It was a calculated and deliberate strategic pivot intended to blunt ETA's strategic narrative centred on independence and autonomy. Consequently, parliament granted autonomy to the 'Basque Autonomous Community' in 1979 and established the conditions for independent elections.[169] A program of amnesty for imprisoned members of ETA was implemented as was a reintegration program for those that had sought sanctuary in France. [170] The Basque government was provided legitimate power having control for the mechanics of government including health, education, taxation and even a police force.[171] In theory, having achieved their original political objective of attaining Basque autonomy ETA's terror actions should have ceased.

---

165 Bew, Frampton, and Gurruchaga, *Talking to Terrorists: Making Peace in Northern Ireland and the Basque Country.* 179-181.
166 Douglas Pike, *The People's Army of Vietnam* (Novato: Presido Press, 1986). 215-220.
167 Burleigh, *Blood and Rage: A Cultural History of Terrorism.* 278.
168 Aly, *Terrorism and Global Security: Historical and Contemporary Perspectives.* 172.
169 Fernando Jimenez, "The Terrorist Challenge and the Governments Response," *Terrorism and Political Violence* 14, no. 4 (1992): 119–20.
170 Burleigh, *Blood and Rage: A Cultural History of Terrorism.* 280.
171 Bew, Frampton, and Gurruchaga, *Talking to Terrorists: Making Peace in Northern Ireland and the Basque Country.* 180-185

The reality was terrorist actions intensified.[172] In part, this shift of tactic had been successful in countering ETA's strategic narrative with popular support and recruitment suffering. To counter this and with a perceived need to retain legitimacy, ETA's terrorist actions now began to target not only elements of the security apparatus but also members of the civilian population.[173] Although actions of this type would logically denude support for ETA, it was, in fact, an attempt to demonstrate the ineffectiveness of Spanish security to maintain control.[174] Often when civilian casualties did occur ETA sought to shift blame onto authorities by claiming they had forewarned the authorities.[175] Although terrorism continued, many of the government's initiatives being enacted including efforts to attain cultural equality and improved policing actions had been successful in reducing popular support for ETA from its traditional middle-class elements within society.[176]

By the mid-1980s support for ETA had waned to the point where even the Basque government openly questioned the terror actions of ETA. Open protests in the hundreds of thousands appealed to ETA to cease their terrorist actions as it was felt it ran counter to progress.[177] The government's counter-terrorism strategy was at a pivotal point, popular support for ETA was falling, the recruitment pool was drying up and importantly their actions continued to exploit the fractures between the leadership within ETA-PM and ETA-M centred on what strategic course of action to employ going forward.[178] At this point, however, the government faltered in its resolve and in essence breathed new life into ETA. Although openly pursuing a 'soft' and inclusive approach to counter-terrorism the Spanish government, due to concerns for the continued levels of violence being enacted by ETA, sought to employ a concurrent coercive para-military counter-terror operation.[179]

---

172 Law, *Terrorism a History*. 242.
173 Law, *Terrorism a History*. 242.
174 Whittaker, *The Terrorism Reader*. 136.
175 Law, *Terrorism a History*. 242.
176 Law, *Terrorism a History*. 242.
177 Whittaker, *The Terrorism Reader*. 135.
178 Whittaker, *The Terrorism Reader*. 135.
179 Argomanz and Vidal-Diez, "Examining Deterrence and Backlash Effects in Counter-Terrorism: The Case of ETA." 164.

The employment of the *Grupos Antiterroristas de Liberacion*, or GAL as it was more broadly known, was an unnecessary strategic failure on behalf of the Socialist government.[180] From 1982 through 1987 GAL engaged in clandestine actions including the assassination of ETA members and, to the determent of counter-terrorism intentions, many individuals who had no relation to ETA.[181] ETA leveraged the actions of GAL to reinforce their strategic message and in essence, enabled the "generational reproduction" of ETA into the 1990s.[182] It is painfully apparent to not recognise how recent counter-terror actions, notably the failings associated with Abu Ghraib and Camp X-Ray in Guantanamo, has likely enabled generational regeneration for those contemporary terrorists drawn to radical Islamist terrorism to counter the United States.[183] In ETA's case popular support prolonged the organisation's longevity.[184]

Own goal

As previously mentioned the need to recognise Basque identity was central to the formation of ETA. The recognition of this unique cultural identity, separate from Spain, drove popular support for ETA and can largely be attributed to the recruitment of members to ETA. The field of Social Identity theory has received increasing levels of attention with regards to contemporary leadership constructs. The premise of the argument being that individuals will act in the interest of the group when the differences of those not considered to be a part of the in-group are emphasised.[185] The salience of this in-group strengthens the more group norms are shared. Individuals therefore are increasingly likely to strive for the attainment of group objectives if they self-affiliate with the group.[186] In short, the individual becomes psychologically linked with

---

180 Argomanz and Vidal-Diez, "Examining Deterrence and Backlash Effects in Counter-Terrorism: The Case of ETA." 164.
181 Woodworth, "Why Do They Kill? The Basque Conflict in Spain." 7.
182 Woodworth, "Why Do They Kill? The Basque Conflict in Spain." 7.
183 Mathew Carr, *The Infernal Machine: A History of Terrorism from the Assassination of Tsar Alexander II to Al-Qaeda* (New York: The New Press, 2006). 312-313.
184 Woodworth, "Why Do They Kill? The Basque Conflict in Spain." 7.
185 Van Dick and Kerschreiter, "The Social Identity Approach to Effective Leadership: An Overview and Some Ideas on Cross-Cultural Generalisability." 364.
186 Van Dick and Kerschreiter, "The Social Identity Approach to Effective Leadership: An Overview and Some Ideas on Cross-Cultural Generalisability." 364.

the organisation. Consequently, success or otherwise for the organisation are reflected as personal outcomes, with this being recognised as a tool of leverage, particularly within military units.[187] The risk to organisational cohesion can however occur on two fronts. Firstly, if the alignment of organisational objectives differs to that of the individual, continued commitment to the group may be compromised. And second, if the organisation engages in actions against its membership then individuals may be forced to question their loyalty to the organisation. For ETA, perhaps more than government counter initiatives, it was a failure to appreciate this aspect of individual and group dynamics that would lead to their demise.

Terror attacks and counteractions continued throughout the 1980s and 1990s however in the early 1990's overt public rejection of ETA as a movement began to occur within the Basque region itself. This culminated with the formation of a grassroots counter movement that adopted its own symbology (a blue ribbon) and emblem.[188] It can be argued that ETA was in effect waging an insurgency against Spain, and as Kilcullen articulates, popular support is a central tenet of an insurgency:

> The centre of gravity of an insurgent movement – the source of power from which it derives its morale, its physical strength, its freedom of action, and its will to act – is its connectivity with the local population in a given area.[189]

ETA was losing control of one of the fundamentals required to achieve its political objective and, importantly, its recruitment and retention abilities suffered.

In addition to this broader rejection occurring throughout the general populace, social reinsertion initiatives were proving successful in degrading ETA's cohesion by affording those individuals that left ETA a life free from prosecution. The actions taken by ETA to counter this membership abandonment is assessed as being central to the organisational demise. This is largely linked to the broader psychological impacts associated with an organisation 'turning' on its membership

---

187 Boas Shamir et al., "Leadership and Social Identification in Military Units: Direct and Indirect Relationships," *Journal of Applied Social Psychology* 20, no. 3 (2000): 612–40.
188 Bew, Frampton, and Gurruchaga, *Talking to Terrorists: Making Peace in Northern Ireland and the Basque Country*. 215-220
189 David Kilcullen, *Counter Insurgency* (Carlton North: Scribe Publications, 2010). 7.

and the cascading effects of individual disillusionment leading to disengagement. ETA sought to increase the costs associated with exiting the organisation. They did this predictably via coercion through threats of and infliction of physical harm (including murder) to those that may have been considering abandoning the organisation.[190] Intimidation also extended to the family unit via a form of social pressure, effectively public shaming the member's extended family.[191] These actions were largely unsuccessful with mistreatment, loss of social support and disillusionment with the group's hypocrisy, being identified as the very reasons contributing to individual disengagement with ETA.[192] In the case of ETA, this cumulative mistreatment of individuals by leadership had in fact compromised the salience of the group and the psychological link integral to effective leadership.[193]

ETA had in large part lost its way. Their political objectives had effectively been achieved, popular support was waning, organisational leadership was fractured and individual disengagement was proving problematic. Although terrorist actions continued throughout the 1990s and into the new millennium, the tide had turned for ETA being revered as viable or effective terrorist organisation seeking political objectives through coercion. Ironically it would be the 2004 *Al-Qaeda* led Madrid train bombings that would signal the end for ETA. This action simply reinforced the Spanish repulsion for terrorism, enabling the security apparatus to arrest the remaining elements of ETA's senior leadership.[194]

Conclusions

Euskadi ta Askatasun will always exist assuming there are pockets of the Basque community that perceive inequities or repression are being

190 Alonso, "Why Do Terrorists Stop? Analysing Why ETA Members Abandon or Continue with Terrorism." 701-702.

191 Alonso, "Why Do Terrorists Stop? Analysing Why ETA Members Abandon or Continue with Terrorism." 701-702.

192 Paul Gill, Noemie Bouhana, and John Morrison, "Individual Disengagement from Terrorist Groups," in *Terrorism and Political Violence*, ed. Caroline Kenndey-Pipe, Gordon Clubb, and Simon Mabon (London: SAGE Publications Ltd, 2015), 243–67.

193 Gill, Bouhana, and Morrison, "Individual Disengagement from Terrorist Groups." 246.; Matthew J. Slater, Andrew L. Evans, and Martin J. Turner, "Implementing a Social Identity Approach for Effective Change Management," *Journal of Change Management* 16, no. 1 (2016): 18–19.

194 Spindlove and Simonsen, *Terrorism Today: The Past, The Players and The Future.* 145-146.

imposed on them. Their effectiveness as a violent political movement, however, has been fractured due to the loss of a legitimate political objective and a rejection of their ideals by the organic Basque and wider population. This is perhaps typified by the surrendering of arms in 2017.[195] For a period ETA was successful in the application of violence to support the attainment of a political objective, in this case, the autonomous recognition of the Basque people. However, a failure to recognise the effectiveness of shifts in government-led counter-terrorist actions triggered the demise of ETA as an effective force. The Spanish government successfully switched to a softer and more inclusive approach to counter-terrorism with the granting of Basque autonomy proving largely successful in delegitimising ETA as an organisation. As popular support and retention of membership suffered, a failure within ETA's leadership led to the implementation of policies aimed at securing retention, with the outcome running counter to intent. The lessons that can be drawn from the Spanish and ETA experience with counter-terrorism provide valuable insights on the effectiveness of government-led counter-terror actions. And it must be said, if viewed from the terrorist perspective, yields valuable insight into the actions that should be taken to guard against membership decay to the betterment of organisational cohesion. The reality relating to this field is that as professional reflection drives improvements to counter terror initiatives a counter-narrative also exists. It is also highly probably the leadership groups with existing and future terror organisations will garner insight from historical reflections on how best to employ violence in support of their political objectives so as to retain organisational legitimacy.

---

195 Powell, "ETA's Weapons Surrender Brings to an End 50 Years of Killing."

Contemporary Terrorism

Essay 4

Contemporary Terrorism - Tactics and Techniques Brief *(Written 2019)*

Executive Summary

As at early March 2019, political leaders are poised to declare the Islamic State (IS) defeated, with President Trump declaring the Caliphate 100 per cent defeated in Syria.[196] Many, however, view these comments with a degree of scepticism, perhaps more accurately with some genuine concern regarding the short-sightedness of such assessments.[197] The reality is that the vast majority of what was the physical terrain once held by IS has been retaken, with only small and functionally dislocated pockets of resistance remaining.[198] This brief will seek first to inform decision-makers about the probable future tactical and operational actions of IS and secondly define how these may present within the operational environment. Historical example as applicable will be used to justify the assessments made.

It is assessed that the IS strategic objective remains extant, being, the replacement of "apostate" regimes with an Islamic State governed by sharia law.[199] However, the result of recent operational successes against IS has triggered a shift in tactical action and operational strategy.[200] It is assessed that probable future trends will include:

---

196 Katie Rogers, Rukmini Callimachi, and Helene Cooper, "Trump Declares ISIS '100%' Defeated in Syria. '100% Not True,' Ground Reports Say.," *New York Times*, February 28, 2019.

197 Rogers, Callimachi, and Cooper, "Trump Declares ISIS '100%' Defeated in Syria. '100% Not True,' Ground Reports Say."

198 Robert Leonhard, *The Art of Maneuver: Maneuver-Warfare Theory and the Airland Battle* (Novato: Presido Press, 1991). 61-77.

199 Fawaz A Gerges, *ISIS: A History* (Princeton: Princeton University Press, 2016). 7

200 Ryan Browne, "Top US General in Middle East Says Fight against ISIS 'far from Over,'" *CNN Politics*, 2019, https://edition.cnn.com/2019/03/07/politics/votel-isis-fight/index.html.

1. A reversion to proven guerrilla and insurgent tactics that seek to challenge the political control within Iraq through subversion and targeted violence.[201] This is being driven by the lack of physical terrain held by IS;

2. It is likely remaining fighters will seek to withdraw into complex terrain, most likely the complex urban terrain, to remain below the security detection threshold as demonstrated by IS leader Abu Bakr al Baghdadi notable absence from the remaining areas of the recognised caliphate;[202]

3. In conjunction with traditional forms of armed attack, it is likely that low cost, low tech actions with high yield potential will be pursued which will enable the continued reinforcement of IS legitimacy within the informational domain;[203]

4. Initial targets within the complex urban terrain may be misconstrued as criminal acts, murder as an example, is more likely to be targeted assassination based on an individual's alignment with given factions and more likely represent moves to dominate an urban area; and

5. The ability for the sovereign security forces to enact independent counter-terrorism actions to self-manage this threat will be critical in avoiding an escalation spiral that will see foreign troops directly targeted and drawn in the ongoing stabilisation actions.[204]

Contextual Background

The Islamic State (IS) as it will be referred to (includes ISIL and ISIS manifestations) came into existence in the early 2000s when Abu Musab al

---

201 Norman Wade, *The Military Engagement Security, Co-operation and Stability Smartbook: Foreign Train, Advise and Assist* (Lakeland: The Lightning Press, 2016). 1-12: Hamdi Malik, "Iraqis Divided over Continued Presence of American Forces," *AL-Monitor*, March 2, 2019: https://iraq.liveuamap.com/en/2019/24-february-the-directorate-of-iraqi-military-intelligence. Bulos, "Iraq's New War against Islamic State: Halting the Groups Budding Rural Resurgence."

202 Chris Massaro, "As Caliphate Crumbles, ISIS Fighters Rage over Absent Leader Al-Baghdadi," *Fox News*, 2019, https://www.foxnews.com/world/as-caliphate-crumbles-isis-fighters-rage-over-absent-leader-al-baghdadi.; https://isis.liveuamap.com/en/2019/17-february-more-than-1000-isis-fighters-have-likely-fled

203 Salih Elias, "Two Dead, 24 Wounded in Blast in Central Mosul," *Reuters World News*, March 1, 2019.

204 Wade, *The Military Engagement Security, Cooperation and Stability Smartbook: Foreign Train, Advise and Assist.* 2-1b.

Zarqawi, the first recognised leader, commenced the training of extremist militants.[205] IS began as a stateless organisation founded on Salafi-jihadism ideology[206]. Due to rapid shifts in regional stability IS effectively exploited power vacuums resulting in significant increases in its membership and standing within the extremist Islamist community. This was aided by an effective informational campaign by al Zarqawi. He sought to position himself as the global leader on Salafi-Jihadist thought by openly dismissing strategic direction from the leadership of Al-Qaeda in Iraq (AQI) and by publishing his thoughts on Salafism on contemporary websites.[207] This is important to appreciate, as IS's maturation, commencing in 2014 is largely attributable to a highly effective information campaign. This campaign identified the proven opportunities for recruitment and support to strategic objectives if the contemporary informational domain was leveraged effectively.[208] This was appreciated by al-Zarqawi and leveraged by recording barbaric acts of torture and death.[209]

The resultant terror that can be generated through these violent acts can enable strategic objectives. It is assessed therefore that the application of terror was deliberate and targeted seeking to generate reactions from multiple audiences all of which combined to enable the rapid rise of IS. When analysing the links from tactical action to strategic objectives a 'threat triad' will be used to contextualise actions and consists of three components:

1. The aim of the Terrorist act
2. Targets of the Terrorist act; and
3. Type of terrorist act.

Aims

As indicated, the strategic objective of the Islamic State was the establishment of a caliphate and appreciating this allows their previous operational and tactical actions to be understood. It also allows likely

205 Stanford_University, "The Islamic State," *Mapping Militant Organisations: The Islamic State*, 2019, web.stanford.edu/group/mappingmilitants/cgi-bin/groups/view/1.
206 Gerges, *ISIS: A History*. 10.
207 Stanford_University, "The Islamic State."
208 Abdel Bari Atwan, "Masters of the Digital Universe," in *Islamic State: The Digital Caliphate* (Oakland: Saqi Books, 2015), 15–32.
209 Atwan, "Masters of the Digital Universe."

actions to be predicted in what could be referred to as a period of retrograde action.[210] For radical change to be successful (in this case governance in Syria and Iraq) popular support and a viable alternative are required.[211] IS, under Abu Bakr al-Baghdadi (real name Ibrahim Awwad Ibrahim Ali al-Badri) appreciated this, and from a change implementation perspective, explains operational actions that occurred during 2012 and 2013.

Popular support can be achieved through coercion or through popular mobilisation and mass complicity.[212] Popular mobilisation can be achieved by discrediting the existing government and security apparatus, whilst simultaneously presenting as a viable alternative.[213]

The "Breaking Down the Walls' campaign in 2012 acted as a key catalyst for IS growth.[214] First, it clearly undermined the legitimacy of the Maliki government in Iraq at the time, whilst also generating popular support and respect for al-Baghdadi as a leader.[215] A secondary campaign referred to as the "Soldiers Harvest" sought to further undermine the legitimacy of the government by demonstrating the ineptitude of the security forces of the time. These operational actions did achieve the intended effect, being to delegitimise the government and generating popular support. This popular support culminated in overt civil disobedience toward security forces in late 2013.[216] It was shortly thereafter that al-Baghdadi rebranded his leadership from AQI to the Islamic State in Iraq and Syria (ISIL).

The key objective of these actions was to provoke action from the global security apparatus, a proven terrorist tactic, which in turn would feed the mobilisation objective by reinforcing the ideological Salafi-jihadist narrative of a clash of civilisations.[217] Clearly, this was successful, when on September 2014 the United States and other willing coalition partners commenced kinetic action against IS.[218] This generated the

210 Browne, "Top US General in Middle East Says Fight against ISIS 'far from Over.'"
211 Martha Crenshaw, "The Logic of Terrorism," in *Explaining Terrorism: Causes, Processes, and Consequences* (New York: Routledge, 2011), 111–112.
212 A K Cronin, "Chapter One: The Strategies of Terrorism," *The Adelphi Papers* 47, no. 394 (2007): 11–22.
213 Cronin, "Chapter One: The Strategies of Terrorism." 19.
214 Stanford_University, "The Islamic State."
215 Gerges, *ISIS: A History.* 122
216 Stanford_University, "The Islamic State."
217 Gerges, *ISIS: A History.* 10: Cronin, "Chapter One: The Strategies of Terrorism." 17
218 Stanford_University, "The Islamic State."

desired response with many globally dislocated Islamist groups pledging allegiance to IS and a flow of voluntary fighters both domestically and internationally responded to the call to arms.[219]

Targets and Types

With the operational conditions set to support the Islamic States strategic objective, their application of terror actions at the tactical level can be analysed in greater detail. It is important to note that this will analyse actions during the organisation's growth phase, as their likely future actions, driven by a loss of physical terrain, are assessed as being different. It does, however, inform intent and provide an indication of likely action.

There are two groups within society that have clearly received deliberate targeting from IS throughout 2012-2017 with these being the military and private citizens with the latter making up 46 per cent of IS targets during this period (as highlighted in figure 1).[220] If the military includes 'police' as representing Iraq's security apparatus, the attacks equate to over 40 per cent of IS actions. This is not unsurprising, as 'conventional warfare' as IS was arguably waging from 2014, sees the operational requirement of seizing terrain.[221] Consequently, militaries will be a primary target, as will the need to coerce, compel or conquer the host populace to support your intent as required.

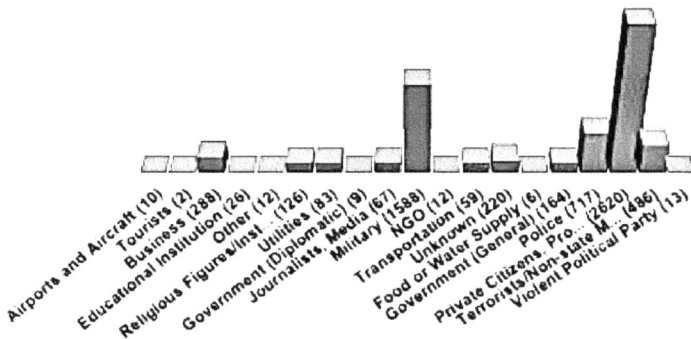

Figure 1: ISIL Targets by Group

219 Stanford_University, "The Islamic State."
220 "Global Terrorism Database: ISIL," *Study of Terrorism and Responses to Terrorism*, 2019.
221 Brandon Webb, Jack Murphy, and Peter Nealen, *The Isis Solution: How Unconventional Thinking and Special Operations Can Eliminate Radical Islam* (New York: St. Martins Press, 2016). 25-36.

Figure 2 highlights the methods of attack used against the groups highlighted above. By a clear margin, the primary method of attack was bombing or explosions, equating to over 65 per cent of kinetic action.[222] Other than 'unknown' actions, the next significant group was hostage taking by kidnapping representing approximately 10 per cent of terror acts.

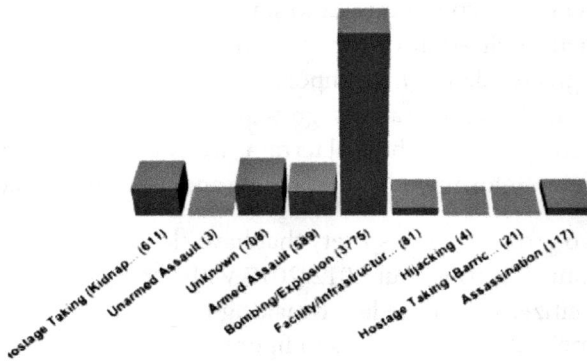

Figure 2: ISIL Targets by Attack Type

One of the smaller groups by frequency, representing less than 1 per cent of terrorist incidents, was the hostage-taking 'Barbaric act'. This, however, became a hallmark of IS tactical action generating global terror, feeding recruitment demand, achieving compliance within host populations and stimulating a response from apostate and infidel regimes (which in turn reinforced their strategic narrative). It is the effect generated by these barbaric acts, particularly with regard to brand identity and relevance that can inform likely IS future actions.

Future Actions

At the height of its power in 2015-2016 IS was functioning as a state. It had recognised systems to generate income to support its ministries and had clearly established their own security organisations that sought to implement Sharia law.[223] This is not unsurprising and indicative of an appreciation of past jihadist theories which articulate the steps required to garner popular support or requirements to coerce doubters to align to

222 "Global Terrorism Database: ISIL."
223 Stanford_University, "The Islamic State."

the jihadist approach.[224] It is only by appreciating this link to established jihadist principals can IS terror targets and their types of attack be understood.

The current ground situation, as highlighted in the media, sees IS largely defeated when it comes to holding physical terrain in either Syria or Iraq.[225] However, the loss of terrain does not equate to the defeat of an ideology with many, rightly, predicting a resurgence of IS.[226] The indicators of tactical shifts and their ability to regroup during a period of retrograde actions will result in a shift in how IS executes kinetic actions. Having lost their ability to engage in what were effectively conventional operations, IS has been forced to sacrifice terrain, for time, reverting instead to proven guerrilla and insurgent actions.[227] It is assessed that this is already occurring and will manifest in the following manner.

1. Defeated IS fighters will seek to withdraw into complex terrain, both complex urban terrain and relatively lawless unpoliced and isolated areas.[228] They will achieve this by presenting as fleeing non-combatants seeking refuge.[229] Those who are successful in this will go through a period of low-level recuperation, gradually re-establishing decentralised networks of contacts and then execute pre-planned tactical action in support of the strategic objective, which remains unchanged.[230]

2. The initial actions are likely to include the targeted assassination of individuals who support those engaged in actions to defeat IS. If viewed in isolation and not recognised as a shift in strategy, these could simply be misconstrued as criminal acts. The recent murder

224 Jarret Brachman, "Strategists," in *Global Jihadism: Theory and Practice* (Routledge, 2009), 79–105.
225 Browne, "Top US General in Middle East Says Fight against ISIS 'far from Over.'"
226 "IS Is Down but Not out," *The Canberra Times*, March 6, 2019.
227 Mao, "Selected Works of Mao Tse-Tung," *Foreign Languages Press* II, no. May 1938 (1967): 1–26. A. Merari, "Terrorism as a Strategy of Insurgency," in *The History of Terrorism: From Antiquity to Al Qaeda*, ed. G Chaliand and A Blin (Berkeley: University of California Press, 2007), 12–54.
228 Arwa Damon et al., "Iraq Defeated ISIS More than a Year Ago. The Group's Revival Is Already Underway," *CNN World*, March 5, 2019.
229 Sarah El Deeb, "Hundreds Leave IS-Held Area in Syria as Fighting Slows down," *AP News*, 2019.
230 Browne, "Top US General in Middle East Says Fight against ISIS 'far from Over.'"

of a respected western aligned journalist in Baghdad and murders of regional local leaders could be indicative of these initial actions.[231]

3. Traditional insurgent targets including government officials or institutions seen to be western in nature or not aligned to IS Salafi ideology are then likely to be targeted.[232] This could occur through targeted assassination or larger high profile attacks employing improvised explosives such as the recent bombing of the Mosul University.[233] These actions achieve the dual effects of continuing to undermine the legitimacy of the perceived apostate governments and security institutions, whilst simultaneously maintaining the organisation's legitimacy through information operations in the media and internet.[234] Perhaps of more risk is that these actions will continue to generate distrust within the Iraqi populace stimulating discord along religious fissures. This, in turn, will severely hinder a return to normalcy within the region.

4. Revenue generation is likely to be sourced through kidnap and ransom. Foreign journalist, diplomats, aid workers, stabilisation professional's or poorly protected military operations aligned to non-combat missions such as the United Nations Assistance Mission Iraq (UNAMI) and NATO Mission Iraq (NMI) may be vulnerable.[235] This group may also be vulnerable to proven low tech targeting techniques such as vehicular convoy ramming followed by armed assault and or the application or IED's (both vehicle borne and suicide).[236] Such attacks and kidnapping will be exploited within the informational domain and in the worst case be associated with

231 "Rights Group Urges Investigations in Murder of Journalist East of Baghdad," *The Baghdad Post*, 2019: https://iraq.liveuamap.com/en/2019/2-february-unknown-armed-men-assassinated-alaa-mashdhub-iraqi:. https://iraq.liveuamap.com/en/2019/3-february-is-militants-claim-house-raid-that-killed-the; https://isis.liveuamap.com/en/2019/28-january-isis-executed-two-men-and-kidnapped-a-third-during
232 Edward H Price, "The Strategy and Tactics of Revolutionary Terrorism," *Comparative Studies in Society and History* 19, no. 1 (1977): 52–66.
233 Elias, "Two Dead, 24 Wounded in Blast in Central Mosul."; Adbul-Zahra Qassim, "Bombs in Iraq's Mosul Kill 1 Person, Injure 17," *AP News*, 2019, https://www.apnews.com/0256fd63080847c89885ae038b31f546.
234 Atwan, "Masters of the Digital Universe." 17-21.
235 "UN Assistance Mission for Iraq," *United Nations Iraq*, 2019.; "NATO Mission Iraq (NMI)," *NATO Factsheet*, 2018.
236 Brian Jenkins and Bruce Butterworth, "An Analysis of Vehicle Ramming as a Terrorist Tactic", *Security Perspective*, 2018.

the 'Barbaric act' as defined by the Global Terrorism Data Base. The counteraction may in fact may achieve the intent of provoking a disproportionate effect from the domestic and foreign security apparatus.

Conclusion

It is assessed that this shift of tactical action in support of the Islamic State's extant strategic objective is currently occurring and in an embryonic state. These are likely the immediate actions in a longer premediated shift in strategy. At the operational level, these actions will likely increase along religious lines to hinder attempts at stabilisation post the conventional defeat of IS. There are long term risks that need to be considered surrounding the management of captured IS fighters and how their treatment by given countries and against what laws can potentially be exploited to reinforce the strategic narrative. The other longer-term risk, which is assessed as an operational line of action, will be the repatriation of 'remorseful' IS members to their country of origin. This may be an unavoidable reality associated with laws relating to individual statelessness. However, it is likely a percentage of these individuals will be well received by disenfranchised pockets of society, held in high regard as successful jihadists, and stimulate radicalised growth for the next iteration of Islamist extremist organisation. Countering this potentiality requires deliberate, and arguably, grand strategic consideration from governments and the global community, as the ability to counter the fervent ideology that exists, is central to the true defeat of IS. The loss of the physical caliphate has done little to negate this reality.

Contemporary Jihadist 'Information Operations'/ Propaganda has proved effective. Discuss, ensuring you define effectiveness *(Written 2019)*

Introduction

It is difficult in the contemporary Jihadist context to approach this question without defining what is first meant by 'Contemporary Jihadists' and secondly what entails Information Operations and or Propaganda. Without defining these aspects, effectiveness cannot be determined. For the purposes of this discussion, the contemporary Jihadist organisation that will be used to guide the discussion will be the Islamic State of Iraq and Syria (ISIS or simply the Islamic State). ISIS is the contemporary darling of the Salafi-Jihadists movement and arguably achieved in two years what Al-Qaeda was unable to achieve in decades.[237] ISIS communicated a clear strategic objective being the replacement of apostate regimes with an Islamic State, a Caliphate.[238] Armed with this concise, exploitable and relatable message, ISIS experienced a meteoric rise in prominence in the years following the United States withdrawal from Iraq in 2011. They established strong brand identification, subsequently connecting with a global audience, eager to support their objectives. This culminated on the 29th of June 2014 when Abu Bakr Al-Baghdadi rose to the pulpit of the grand Mosque in the recently conquered city of Mosul and self-declared as leader of the newly established caliphate.[239] He was the caliph and hence the true leader of contemporary Jihadists globally. Previous frictions and power-

---

237 Fawaz A Gerges, *ISIS: A History* (Princeton: Princeton University Press, 2016). 24; Benjamin Hall, *Inside ISIS: The Brutal Rise of a Terrorist Army* (New York: Hachette Book Group, 2015). 5.
238 Gerges, *ISIS: A History*. 7.
239 Hall, *Inside ISIS: The Brutal Rise of a Terrorist Army.*

plays within the contemporary Jihadists' political architecture should cease. Televising this address was a deliberate action to communicate to multiple audiences.

This paper, however, will argue that the effectiveness of ISIS's Information Operations campaign, although operationally effective, has ultimately run counter to the organisation's strategic objectives. As of early 2019 the physical caliphate, trumpeted by the ISIS media machine as a call to arms, has dissolved. ISIS is not conquered as such, however, their inability to retain this terrain, replace regimes, and build a Caliphate for the loyal contemporary jihadist is clear. [240] As it currently stands, the organisation has unambiguously failed in achieving its strategic objective of establishing a physical caliphate. It is assessed that their failure to effectively employ a balanced and integrated Information Operations campaign was a central pillar in this failure.

Operations and Information

When examining terrorism strategies, it is prudent to view them in the context of the intersection between objective, target and audience.[241] In the case of ISIS, the strategic objective is clear, the establishment of an Islamic State. How this is to be achieved at an operational level and the roles that various audiences play is ultimately what forms a central component of any military strategy (terrorist or conventional). The ability to effectively leverage information to shape opinion in the interests of a desired strategic objective is hardly a revolutionary concept; the criticality of this is increasingly appreciated in contemporary military activities.[242] The ability to achieve this is known as Information Operations, which employs several information related capabilities to gain and maintain information superiority allowing commanders to seize, retain and exploit the initiative.[243] Militaries (and militants) are

240 Katie Rogers, Rukmini Callimachi, and Helene Cooper, "Trump Declares ISIS '100%' Defeated in Syria. '100% Not True,' Ground Reports Say.," *New York Times*, February 28, 2019.

241 A K Cronin, "Chapter One: The Strategies of Terrorism," *The Adelphi Papers* 47, no. 394 (2007): 11–22.

242 Leigh Armistead, *Information Operations Matters* (Virginia: Potomac Books, 2010). 45-54

243 No Author, "FM 3-13 Information Operations: Doctrine, Tactics, Techniques, and Procedures" (Fort Leavenworth: Department of the Army (US), 2003). 11.

increasingly aware of the need for Information Operations to be integral in any military campaign and fully harmonised in support of other military actions, such as combat actions.[244]

In the case of ISIS, they were acutely aware of this requirement employing several information related capabilities to great effect. They did this in a deliberate and concurrent manner with messaging tailored to suit specific audiences. What components combine to constitute an Information Operations campaign will vary dependant on what source document is employed. However, there are several widely recognised information related capabilities that will be used to demonstrate levels of effectiveness by ISIS at varying times of their campaign. Their ability to employ Operational Imagery in support of a deliberate Public Affairs campaign is an example of effectiveness with regards to the recruitment of foreign fighters.[245] Additionally, they employed elements of Civil-Military co-operation and Key Leader Engagement to establish support from host (or conquered) communities.[246] The importance of this line of effort cannot be understated. A proven tool in counter-terrorism or counter-insurgent operations is the ability for legitimate forces to garner support from the host populace.[247] It is a prized treasure of the belligerent. ISIS identified this likely counter-action and sought to blunt the security response prior to inception. They also employed other information related capabilities such as Counter Intelligence, Posture presence and Profile, Information assurance, Electronic Warfare and Operations Security.[248]

These, when combined, allowed ISIS to generate waves of propaganda in support of their operational and strategic objectives. An individual's response to this informational campaign is dependent on where and within what audience an individual resides. For the host populace in the conquered areas of the Caliphate, it may well equate

---

244 Author, "FM 3-13 Information Operations: Doctrine, Tactics, Techniques, and Procedures." 11.

245 No Author, "Operation Series: Information Activities," *Australian Defence Doctrine Publication 3.13*, 2013, http://www.defence.gov.au/FOI/Docs/Disclosures/330_1314_Document.pdf. 1-3: James P Farwell, "The Media Strategy of ISIS," *Survival: Global Politics and Strategy* 56, no. 6 (2014): 49.

246 Aymenn Jawad Al-Tamimi, "The Dawn of the Islamic State of Iraq and Ash-Sham," *Current Trends in Islamist Ideology* 16 (2014): 5–15.

247 David Kilcullen, *Counter Insurgency* (Carlton North: Scribe Publications, 2010). 221.

248 Author, "Operation Series: Information Activities." 1-13

to compliance through coercion and fear. For the willing jihadist both internal and external to the Caliphate this clearly resulted in a form of popular mobilisation.[249] Provocation may have also been sought from Syrian, Iraqi and international security forces to undermine government legitimacy and advance ISIS Salafi ideology.[250] For ISIS however, despite their efforts to learn from historical precedent, the effectiveness of this provocation action has ultimately led to strategic failure.

Context

ISIS's ability to integrate Information Operations into their military campaign across Syria and Iraq did not simply materialise by chance, they did not create the concept. Historical precedence played a role in developing the organisational understanding of its importance. It would be inaccurate to simply view Abu Bakr Al-Baghdadi, the self-proclaimed caliph of IS, as simply a thug and murderer who managed to lead a collective group of savages. On the contrary, he was raised in a religious household on the outskirts of Baghdad, studied at the Islamic University of Baghdad and reputedly holds a Bachelors, Masters and PhD in Sharia law.[251] He commenced these studies prior to Operation Desert Storm, the United States invasion of Iraq in 1991.[252] This is important to appreciate as it helps contextualise Al-Baghdadi's ability to employ Information Operations in support of a military strategy. First, due to the field of his studies, he likely holds a deep understanding of theological Islamic texts. Consequently, he could identify what components could be leveraged for recruitment when centred on Salafi-jihadist ideology. Secondly, throughout his entire adult life, he has witnessed foreign incursion into countries and areas he would consider Muslim lands, continuing to fuel an anti-west sentiment.[253] And finally, he has witnessed the ebb and flow of numerous Jihadists organisations. Therefore, given his demonstrated ability to learn, he can likely adjust his proposed operational strategies based on proven historical failures.

---

249 Cronin, "Chapter One: The Strategies of Terrorism." 19-20.
250 Cronin, "Chapter One: The Strategies of Terrorism." 17-18.
251 Hall, *Inside ISIS: The Brutal Rise of a Terrorist Army*. 23.
252 Andreas John. Olsen, "Operation Desert Storm 1991," in *A History of Air Warfare*, ed. John Andreas Olsen (Washington D.C.: Potomac Books, 2010), 177–200.
253 Gerges, *ISIS: A History*. 131.

The application of espionage and propaganda can be gleaned from the Koran with sword verses highlighting the following 'Slay the Pagans wherever ye find them, and seize them, beleaguer them, and lie in wait for them in every stratagem of war'.[254] The prophet Muhammed (PBUH) is also reported to have employed a network of spies who utilised espionage and counter-espionage. The application of these capabilities is assessed as being integral to the conquest of the Arabian Peninsula.[255] In addition to countering assassination attempts, propaganda was also a tactic employed by the prophet Muhummad (PBUH) to generate friction amongst the factions of his enemies.[256] The 'Isma'ilis' sect established an intelligence service that would infiltrate normal society to nurture anti-government sentiment; this would effectively create instability through the dissemination of information (or misinformation).[257]

It is not surprising then that ISIS had its own internal intelligence apparatus known as the '*Emni*' who sought to spread ISIS propaganda and fear to an internal ISIS audience and a wider external audience.[258] Additionally, they deployed a network of spies to monitor the actions of fleeing refugees and also vetted new recruits.[259] This is effectively the application of counter-intelligence, being the ability to detect, identify, assess, counter, neutralise or exploit hostile intelligence and is a key Information Operations capability.[260] It is highly probable that Al-Baghdadi's incorporation of the ISIS *Emni* into Caliphate business was in large part informed by his understanding of these ancient historical precedents.

More recently, however, the actions of earlier manifestations of ISIS have proven productive in informing contemporary Information Operations, particularly in the field of public relations. In the late 1990's, Al Zarqawi, the godfather of IS, was introduced to a Kurdish Jihadist group known

254 Patrick Sookhdeo, *Understanding Islamist Terrorism: The Islamic Doctrine of War* (McLean: Isaac Publishing, 2009). 52-52
255 Sookhdeo, *Understanding Islamist Terrorism: The Islamic Doctrine of War*. 52-53
256 Sookhdeo, *Understanding Islamist Terrorism: The Islamic Doctrine of War*. 52-53
257 Sookhdeo, *Understanding Islamist Terrorism: The Islamic Doctrine of War*. 91-92
258 Anne Speckhard and Ahmet Yayla, "The ISIS Emni: Origins and Inner Workings of ISIS's Intelligence Apparatus," *Perspectives on Terrorism* 11, no. 1 (2017): 1–15.
259 Speckhard and Yayla, "The ISIS Emni: Origins and Inner Workings of ISIS's Intelligence Apparatus." 2-10.
260 Author, "FM 3-13 Information Operations: Doctrine, Tactics, Techniques, and Procedures." 82.

as 'Ansar Al-Islam'. Ansar Al-Islam was employing initiatives that would later become central tenets in ISIS approach to operations. First, they sought to enforce their principles of governance in areas that they controlled including banning music and enforcing the wearing of veils for women. They had a reputation for beheading prisoners and were actively involved in information sharing through the internet, including a tri-lingual website.[261] It is assessed that Zarqawi recognised the potential benefits of online distribution identifying it as an opportunity to gain and maintain information superiority to seize, retain and exploit the initiative; which is the intent of Information Operations. It is apparent that this was communicated through the evolving leadership of IS including, ultimately, Al-Baghdadi. It became modus operandi in ISIS operations. As an example, when introducing governance practices into areas that ISIS had conquered it was standard practice for ISIS to do this following the opening of a *dawa*, for the sole purpose of gaining popular support for their actions.[262] This was done through key leader engagement (KLE), a proven information related capability. ISIS was attempting to employ historical precedent from ancient practice and also more contemporary actions. As will be shown, in the short term, these proved highly beneficial, but due to overreach and an inability to recognise previous failure, ISIS ultimately failed in achieving their strategic objective.

Branding

If information operations generate opportunities for a commander to seize the initiative, then Al Baghdadi's ability to employ these to exploit his position within competing jihadist networks was calculated, precise and highly effective.[263] Up until his public unveiling on the 29th of June 2014 the leadership associated with Jihadists networks, not only within the Middle East but globally, was in a state of flux.[264] This had in fact been

261 Brian H Fishman, *The Master Plan: ISIS, Al-Qaeda, and the Jihad Strategy for Final Victory.* (Yale: Yale University Press Books, 2016). 23-25
262 Speckhard and Yayla, "The ISIS Emni: Origins and Inner Workings of ISIS's Intelligence Apparatus." 4.
263 Author, "FM 3-13 Information Operations: Doctrine, Tactics, Techniques, and Procedures." 20.
264 G Weimann, "Emerging Trends," in *Terrorism in Cyberspace: The Next Generation* (New York: Columbia University Press, 2015), 2–71.

caused by the absence of effective personnel in key leadership positions caused by the death of Abu Musab Al-Zarqawi and a lack of dominant scholars within the Middle East.[265] Consequently the Al-Qaeda 'brand' was under threat from as early as 2006. The resultant was vocal insubordination from affiliate organisations whose ideological position, Salafi-Jihadist or otherwise, differed from Al-Qaeda's position.[266]

Al-Baghdadi most likely sensed the opportunity to extricate himself from the Al-Qaeda brand following Osama Bin Laden's death in 2011 and the appointment of the less revered Al-Zawahiri.[267] As such, frictions between Al-Qaeda in the Arabian Peninsula (AQAP), Al-Qaeda in Iraq (AQI and what would become ISI, ISIL, ISIS then ultimately the Islamic State) and Al-Qaeda in the Islamic Maghreb (AQIM) were ripe for exploitation. The opportunity was presented to remove 'his' organisation from the hierarchical constraints of Al-Qaeda proper, free of the assumed loyalties and constraints of a lesser subordinate affiliate.[268]

For Al-Baghdadi, the seeding of his intent came via overt insubordination of direction provided by Al-Zawahiri, the global head of Al-Qaeda writ large. In the audio message, naturally released online, Al-Baghdadi defied direction to disband the Islamic State of Iraq and the Levant (ISIL).[269] The crux of the issue was that Al-Baghdadi had expanded his operations from the Islamic State in Iraq (ISI) to now include geographical regions within Syria resulting in his organisation, ISIL, encroaching on another Al-Qaeda affiliate's terrain, being the Al-Nusra front.[270] From a leadership perspective, the management of this issue was poor; Ayman Al-Zawahiri was tested, and he failed. Significant amounts of online chatter associated with the recording, Al-Zawahiri's mismanagement of the issue and his inability to control subordinates resulted in doubts around his capacity to

---

265 Weimann, "Emerging Trends." 32.

266 Weimann, "Emerging Trends." 32-33.

267 Bruce Hoffman and Fernando Reinares, "Conclusion," in *The Evolution of the Global Terrorist Threat: From 9/11 to Osama Bin Laden's Death.*, ed. Bruce Hoffman and Fernando Reinares (New York: Columbia University Press, 2014), 635.

268 Barak Mendelsohn, "Formal Organisational Expansion," in *The Al-Qaeda Franchise: The Expansion of Al-Qaeda and Its Consequences* (Oxford: Oxford University Press, 2009) 9. Hoffman and Reinares, "Conclusion." 621.

269 Weimann, "Emerging Trends."33.

270 Hall, *Inside ISIS: The Brutal Rise of a Terrorist Army.* 46-52.

act as leader for the global Jihadist cause.[271] Al-Qaeda's sparkle was fading and Al-Zawahiri sensed it. In a final attempt to exert control and re-establish command over Al-Qaeda's various branches and affiliates, ISIL and Al-Baghdadi were disavowed and their actions, (read strategic intent and operational methodology) rejected.[272]

This outcome most likely served Al-Baghdadi's intent, as although he disobeyed direction, he had never vocally challenged Al-Zawahiri's leadership. Now, as an outcast, if he were to pose an alternate global organisation, it would be done from the moral perspective of an individual offering an alternative, and not seeking necessarily to usurp or destabilise the leadership. It is assessed as a deft political move that could offer individuals and organisations dissatisfied with Al-Qaeda's leadership and vision, a viable alternative that would allow expansion under a unification strategy.[273]

With the cracks present, Al-Baghdadi sought to exploit the sectarian divisions to generate increased levels of support in Iraq and Syria.[274] Leading from the front, or within battle is central to the Islamic State brand.[275] Al-Baghdadi understood this, arguably cultivated it, and sought to exploit the remoteness of Al-Zawahiri whilst simultaneously leveraging historical precedent and apocalyptical messaging to build his brand. The most notable form of ISIS branding, the Black flag, leveraged historical linkages to the Prophet Muhammad's flag.[276] This, when coupled with a narrative articulating that the apocalypse or end of days is under way within the holy lands of Syria and Iraq, becomes a powerful tool in fomenting support.[277]

Thus, on the first night of Ramadan 2014, Al-Baghdadi announced himself as Caliph of the re-established Caliphate.[278] It mattered not that a large portion of the Muslim world saw this as void under sharia law;

271 Daniel Byman, *Al Qaeda, the Islamic State and the Global Jihadist Movement* (London: Oxford University Press, 2015). 6.
272 Al-Tamimi, "The Dawn of the Islamic State of Iraq and Ash-Sham." 5-6.
273 Barak Mendelsohn, "Formal Organisational Expansion," in *The Al-Qaeda Franchise: The Expansion of Al-Qaeda and Its Consequences* (Oxford: Oxford University Press, 2009), 14-15.
274 Daniel Byman, *Al Qaeda, the Islamic State and the Global Jihadist Movement* (London: Oxford University Press, 2015). 171.
275 Byman, *Al Qaeda, the Islamic State and the Global Jihadist Movement*. 171.
276 Byman, *Al Qaeda, the Islamic State and the Global Jihadist Movement*. 171.
277 Byman, *Al Qaeda, the Islamic State and the Global Jihadist Movement*. 171-172.
278 Byman, *Al Qaeda, the Islamic State and the Global Jihadist Movement*. 165.

the fact was he had positioned himself as a religious leader and support via religious channels was not only implicit but expected.[279] He further cemented his position as legitimate Caliph during his address from the Mosul Grand Mosque on the 29th of June 2014.[280] Prior to its fall, Mosul represented what a religiously diverse city could achieve, including cohabitation of various religions and co-ed schools.[281] Its fall, and the subsequent destruction of Christian Churches, Shia Mosque's and summary executions fed the propaganda machine. The video files of this address spread through predictable and rampant online dissemination, proclaiming that the Caliphate was real. Al-Baghdadi's transition to Caliph was complete and his support base stimulated.

The Communication process is thought to have six components, the source of the message, the message itself, the audience, communication mediums, the purpose of the message and the effect of the message.[282] From a strategic communication and Information Operation perspective, Al-Baghdadi could be commended. The effects he achieved, by generating the opportunity to seize command of a fracturing Jihadist community and position himself as the existing authority was the execution of a highly efficient absorption strategy.[283] It was clear to all audiences, the disenfranchised potential recruit, the self-revered Jihadist scholar, the proclaimed leader of lesser Jihadist organisations and clearly the global intelligentsia, that the one and only, the preeminent authority on the Salafi-Jihadists movement was the Islamic State. There was but one authoritative voice. The Caliph, Abu Bakr al-Baghdadi.[284]

By identifying as the Caliph, Al-Baghdadi was claiming authority 'by the order of God' and as Mendelsohn rightly states, an absorption strategy is 'less a merger than an acquisition' and individuals harbouring a version of Salafi-Jihadist Grand Strategy were obliged to fall into line with his intent.[285] This was a precise and deliberately

---

279 Hall, *Inside ISIS: The Brutal Rise of a Terrorist Army.* 63.

280 Hall, *Inside ISIS: The Brutal Rise of a Terrorist Army.* 63.

281 Fishman, *The Master Plan: ISIS, Al-Qaeda, and the Jihad Strategy for Final Victory.* 199-200

282 P Seib and D Janbek, "Terrorists' Online Strategies," in *Global Terrorism and the New Media* (New York: Routledge, 2011), 45.

283 Mendelsohn, "Formal Organisational Expansion." 10-11.

284 Hall, *Inside ISIS: The Brutal Rise of a Terrorist Army.* 62-65.

285 Hall, *Inside ISIS: The Brutal Rise of a Terrorist Army.* 63. Mendelsohn, "Formal Organisational Expansion." 10-11.

orchestrated communication strategy that leveraged the information related capabilities of public affairs, operational imagery, psychological operations and posture, presence and profile.[286] The results generated ideological uniformity, leveraged public appeal, centralised power and achieved the resultant condition for absolute domination of the Jihadist terrorism narrative. The conditions were set for the execution of his grandiose vision.

Appeal

Having established the conditions to build his vision, Al-Baghdadi needed to focus efforts on the recruitment of an employable workforce. When considering this, the reality is both internal (to Iraq and Syria) and external sources of recruitment need consideration. Al-Baghdadi's strategy differed from previous Al-Qaeda strategies, such as targeting the near or the far enemy, which largely focused on attacking interventionist countries.[287] ISIS, rather, had an intent to firstly establish a state, then purge it of perceived enemies, be that incongruent government or any religious organisation that differed from the Caliph's view.[288] From here expansion would come. The far enemy could wait. In large part, internal recruitment sources such as smaller affiliates or the disenfranchised within Iraq and Syria willingly offered their support based on Al-Baghdadi's well-executed communication strategy. In short, those that could be swayed based on the apocalyptical message being communicated to an audience in proximity to the 'action', were.[289]

His vision, however, demanded more. It needed a commitment from individuals geographically dislocated from the Caliphate. This audience needed to become willing participants and offer support on multiple fronts, be that through financial support or individual commitment to the Jihad. The message was clear, 'the Caliphate is re-established, come and fulfil your religious duty of advancing Salafi-Jihadist ideals'.[290] To achieve market reach into these external audiences and stimulate the motivational drivers for commitment, an effective engagement

---

286 Author, "Operation Series: Information Activities." 13.
287 Fawaz Gerges, *Rise and Fall of Al-Qaeda* (New York: Oxford University Press, 2011). 48.
288 Byman, *Al Qaeda, the Islamic State and the Global Jihadist Movement.* 170.
289 Byman, *Al-Qaeda, the Islamic State and the Global Jihadist Movement.* 171.
290 Farwell, "The Media Strategy of ISIS." 49.

strategy would be required.[291] It is no surprise then that the Islamic State's recruitment drive leveraged the online medium and was hugely successful. They had several factors playing to their advantage.

First, as previously discussed, they had learnt from historical precedent be that from Al-Zawahiri, or Al-Zarqawi or Al-Awlaki. Al-Baghdadi appreciated the importance of a focused recruitment strategy anchored in contemporary mediums which could be framed in easily digestible content.[292] Islamic State consequently sought out technical specialists with online marketing expertise who could develop campaigns which would appeal to their primary target audience; males in their late teens or early twenties.[293] This audience, the fighting aged male, is highly active in the online medium.[294] The outcome was a deliberate and highly orchestrated media campaign managed by the head of the IS media arm, Ahmed Abousamra.[295] Under his direction several highly professional multi-lingual media productions exemplifying the *mujahedeen* warrior ethos, or barbaric executions, were released on the world.[296] This deliberate line of effort was mutually supported by the equally effective, albeit less controllable, social media front. As such, jihadists engaging in battle within the Caliphate would communicate their actions through contemporary media platforms, crafting an image of 'jihadi cool' to an insatiable and growing audience.[297] To the geographically dislocated, these supporting lines of communication combined to deliver a powerful recruitment pull and in contemporary parlance, a severe case of FOMO.

It would be a failure of analysis to suggest this was the only target audience ISIS sought to recruit; after all, what better way to build a future force than through self-generation. Thus, deliberate campaigns that sought to target women and children or 'cubs of the caliphate' were developed. This methodology in the online medium is known as narrow-casting.[298] Forums dedicated to women and Islamic families existed, purely with

291 Seib and Janbek, "Terrorists' Online Strategies." 45.
292 Abdel Bari Atwan, "Masters of the Digital Universe," in *Islamic State: The Digital Caliphate* (Oakland: Saqi Books, 2015), 17.
293 Atwan, "Masters of the Digital Universe." 16-18.
294 Atwan, "Masters of the Digital Universe." 16-18.
295 Atwan, "Masters of the Digital Universe." 21-22.
296 Atwan, "Masters of the Digital Universe." 21-22.
297 Atwan, "Masters of the Digital Universe." 20.
298 Weimann, "Emerging Trends." 2.

a view to inculcate the importance of their role in supporting the development of the caliphate.[299] For the women of ISIS, their role in supporting their husband fighters and building a supporting family base was leveraged to generate the appropriate recruitment pull.[300] Again when overlaid with imagery of textile finery and BMW associated riches 'jihadi cool' is now a stimulant that can be experienced by both sexes.[301]

The above points illustrate how contemporary mediums were leveraged effectively by ISIS to deliver public-relations and marketing campaigns within its broader information operations campaign. Is does little however to explain the effectiveness of these strategies in supporting the intent of the communication strategy, in this case, recruitment. That is assessed as being the second pivotal aspect that played to their favour, their ability to leverage influence to achieve their agenda based on emotional drivers, this being central to the aim of Propaganda.[302]

ISIS was effective in recruitment not simply through slick marketing, rather it tapped into the core of human identity, a need to belong and the inherent human drive to sense that life has served some higher purpose. Any number of motivational theories recognise these inherent human needs be it Maslow's Hierarchy of Needs or Alderfer in his Existence Relatedness and Growth motivational construct.[303] More recently however is the leader-follow concept known as Social Identity Theory. In short, the hypothesis of this concept is that humans are more likely to support a leader's objectives if they feel like they are part of the in-group and the group's strength (salience) is reinforced by highlighting differences of those not of the shared collective.[304] No clearer delineation of in-group out-group dynamics than that of the believer or *Kafir*. This is assessed as a central aspect of ISIS identify. It is in the organisation's DNA having been embedded in Abu Al-Zarqawi's vision for Al-Qaeda in Iraq (AQI) which centred on concepts underpinned by shared identity

---

299 Weimann, "Emerging Trends." 6-7.

300 Atwan, "Masters of the Digital Universe." 20.

301 Atwan, "Masters of the Digital Universe." 6.

302 Author, "FM 3-13 Information Operations: Doctrine, Tactics, Techniques, and Procedures." 26.

303 Kathryn M Bartol et al., *Management: A Pacific Rim Focus* (North Melbourne: McGraw-Hill Book Company Australia Pty Limited, 1995). 344-369.

304 Rolf Van Dick and Rudolf Kerschreiter, "The Social Identity Approach to Effective Leadership: An Overview and Some Ideas on Cross-Cultural Generalizability," *Front. Bus. Res. China* 10, no. 3 (2016): 363–84.

and communal politics.[305] It is this aspect of ISIS which is an enabling action empowering those within the organisation to commit abhorrent and extreme violence. Individuals with a shared identity are more likely to engage in acts of violence in the interest of the organisation if organisational membership is highly salient.[306]

People didn't join ISIS as such, they simply identified with what was on offer, interpersonal bonds and sense of purpose.[307] For Al-Baghdadi the benefits associated with high levels of group identity when facing a unified threat would soon support his operational objectives. His followers would increasingly respect his leadership, idealise in-group values and enforce sanctions for deviance from excepted in-group norms.[308] Al-Baghdadi had delivered more than simply propaganda, he had executed a global Psychological Operation by conveying selected information to foreign audiences with a view to alter behaviour favourable to his objectives.[309]

Influence

There are several paradigms that can be used to implement intent; one of the most widely recognised is the DIME paradigm that recognises the requirement to leverage all elements of state power. In the DIME paradigm, diplomatic channels are pursued, information is leveraged, economic sanctions or incentives are employed and clearly, when required, the military component of state power can be flexed.[310] Equally important in understanding contemporary conflict and power projection is perhaps Joseph Nye Jnr's concept of soft and hard power. Soft power is the ability to attract and persuade followership through attraction to shared ideals and cultural expectations, whereas hard power employs the proven tool of coercion.[311] On reflection, it is difficult to not recognise

---

305 Gerges, *ISIS: A History*. 10.

306 Clark McCauley and Sophia Moskalenko, *Friction: How Radicalisation Happens to Them and US* (New York: Oxford University Press, 2011). 84.

307 McCauley and Moskalenko, *Friction: How Radicalisation Happens to Them and US*. 84.

308 McCauley and Moskalenko, *Friction: How Radicalisation Happens to Them and US*. 118.

309 Arturo Munoz, *U.S. Military Information Operations in Afghanistan: Effectiveness of Psychological Operations 2001-2010* (Santa Monica: RAND Corporation, 2012). 31

310 Dean S Hartley, "The DIME/PMESII Paradigm," in *Unconventional Conflict*, ed. Dean S Hartley (New York: Springer International Publishing, 2017), 99–106.

311 Joseph S Jnr Nye, *Soft Power: The Means to Success in World Politics* (New York: PublicAffairs, 2009). 17-20.

the application of these tools of statecraft being employed by ISIS during its metamorphosis from a terrorist organisation to 'recognised' state.

Al-Baghdadi's ability to generate high levels of followership did not simply occur through the threat of violence to generate individual acquiescence. On the contrary, followers were drawn not only to his charismatic leadership positioning as the new caliph but more so for the opportunity to experience affiliation with an increasingly connected community with shared cultural norms. The allure was kinship. Therefore, to protect the salience of this group, ISIS members displayed high levels of commitment on the battlefield including a willingness to commit to risky behaviour, engage in suicide attacks, and as history will show engage in abhorrent acts of murder and torture.[312]

ISIS seemed to effortlessly sweep across and claim control over large geographical areas in both Syria and Iraq. The intent was to establish the state, purify, then expand.[313] For those who aligned to the ISIS vision, their arrival was welcomed and membership assured. For the remainder, of what could now be referred to as the host populace, their support was still required, tacit or otherwise. Violence, or the threat of violence, gets to the core of terrorism. In its purest form, the calculated employment of these actual or perceived threats of violence is intended to inculcate fear, coerce a population and generate support for organisational objectives (religious, ideological or otherwise).[314]

ISIS was surgical in its application of terror to generate support. These acts of violence, beheadings, rape and immolation were recognisable globally. Within the Caliphate these were exploited by the *Emni* to generate fear and obedience.[315] As such, when low tech mobile footage or the professional productions of terrorist acts were shared within the host populations, fear became palpable and beleaguered support for ISIS was the outcome.[316]

It was, however, ISIS's ability to integrate softer forms of influence including diplomatic and economic lines of effort that would prove decisive. Support of a host population is central to an effective guerrilla campaign and it could

---

312 Byman, *Al Qaeda, the Islamic State and the Global Jihadist Movement*. 174.
313 Byman, *Al Qaeda, the Islamic State and the Global Jihadist Movement*. 170.
314 Bruce Hoffman, *Inside Terrorism* (New York: Columbia University Press, 2006). 31.
315 Speckhard and Yayla, "The ISIS Emni: Origins and Inner Workings of ISIS's Intelligence Apparatus." 3.
316 Farwell, "The Media Strategy of ISIS." 50.

be argued ISIS was employing elements of Mao's protracted warfare were 'weapons are an important factor in war, but not the decisive factor; it is people, not things, that are decisive'.[317] As a result, when approaching a new region or town ISIS would employ a deliberate community engagement line of effort that ran in parallel to the terror line of effort.[318]

Community outreach actions were implemented or *Dawa* forums were co-ordinated that communicated the benefits of sharia law, the religious requirement of jihad and the virtuous actions of the mujahedeen.[319] Old tech communication mediums were leveraged to convey these strategic messages such as the dissemination of pamphlets and the tried and tested word of mouth communication medium.[320] Perhaps more importantly, ISIS just didn't 'talk the talk', they implemented initiatives that were of immediate benefit to communities. Social outreach programs were initiated such as food distribution, the running of schools (importantly catering to both genders) and also establishment of Islamic courts.[321] The outcome when these mutually supporting lines of effort were communicated via a deliberate informational campaign was an explosion of support within conquered territories. This support came in many forms, fighting age males willingly offering support to wage jihad, safe harbour within communities was afforded, funding was provided and many willing female supporters offered to play their role. In hindsight, it is clear to see why this occurred, the vision of an Islamic Caliphate 'was' being achieved, the Caliph 'was' providing for the community and the punishment for not adhering to the new religious order 'was' clearly being delivered. The question is not 'why support ISIS' but rather 'why would you not support an Islamic State'?

Overreach

The ISIS propaganda machine was proving to be highly effective and their low-tech communications mediums were effective in generating

---

317 Mao, "Selected Works of Mao Tse-Tung," *Foreign Languages Press* II, no. May 1938 (1967): 21.

318 Brandon Webb, Jack Murphy, and Peter Nealen, *The Isis Solution: How Unconventional Thinking and Special Operations Can Eliminate Radical Islam* (New York: St. Martins Press, 2016). 20.

319 Webb, Murphy, and Nealen, *The Isis Solution: How Unconventional Thinking and Special Operations Can Eliminate Radical Islam.* 20.

320 Al-Tamimi, "The Dawn of the Islamic State of Iraq and Ash-Sham." 10.

321 Al-Tamimi, "The Dawn of the Islamic State of Iraq and Ash-Sham." 9-12.

support within host communities. The efforts they invested in professional communication mediums such as *Dabiq* were stimulating increasing levels of support from foreign audiences.[322] This drove support and a foreign recruitment pull which increasingly fomented hate in the Jihadi who was dislocated from the recognised caliphate, the home-grown terrorist or lone wolf.[323] It was these tactical and operational level successes within the information domain that would ultimately be the Islamic States' strategic downfall, triggering the collapse of their caliphate. Thucydides talks of fear, honour and interest as being the primary motivators compelling nations to engage in war.[324] For the global community, in particular the United States, the operational success of the Islamic State in Iraq and the effectiveness of their communication strategy struck a chord with all three.

Barbaric acts committed against both captured US and UK civilians were designed to generate a recruitment pull, but also increasingly to communicate to the populations of both countries (and their government) to stay out of the conflict.[325] A given US action will be met with a counteraction, likely the beheading of captured personnel. The risk, however, is over-reach. Al-Baghdadi failed to fully appreciate this risk, a risk appreciated by Al-Qaeda's commander and chief Al-Zawahiri and previously conveyed to Al-Zarqawi.[326] Perhaps Al-Baghdadi's disdain for Al-Zawahiri or his personal hubris contributed to this strategic blunder? The fear for the United States was not so much the risk of foreign fighters returning and becoming a domestic threat, although real, this was a tertiary concern. The true fear that drove intervention was the fact that the United States' interests, being a stable and secure Iraq and their honour, through an inability to protect this interest was in question. The Yazidi incident associated with the potential mass slaughter (all to be televised) was the inconvenient tipping point.[327] Thucydides motivational principles had stimulated the coalition war machine.

---

322 Robert Manne, *The Mind of Islamic State* (Carlton: Redback Quarterly, 2016). 108-109
323 Byman, *Al Qaeda, the Islamic State and the Global Jihadist Movement.* 172.
324 Robert B. Strassler, *Thucydides: A Comprehensive Guide to the Peloponnesian War* (New York: Schuster Inc, 1996). 43.
325 Byman, *Al Qaeda, the Islamic State and the Global Jihadist Movement.* 176.
326 Byman, *Al Qaeda, the Islamic State and the Global Jihadist Movement.* 178.
327 Byman, *Al Qaeda, the Islamic State and the Global Jihadist Movement.* 185.

What followed, although untidy both with regards to military alliances and execution, was the predictable inevitability of a 'conventional' military defeat when military capabilities are disproportionately skewed toward a given belligerent. The military forces committed to the defeat of the Islamic State include the United States Military, Russian Military, Syrian Army, Turkish military, a global coalition of 70 plus countries and a homogenised mix of forces including the Syrian Democratic Forces, Kurdish Peshmerga and Iraq Shia militias.[328] At best Al-Baghdadi may have planned on his Information Operations dissuading US interference, and at worst illicit US involvement through the concept of provocation; after all, this would reinforce his strategic narrative.[329] His great strategic misstep, however, was failing to appreciate the scale of commitment from a multitude of nations and religiously diverse stakeholders. The fear was real and the interest global. This Caliphate had become unpalatable.

Throughout the five years following the Yazidi tipping point, military action was often recognisable as conventional warfare. That is, having secured terrain, claimed a Caliphate and literally staked a flag, the Islamic State had a requirement to hold this terrain. Their belligerents were obliged to dislodge and retake this terrain. The military actions therefore centred on classical principles of warfare, namely, offensive and defensive actions. Although clearly superior from a military standpoint, those opposing the Islamic State also identified the need to augment the military effort with actions throughout the informational domain. The defeat of the Islamic State required actions across the entire DIME continuum. Consequently, counter-narrative campaigns, and Information Operations campaigns ran in parallel to the military line of effort. Video campaigns, social media campaigns and traditional print campaigns some overt, many covert, were employed to blunt the Caliphs message, sow discontent, degrade recruitment and ultimately contribute to the Islamic States defeat.[330] The result, as history will attest, was the declaration by the United States President that the Islamic States

---

328 Richard Hall, "ISIS Caliphate Defeated: How Did It Happen and Do They Still Pose a Threat?," *Independent*, 2019.

329 Cronin, "Chapter One: The Strategies of Terrorism." 15-18.

330 Anne Speckhard, Ardian Shajkovci, and Neima Izadi, "Using Counter-Narrative Campaigns to 'Break the ISIS Brand' in Iraq," *Government Technology and Services Coalitions: Homeland Security*, 2018.

Caliphate was one hundred per cent defeated. This occurred on the 28th February 2019.[331] Al-Baghdadi purportedly ceded as much via a televised interview on 29th April 2019 during which a shift in strategy was discussed. What is clear, however, is that the strategic objective originally sought, being a physical caliphate, has to date eluded Al-Baghdadi and the Islamic State.

Conclusion

One cannot deny the existence of individuals who align themselves to the ideals espoused within the Salafi-Jihadists objectives of the Islamic State. Abu Bakr Al-Baghdadi remains the organisation's leader, who through charismatic leadership and an apocalyptic end of day's message has been able to generate high levels of global followship. The organisation's ability to leverage the contemporary media landscape resulted in a co-ordinated and deliberate Information Operations campaign that enabled both local and foreign recruitment. If willing commitment was not gained within the host populace, the promulgation of barbaric acts of violence coerced host populations within Iraq and Syria to yield to the Islamic State. To a large extent, the organisation sought to employ lessons learnt from previous failures, notably the application of excessive violence, and implemented governance initiatives as a supporting line of effort to garner support.

Even with all these measures in place, the Islamic State has failed to achieve its strategic objective of establishing (and retaining) a Caliphate. Al-Baghdadi cannot currently be referred to as Caliph, as the retention of terrain for which to govern predicates this title. He clearly remains the leader and the Islamic State remains a global threat, however, it is evident that their Information Operations campaign has been ineffective in realising strategic intent. The physical caliphate is gone. The Islamic State ultimately lost control of its Informational Campaign, it became too effective. It stimulated seemingly universal levels of admonishment, which in turn focused the actions of multiple stakeholders who previously had competing interests. Perhaps it was an unintended consequence associated with the uncontrolled dissemination of violence. After all, media devices are ubiquitous on the modern battlefield and

---

331 Rogers, Callimachi, and Cooper, "Trump Declares ISIS '100%' Defeated in Syria. '100% Not True,' Ground Reports Say."

the membership demographic of the Islamic State craves 'Insta' fame. There must have come a point where this became a cause of concern for the leadership of the Islamic State. The Islamic State may have lost 'the battle for the Caliphate of 2014-19' as it may well be referred in history. The war however continues, followship remains, leadership remains and the vision is steadfast. Moving forward, the ability for Islamic State to be effective may well be dependent on a more balanced application and dissemination of violence across the information spectrum. If, as intimated by his measured address on the 29th April 2019, Abu Bakr al-Baghdadi is alert to this requirement, the future in the Middle East and global stability writ large remains dire.

Radicalisation

Essay 6

'Select one of the theoretical or conceptual explanations of the radicalisation process and provide a written critique of the strengths and weakness of this theory or conceptualisation of the radicalisation process'. *(Written 2018)*

Introduction

An increasingly focal area for combating or defeating terrorism is preventing the radicalisation process from the outset. Prevention, after all, is better than cure, with counter-radicalisation efforts increasingly being viewed as a complementary effort to the policing or military actions executed by security organisations.[332] Driven in large part by rising levels of religious centric terrorism, recent studies by the counter-terrorism fraternity have attempted to 'solve' the problem of violent extremism and develop new theories. Regardless of whether they are founded on empirical research or rooted in social psychology theories, all have the well intended aim of countering the process that may see an individual progress from radicalisation of thought, into terrorist practitioner.[333]

Moghaddam's Staircase to Terrorism, to be clear from the outset is a metaphor, an opinion piece almost. It is, however, a well-structured argument that seeks to articulate the radicalisation process.[334] It is founded on academic insights, not empirical data, and has led to the development

---

332 Anthony Bergin et al., "Gen Y Jihadists: Preventing Radicalisation in Australia" (Canberra, 2015). 51-56.

333 Randy Borum, "Radicalization into Violent Extremism II: A Review of Conceptual Models and Empirical Research.," *Journal of Strategic Studies* 4, no. 4 (2011): 37–63.

334 Fathali M Moghaddam, "The Staircase to Terrorism," in *Psychology of Terrorism*, ed. Bruce Bognar et al. (New York: Oxford University Press, 2007), 69–80.

of more contemporary models in use by security organisations such as the New York Police Department.[335] This conceptual model has been chosen as the focus of this critique for three main reasons. Firstly, by order of importance, is how it positions itself with regards to terrorism, which is clearly articulated being:

> Politically motivated violence that is perpetrated by individuals, groups, or state-sponsored agents and intended to bring about feelings of terror and helplessness in a population in order to influence decision making and to change behaviour.[336]

Importantly this definition, and the model, removes any religious connotation associated with other models such as Precht's Model of Radicalisation.[337] The Staircase to Terrorism metaphor is equally applicable to left-wing, right-wing, separatist and, clearly, Religious Terrorism.[338] This is a standout strength of this model in comparison to others.

Second, engagement is viewed as a rational choice on behalf of the individual with psychopathic tendencies discounted.[339] This is assessed as critical to an effective theoretical analysis. Finally, Moghaddam (and increasingly others) view engagement as a graduated procedural indoctrination into violence.[340] The model views the issue of radicalisation as a socio-psychological problem and hence to effectively counter it, an appreciation of these graduations is required.[341]

---

335 Borum, "Radicalization into Violent Extremism II: A Review of Conceptual Models and Empirical Research." 41.

336 Moghaddam, "The Staircase to Terrorism." 69

337 Borum, "Radicalization into Violent Extremism II: A Review of Conceptual Models and Empirical Research." 42.

338 Zeynep Sutalan, "Major Ideologies Motivating Terrorism and Main Characteristics of Terrorism," in *Centre of Excellence Defence Against Terrorism. Organisational and Psychological Aspects of Terrorism* (Ankara: IOS Press, 2008), 13–23.

339 Moghaddam, "The Staircase to Terrorism." 70.

340 Moghaddam, "The Staircase to Terrorism." 70-71; John Horgan, *The Psychology of Terrorism* (New York: Routledge, 2006). 107-110.

341 Bradley McAllister and Alex P Schmid, "Theories of Terrorism: Social Identity Theory," in *The Routledge Handbook of Terrorism Research* (London: Routledge, 2011), 214–215.
Todd C Helmus, "Why and How Some People Become Terrorists," in *Social Science for Counter-Terrorism: Putting the Pieces Together*, ed. Paul Davis and Kim Cragin (New York: RAND Corporation, 2009), 71–112.

Small steps

To understand and counter an individual's transition to terrorism Moghaddam employs a metaphor of the transition being like ascending through five flights of stairs, six including the ground. Regardless of professional insight into the issues of terrorism, counter-terrorism or countering violent extremism his metaphor is rational, easy to appreciate and considered. Of note is his emphasis on how options for descending the building, that is disengaging from the radicalisation process, decrease as an individual ascends through the various floors.[342] This is a rational hypothesis that does pose thought for further empirical based research that may ultimately drive policy.

On the 'ground floor' an individual may question their material conditions in life and if a 'perceived' inequity exists commence the radicalisation process. The issue of inequality has been identified by other professionals relating to how poverty, repression, a threat to identity, or illegitimacy of the ruling regime may act as a catalyst for an individual to commence the radicalisation process.[343] Other writers and scholars also highlight how this may simply be a perception of inequality from an individual's interpretation of the situation, and adds weight to Moghaddam's metaphor and his hypothesis that what matters most on the ground floor is individual 'perception' on fairness.[344] If an individual now wishes to fight the perceived unfair treatment through improving their own personal situation or fighting injustice then they are considered to have transitioned into the 'First Floor'. This, however, can be problematic due to issues associated with an individual's ability to engage in the decision making apparatus of a country which can further compound the issues already highlighted on the ground floor. Importantly if the reasons for this inequality and failure can be shifted

342 Moghaddam, "The Staircase to Terrorism." 70.

343 Darcy Noricks, "The Root Causes of Terrorism," in *Social Science for Counter-Terrorism: Putting the Pieces Together*, ed. P Davis and K Cragin (New York and London: RAND Corporation, 2009), 19–21.

Edward Newman, "Exploring the 'Root Causes' of Terrorism," *Studies in Conflict and Terrorism* 29, no. 8 (2006): 750-753.

344 Newman, "Exploring the 'Root Causes' of Terrorism." 753: Horgan, *The Psychology of Terrorism*. 102-103: Bergin et al., "Gen Y Jihadists: Preventing Radicalisation in Australia." 6: Moghaddam, "The Staircase to Terrorism." 72.

to another entity then it is likely that an individual may transition to the 'Second Floor'.[345]

Throughout his discussion on the Second Floor, Moghaddam touches on a critical aspect of contemporary theory relating to intergroup behaviour, that being in-group/out-group dynamics. However, it is assessed that the effectiveness of the argument is blunted by his use of Freudian citations. Although the concepts and argument are correct, it seems dated and out of place. The contemporary relevance of the metaphor would have been enhanced if the Social Identity Theory on leadership had been used as the medium in which to highlight the importance of in-group/out-group relations.[346] Highlighting how in-groups responding to out-groups and how this focuses actions toward the interest of the group (potentially a terror group) would add more weight than what Freud refers to as targets for displacement.[347] The argument is sound and justifies a move to the 'Third Floor' being Moral Engagement.

The Third Floor centres on the issue of moral engagement raising the enduring issue associated with perspective and which group is actually the terrorist organisation.[348] Again there is a missed opportunity during this floor as although it highlights how recruits are persuaded to commit terrorist acts it fails to articulate how governments can counter this alternate viewpoint. Discussion on what actions could be taken by governing institutions (not simply governments) to provide an 'off-ramp' into the stairwell for individuals would have been highly beneficial. This would have added valuable consideration to the metaphor as when an individual ascends to the 'Fourth Floor', being the perceived legitimacy of the Terrorist organisation, the opportunities for disengagement greatly decrease.[349]

Moghaddam briefly discusses the importance of cell structures during the Fourth Floor and how this enables security associated

---

345 Moghaddam, "The Staircase to Terrorism." 73.

346 Alexander S. Haslam, *Psychology in Organisations: The Social Identity Approach* (London: SAGE Publications Ltd, 2004). 64-70.

347 Rolf Van Dick and Rudolf Kerschreiter, "The Social Identity Approach to Effective Leadership: An Overview and Some Ideas on Cross-Cultural Generalisability," *Front. Bus. Res. China* 10, no. 3 (2016): 363–84.

348 Moghaddam, "The Staircase to Terrorism." 74.

349 Moghaddam, "The Staircase to Terrorism." 74.

with operations leading to group affiliation. The metaphor at this stage again feels a bit dated with cell structures originally forming as a method to wage Guerrilla Operations.[350] Some discussion on the evolution of terrorist's structures including the impact of umbrella organisations and technological advances would have strengthened the article, particularly if linked to counter strategies.[351] The strength of his metaphor at this stage relates to the focus on social categorisation and the importance this plays with regards to an individual's shifting psychological processes. He highlights the 'us versus them' argument which could be further reinforced if a more effective link to Second Floor and Freudian concepts (or ideally Social Identity Theory) had been made. An individual's commitment to the group occurs through a socialisation process centred on traditions and shared goals.[352] The need for identity and belongingness are characteristics prevalent in people who radicalise, so Moghaddam's hypothesis at this stage is valid.[353] How this belongingness is achieved via a socialisation process which emphasises the uniqueness of the group through symbology and ritual would have been beneficial at this stage.[354] Arguably this ability to create a strong in-group and 'us' identity is becoming a critical component needed by contemporary terrorist organisations; an ability to establish their own 'brand' becomes central to providing purpose to the common enemy, but importantly may also limit the effects of personnel drain to other similar organisations.[355]

The final floor in Moghaddam's metaphor is the 'Fifth Floor' and relates to the terrorist act and the ability of individuals to side-step mechanisms that may inhibit violent actions toward individuals. He raises some valid points associated with how civilians (or the targets, which could be security personnel) are emphasised as being outsiders of the group, the

---

350 Jonathan R. White, *Terrorism and Homeland Security* (New York: Thomson Wadsworth, 2006). 40-41.
351 White, *Terrorism and Homeland Security.* 40-41.
352 Moghaddam, "The Staircase to Terrorism." 74.
353 Bergin et al., "Gen Y Jihadists: Preventing Radicalisation in Australia."
354 Boas Shamir et al., "Leadership and Social Identification in Military Units: Direct and Indirect Relationships," *Journal of Applied Social Psychology* 20, no. 3 (2000): 612–40.
355 Brandon Webb, Jack Murphy, and Peter Nealen, *The Isis Solution: How Unconventional Thinking and Special Operations Can Eliminate Radical Islam* (New York: St. Martins Press, 2016). 12-13.

out-group in Social Identity vernacular.[356] This aspect of dehumanising or demonising the enemy has been recognised as enabling contemporary terror actions by the Islamic State in Iraq and al-Sham giving legitimacy to Moghaddam's claims.[357] He raises an interesting point relating to the concealed nature of most terrorist actions and how an individual's inability to show fear to the terrorist may enable the terrorist to actually initiate the violent action. This is an interesting aspect and may have benefited from increased focus.

Fire escapes?

Moghaddam's staircase metaphor provides an easily consumable concept that in large part provides a valid hypothesis on the radicalisation process an individual may progress through in the process of becoming a terrorist. However, the greatest shortfall of his argument relates to the options for countering this process and providing options for individuals to disengage from the process. He provides four key policy implications that appear to be based on opinion rather than factual knowledge of the counter violent extremism process. His first implication is that prevention must come first, of which it is hard to disagree.[358] He emphasises the need to change the conditions for those situated on the first floor, however this does little to counter a central premise of his metaphor, being the issue of perception. A society may, in fact, be void of repression, provide the conditions for individual expression and be democratic, however individuals may still 'perceive' a sense of injustice and inequality. This may actually be linked to the practice of democracy that runs counter to sharia law and is hence an attack on their cultural ideology.[359] The metaphor does little to address this wicked problem which appears to erode that cohesion central to a western democratic society. He also makes sweeping accusations that counter-terrorism is skewed toward security organisations that target 'bad apples' after the radicalisation process has occurred. At best this is a dated viewpoint, as contemporary counter radicalisation programs are very much aligned

---

356 Moghaddam, "The Staircase to Terrorism." 75.
357 Webb, Murphy, and Nealen, *The Isis Solution: How Unconventional Thinking and Special Operations Can Eliminate Radical Islam*. 21.
358 Moghaddam, "The Staircase to Terrorism." 76.
359 Newman, "Exploring the 'Root Causes' of Terrorism." 753.

to the need for collaboration and engagement with minority groups susceptible to radicalisation.[360]

His second policy implication relates to procedural justice and his belief that existing cultural practices and symbolic systems need to be incorporated to provide mobility opportunities, which in theory would positively influence the perception of community engagement.[361] Western societies have, and continue to make, concerted efforts to support cultural identity and freedom of religion, yet continue to suffer the effects of Islamist terrorism.[362] Additionally, concerted efforts relating to the inclusion of cultural identity relating to ethno-nationalists terrorism groups has failed to eradicate terrorism. This is exemplified by *Euskadi Ta Askatasuna* (ETA) who even when granted autonomy for self-governance, their own flag and national anthem continued to engage in terrorist acts against Spain.[363] He also suggests that the need for democratic process is integral to countering violent extremism, however, this assumes equal rights for all is supported (as in the west) whereas this may ultimately run counter to cultural norms. Social engineering is not an effective counter radicalisation process and as illustrated by ETA, an increase in democratic rights may lead to increased levels of terrorism.[364]

Perhaps the biggest quandary relating to his metaphor and policy implications relates to the issue of 'us versus them'.[365] Although a logical, almost motherhood statement, it runs counter to his previous policy implication. If conforming to the norm and the social integration of individuals to existing societal norms is not seen as viable, does this not create an 'us and them' scenario? Demographic shifts driven by globalisation and modernisation drive this issue defined as a clash of

360 Bergin et al., "Gen Y Jihadists: Preventing Radicalisation in Australia." 51-56.

361 Moghaddam, "The Staircase to Terrorism." 76.

362 Clive Walker, "United Kingdom," in *Counter-terrorism Yearbook 2018*, ed. Isaac Kfir, Sofia Patel, and Micha Batt (Canberra: Australian Strategic Policy Institute, 2018), 141–49.

363 Rogelio Alonso, "Why Do Terrorists Stop? Analyzing Why ETA Members Abandon or Continue with Terrorism," *Studies in Conflict and Terrorism* 34, no. 9 (2011): 696–698.

364 Woodworth, "Why Do They Kill? The Basque Conflict in Spain." 5-6: Noricks, "The Root Causes of Terrorism." 22-26.

365 Moghaddam, "The Staircase to Terrorism." 76.

identities and is a contributing variable to terrorism.³⁶⁶ His final point relating to *inter-objectivity* is simply an extension of 'us vs them' issues and provides little with regards to policy implication.³⁶⁷ It simply highlights that existing cultural divides impact on the cohesiveness of societies throughout the world. It also assumes that the custodians and members of these cultures share his level of desire to understand and coexist with others, whereas this may not be the case.

Conclusion

Moghaddam's Staircase to Terrorism metaphor provides a sound conceptual framework that seeks to highlight the radicalisation process. If various terrorist organisations are viewed with regards to his staircase metaphor, worthy linkages can be found relating to perceptions of inequality and how this may trigger the radicalisation process. Unfortunately, his metaphor does little to inform relevant shifts to policy, and when he does offer recommendations, they often run counter to proven historical example as highlighted by ETA. It is an effective theory in triggering thought and has informed more recent pathway concepts. If viewed in the context of being a source of stimuli regarding the formation of actual counter-terrorism and counter violent extremism policy, the staircase metaphor can still provide valuable insight to both practitioner and academic alike. An attempt to incorporate more contemporary examples and include existing empirical data would likely strengthen his argument, however, at this stage, it provides limited tangible benefit.

366 Newman, "Exploring the 'Root Causes' of Terrorism." 754-756.
367 Moghaddam, "The Staircase to Terrorism." 77.

'Religion is a major contributor to the radicalisation of terrorists. Discuss'. *(Written 2018)*

Introduction

Religion has played a critical role in shaping societies for millennia, not only as a medium in which to establish societal norms and expectations but equally so as a medium in which to inspire violence.[368] Today it is increasingly apparent that religion is a divisive issue that if leveraged correctly can have a negative impact on the cohesion of society. This paper will discuss the role that religion plays in the radicalisation of individuals that actively choose to engage in violent acts of terrorism. The premise of the argument is that religion acts as a catalyst for individual's which triggers psychological commitment toward, and through, the radicalisation process. This is assessed to occur in three key areas. Firstly, misinterpretation of guiding texts can lead to an intentional or unintentional biased form of indoctrination which stimulates personal grievance for those individuals susceptible to radicalisation. The result may ultimately be violent action. Secondly, the belonging, sense of identity and group cohesion contributes to a form of group grievance that sanctions violent actions toward individuals and groups not sharing similar social norms and religious expectations. And finally, many religions, afford a degree of absolution to individuals who engage in acts of terrorism through a perception of religious duty.

To bind the discussion, however, it is critical that an appreciation of what may constitute religious terrorism is articulated. In doing so the following definition of terrorism has been used, as although religion is not mentioned per se in the definition, it has broad utility across multiple religions:

---

368 Richard B Miller, *Terror, Religion and Liberal Thought* (New York: Columbia University Press, 2010). 1

'A premeditated and unlawful act in which groups or agents of some principal engage in a threatened or actual use of force or violence against human or property targets. These groups or agents engage in this behaviour intending the purposeful intimidation of governments or people to affect policy or behaviour with an underlying political objective'.[369]

If viewing the Islamic State of Iraq and the Levant (ISIL) through this lens the utility of this definition is clear. ISIS had an initial political objective post 9/11[370] of resisting US intervention in Afghanistan and Iraq. This was to be achieved through the application of violence. Abu Musa al-Zarqawi then leveraged the divide between non-Muslims and apostates to imbue a religious aspect to this terrorist organisation.[371] In comparison, several extreme right-wing terrorist's organisations, such as the Militia of Montana, seek change to the existing norms associated with US society.[372] Like ISIS, the Militia Men of Montana leverage religious ideology, including the perception of an impending apocalypse, to generate recruitment and focus its members.

This is important to appreciate in the context of this discussion as it clarifies the misconception and assumption that religious terrorism is an Islamist phenomenon, it is not. The end-state of any terrorist organisation remains the attainment of a political objective. The underlying premise of this argument is that the leadership of a given terrorist organisation may leverage religion to focus recruitment and project violence to achieve a politico-religious objective in the name of God.[373]

Glue

If as shown above terrorist organisations from various faiths utilise religion within their terrorist ideology, what is it about religion that makes it such a powerful, divisive and effective motivational

---

369 Gus Martin, *Essentials of Terrorism*, 3rd ed. (London: SAGE Publications Ltd, 2014). 8.

370 9/11 refers to the terrorist attacks against the World Trade Centre in New York, executed on the 11th of September 2001.

371 Wayne F Jnr Lesperance, "The Rise of the Islamic State," in *The New Islamic State: Ideology, Religion and Violent Extremism in the 21st Century*, ed. Jack Covarrubias and Robert J Jnr Pauly (Oxon: Ashgate, 2016), 1.

372 Bruce Hoffman, *Inside Terrorism* (New York: Columbia University Press, 2006). 104-105.

373 Aref M Al-Khattar, *Religion and Terrorism: An Interfaith Perspective* (Westport: Praeger, 2003). 5.

tool? Ultimately the answer to this lies with what religion offers an individual and by extension, society. Religion acts as a moral ballast for societies. Christianity has the ten commandants which guide individual behaviour, and Christians' Holy Scripture, the Bible, provides direction on how to lead a morally disciplined life.[374] Islam is a religion that expects complete submission and obedience to Allah, is guided by the Six Articles of Faith, the Five 'Pillars of Islam' and the core teachings of the Prophet Muhammad (PBUH) as contained in the Quran.[375] On reading these principles they all seem like sound belief systems for an individual to live by. Sins to avoid are highlighted and virtuous positive behaviour articulated. As such, religion acts as a mechanism that maintains a form a social control with real and perceived punishment available for those that stray from expected behaviours.[376] Upon committing to a given religion and their guiding principles, the individual also becomes a member of the wider collective who also seeks to adhere to these guiding principles.[377] This unity of a collective who adhere to common societal norms is the essence of a healthy and functioning society.[378]

Religion plays a central role in maintaining the stability of many societies. The 'value' of religion with regards to terrorism gets to the heart of individual human motivation and resides in the field of social-psychological being:

> 'the study of how people interact with each other and how their thoughts, feelings behaviours or intentions are influenced by the actual or implied presence of others.'[379]

Key within this definition is the term 'implied'. This has implications with regards to much of the literature relating to individual radicalisation, as many theories refer to the 'perception' of injustice as being a central

---

374 Kenneth Barker, ed., *The New International Study Bible* (Michigan: Zondervan Publishing House, 1995). Exodus 20: 1-17: Al-Khattar, *Religion and Terrorism: An Interfaith Perspective*. 12.

375 Imam Kamil, "Core Values of Islam," *Islam Religion*, 2013.

376 Al-Khattar, *Religion and Terrorism: An Interfaith Perspective*. 9-10.

377 Al-Khattar, *Religion and Terrorism: An Interfaith Perspective*. 9-10.

378 Society: an organisation to which people who share similar interests can belong (https://dictionary.cambridge.org/dictionary/english/society)

379 Joseph P. Forgas, *Interpersonal Behaviour: The Psychology of Social Interaction* (Sydney: Pergamon Press, 1989). 3-4.

contributor.[380] This then is the value of religion relating to terrorism. Firstly, any action committed by an individual, group or state that may be perceived as a threat to the sanctity of a given religion is ultimately an attack on the individual's belief system. This then may act as the catalyst that results in an individual engaging in the radicalisation process and may see them evolve to the point where they are prepared to commit terrorist acts. This threat to identity has been identified by Moghaddam in his 'Staircase to Terrorism' metaphor and is assessed as a primary contributor as to why individuals may commence the radicalisation process.[381]

The other potential contributing factor is how an attack on the now shared collective to which an individual has committed can be leveraged by the leadership of religious terrorist organisations and stimulate action.[382] To remain identifiable with the group, individuals, in general, seek to care for and show interest in the welfare of others who are a member of this shared collective.[383] For religion, the salience of these common societal norms removes the barrier of geographic separation. Consequently, an affront to a given religion in region 'x' is not only perceived as slight by individuals in that area, it is felt by the group at large regardless of geographical positioning. These two contributing factors of personal grievance and shared collective identity are assessed as the primary contributors to the radicalisation of terrorists. For many, religion and the associated structures, routines and symbology provide much-needed grounding and purpose in a chaotic world. Any threat to this centring aspect of their life is likely to result in retaliatory action.

Individual purpose and grievance

Moghadam and other theorists relating to the radicalisation process have identified personal grievance as a primary contributor for radicalisation. McCauley and Moskalenko delve deeper into this aspect

---

380 Anthony Bergin et al., "Gen Y Jihadists: Preventing Radicalisation in Australia" (Canberra, 2015). 6.
381 Fathali M Moghaddam, "The Staircase to Terrorism," in *Psychology of Terrorism*, ed. Bruce Bognar et al. (New York: Oxford University Press, 2007), 70-71.
382 James J F Forest, *The Terrorism Lectures* (Orange County: Nortia Press, 2012). 242.
383 Clark McCauley and Sophia Moskalenko, *Friction: How Radicalisation Happens to Them and US* (New York: Oxford University Press, 2011). 28.

of personal grievance linking it to Aristotle's hypothesis' that specifies that the outcome of such grievance can be anger and the desire for revenge.[384] Importantly what constitutes a slight, insult or grievance is deeply rooted in cultural norms where a seemingly innocuous action by one group can be perceived as a deeply insulting action by another.[385] Perhaps the most contemporary example of this was the Charlie Hebdo cartoon which was perceived as highly insulting by one group and did trigger retaliatory terrorist action based on religious slight.[386] The full impact of this publication in acting as a trigger for individuals to commence the radicalisation process will never fully be known and is most likely still acting as a source for recruitment.

It does, however, provide a simple example of religious ideology and positioning that is played out through Islamist terrorist recruitment, most notably Al-Qaeda. Propaganda for Al-Qaeda consistently emphasised the oppression of Muslims by non-Muslims highlighting America's occupations in Iraq and Afghanistan as an attack on the Muslim faith.[387] If this message is received by an individual then it may well be interpreted as a threat to the individual's belief system and by extension the shared collective. This introduces an additional layer of complexity surrounding religion and the nurturing of individual grievance, that being messaging, or perhaps more accurately, miss-messaging.

The process of transferring information involves the development of the message by the source, disseminating the message, receipt of the message, the interpretation of the message and then action by the receiver.[388] Risk exists on several fronts. Firstly, the message may simply be incorrect in the first instance, with this error then being compounded the more it is received and subsequently transmitted. Secondly, the message may be intentionally misleading with the view of stimulating the desired response in the receiver as designed by the message transmitter. And finally, the receiver may simply misinterpret

---

384 McCauley and Moskalenko, *Friction: How Radicalisation Happens to Them and US.* 17.

385 McCauley and Moskalenko, *Friction: How Radicalisation Happens to Them and US.* 17.

386 Mathew Moran, "Terrorism and the Banlieues: The Charlie Hebdo Attack in Context," *Modern and Contemporary France* 25, no. 3 (2017): 315–32.

387 Daniel Byman, *Al Qaeda, the Islamic State and the Global Jihadist Movement* (London: Oxford University Press, 2015). 100-104

388 Stephen Robbins et al., *Organisation Behaviour: Concepts, Controversies and Applications* (Sydney: Prentice Hall, 1994). 422-423.

the message and initiate action on poorly formed assumptions. This is problematic for the propagation of religious terrorism, as the rubric that an individual may employ to identify a slight (and hence develop a personal grievance) may be corrupted (intentionally or unintentionally) from the outset. This can occur through what have been identified as two primary communication mediums being Directed Communication Mediums and Indirect Communication Mediums.[389]

Directed Communication Mediums (DCM) are ultimately those elements of the religious architecture that can be used to disseminate a message to a targeted and known audience. These could include such things as the Church in a Christian context, the Mosque in an Islamist context and the Synagogue in a Jewish context. More so, however, it relates to those institutions that can inculcate messaging into those within society vulnerable or susceptible to the receipt of intentionally biased religious worldviews. The messaging being communicated in the *Pesantren*[390] throughout Indonesia have increasingly been viewed with a level of scepticism as many perpetrators of terrorist bombings within Indonesia have been executed by those with an affiliation to the *Pesantren* system or similar Islamic Institutions.[391] Violent Muslim groups within Indonesia seek to fracture Indonesia's concept of *Pancasila*, which is the cornerstone of Indonesian multiculturalism and religious tolerance.[392] The point is that the governance of curriculum throughout these institutions is tenuous at best. Messaging, including inflammatory anti-Christian rhetoric, can be used to generate deep personal grievance within the congregation and student body. The risk of DCM intentionally misinterpreting texts for their own agenda is not unique to Islamist Institutions with Christian and Jewish institutions all having their own form of indoctrination that in some way skews the guiding texts for a positive outcome.

Indirect Communications Mediums (ICM) relate to those tools where the receiver is dislocated from the messenger and could include bookstores, but more likely, internet communication mediums. There are many opinions relating to the role of the internet in the radicalisation

---

389 Author's own titles.

390 Pesantren is the Indonesian Equivalent of the Madrassa

391 Dina Afrianty, "Islamic Education and Youth Extremism in Indonesia," *Journal of Policing, Intelligence and Counter Terrorism* 7, no. 2 (2012): 134.

392 http://www.oxfordislamicstudies.com/article/opr/t125/e1818

process, however, one which has been supported by a RAND study is that the internet creates more opportunities for individuals to become radicalised.[393] Central to supporting this hypothesis is the fact that almost all studies reviewed in the RAND report agree on one point, being, that the internet promotes radicalisation.[394] Stevens and Neuman go further highlighting that:

> The internet can be used by extremists to illustrate and reinforce ideological messages and/narratives. Through the internet, potential recruits can gain… access to visually powerful video and imagery which appear to substantiate the extremist's political claims'.[395]

A cursory search of the internet will provide examples from multiple religions that highlight their proficiency in employing electronic media products to support their objectives.[396]

Most recently, however, has been ISIS's use of professionally developed propaganda tools to support their cause. In fact, under the organisational structure of the 'Islamic State,' the group had a dedicated Ministry of Media that focused on the Internet, filming, documenting and the print media.[397] This branch focussed on generating highly effective propaganda campaigns that exacerbated the religious divide between those committed to ISIS and those opposed, in particular, the United States.[398] In being more specific, the media campaigns executed by the Ministry of Media ultimately reflect an intentional psychological operation, being:

> A planned operation to convey selected information and indicators to foreign audiences to influence their emotions, motives, objective reasoning, and ultimately the behaviour of foreign governments, organisations and individuals. The purpose

---

393 Ines Von Behr et al., "Radicalisation in the Digital Era: The Use of the Internet in 15 Cases of Terrorism and Extremism" (Brussels, 2013). XI.

394 Von Behr et al., "Radicalisation in the Digital Era: The Use of the Internet in 15 Cases of Terrorism and Extremism." 17.

395 Tim Stevens and Peter R Neumann, "Countering Online Radicalisation: A Strategy for Action" (London, 2009). 16

396 Martin, *Essentials of Terrorism*. 156.

397 Rachael Yon, "The USe of Propaganda and Social Media," in *The New Islamic State: Ideology, Religion and Violent Extremism in the 21st Century*, ed. Jack Covarrubias, Tom Lansford, and Robert J Jnr Pauley (Oxon: Ashgate, 2016), 43–60.

398

of psychological operations is to induce or reinforce foreign attitudes and behaviour favourable to the originator's objectives.[399]

ISIS's actions throughout various ICM was far more than propaganda. Rather, it was a deliberate planned action executed in the cyber realm with the clear intent of eliciting individual support via divisive religious messaging to support strategic goals. It worked, with large numbers of foreign individuals dislocated physically from ISIS developing a deep personal grievance founded on a perceived attack on their guiding religious beliefs.

Once the personal grievance has been founded, in this case, centred on a religious slight, individuals may pursue radicalising action, be it engaging in online forums or the propagation of radicalised religious ideas to peers. In Moghaddam's Stairway to Terrorism metaphor, an individual that has committed to engaging in this type of behaviour is assessed as having transitioned to the 'first floor' which involves becoming actively engaged in opposing the perceived slight or inequity.[400] Why individuals are motivated to make this transition from a passive passenger to an active participant is increasingly being recognised as a social psychological phenomenon. One of the most recognisable theorists on human motivation, Abraham Maslow, discusses human motivation with regards to needs theories. One higher order need is defined as 'esteem needs'; with the hypothesis being that humans, in general, have an inherent desire to satisfy self-esteem drivers which can be achieved when respect is transferred from others.[401] In this case, if an individual has made a conscious decision to transition toward active engagement, they will likely satisfy individual esteem needs through both a sense of religious fulfilment and also through group aggrandizement if actively engaging in DCM and or ICM. Satisfying this 'quest for significance' is increasingly identified as a driver that placates individual involvement in suicide terrorism, coincidently an increasing trend due to religious overtones.[402]

---

399 Arturo Munoz, *U.S. Military Information Operations in Afghanistan: Effectiveness of Psychological Operations 2001-2010* (Santa Monica: RAND Corporation, 2012). 31.
400 Moghaddam, "The Staircase to Terrorism." 73.
401 Abraham Maslow, *A Theory on Human Motivation*, 1943rd ed. (Mansfield Centre: Martino Publishing, 2014). 15-16.
402 Arie E Kruglanski and Edward Orehek, "The Role of the Quest for Personal Significance in Motivating Terrorism," in *The Psychology of Social Conflict and Aggression*, ed. Arie W Kruglanski and K Williams (New York: Psychology Press, 2011), 153–64.

Until this point, religion's role in being a contributing factor in the radicalisation of terrorists has focused on how an individual may generate a personal grievance founded on a perceived slight by another who does not share their worldly view. However, the reality is the success of a terrorist group or organisation relies on the direct actions of a collection of individuals who share the same worldview. The ability to truly affect behaviour and achieve policy change comes when the latent power of this collective group can be harnessed against another.

Belonging, identity and empowerment

The motivational driver for humans to seek out like groups to find affiliation is an established human concept. Maslow discusses this as a higher order need, as does Alderfer in his Existence, Relatedness and Growth theory on human motivation.[403] These higher order needs are deeply intrinsic motivational drivers for individuals. The fundamental premise of these theories is that humans will continue to search for a collective group that satisfies this deep interpersonal relationship need, and until this is achieved, the individual will remain dissatisfied with their lot in life. Clearly then if an individual is aligned to a given religion, adheres to the prescribed social expectations and partakes in the symbolic actions unique to that religion; then they are likely to satisfy these belonging needs if they are accepted into the membership of a group which also adheres to the practices of that religion. This distinctiveness between religions is assessed as being a fundamental contributor in the radicalisation of terrorists. Religions, rhetoric and niceties aside, are different, and by extension, as will be the character of that membership. To satisfy this belongingness requirement individuals are either fully committed and recognised as 'in the group' or they are 'out'.

This concept of the in-group and out-group is central to Social Identity Leadership theory and is a more contemporary social-psychological approach to group dynamics. Appreciating the nuances of this theory allows the consequent actions which result in the personal grievance to be understood in the context of religious radicalisation. Central to the social identity theory is how individuals view themselves in relation to

---

403 Kathryn M Bartol et al., *Management: A Pacific Rim Focus* (North Melbourne: McGraw-Hill Book Company Australia Pty Limited, 1995). 344-359

the group. Firstly, individuals see themselves and others within the in-group as effectively interchangeable and dismiss the differences through a process of depersonalisation.[404] Conversely, they will exaggerate and emphasise the differences of those not in their group, hence the term outgroup.[405] When this occurs a common perspective begins to emerge. Individuals then increasingly strive to achieve the objectives of the group as a failure for the group is also perceived as a failure at the individual level.[406] This is an established and proven method for developing effectiveness in military units where this sense of unique group membership is further amplified through military symbology, unit flags, uniform patches and ritual acts.[407] The parallel to any number of terrorist organisation's use of symbology is evident, most notably being ISIS's haunting use of ritual murder complete with resplendent matching uniforms for victim and practitioner alike and the seemingly ubiquitous presence of the 'Black Standard' in associated imagery.[408]

Group grievance then becomes central with regards to the radicalisation of individuals to terrorism. It has already been highlighted that exposure to messaging which suggests a given religion is being repressed can result in a personal grievance and the need to direct hostility toward the offending group.[409] Furthermore, if the messaging is recognised through a form of religious endorsement, such as the fatwa issued below from Osama Bin Laden, it becomes obvious as to how a religious overtone is a powerful tool for action:

> The ruling to kill the Americans and their allies-civilian and military is an individual duty for every Muslim who can do it in any country in which it is possible to do it, in order to liberate the al-Aqse Mosque and the holy mosque (Mecca) from their grip,

404 Rolf Van Dick and Rudolf Kerschreiter, "The Social Identity Approach to Effective Leadership: An Overview and Some Ideas on Cross-Cultural Generalisability," *Front. Bus. Res. China* 10, no. 3 (2016): 364.
405 Van Dick and Kerschreiter, "The Social Identity Approach to Effective Leadership: An Overview and Some Ideas on Cross-Cultural Generalszability." 364
406 Matthew J. Slater, Andrew L. Evans, and Martin J. Turner, "Implementing a Social Identity Approach for Effective Change Management," *Journal of Change Management* 16, no. 1 (2016): 21.
407 Boas Shamir et al., "Leadership and Social Identification in Military Units: Direct and Indirect Relationships," *Journal of Applied Social Psychology* 20, no. 3 (2000): 614-616.
408 Benjamin Hall, *Inside ISIS: The Brutal Rise of a Terrorist Army* (New York: Hachette Book Group, 2015). 151-153.
409 McCauley and Moskalenko, *Friction: How Radicalisation Happens to Them and US.* 117.

and in order for their armies to move out of all the lands of Islam, defeated and unable to threaten any Muslim.[410]

On receiving the above message either through a DCM or ICM an individual may make the conscious decision to become a passive non-violent participant. Their thoughts may become more radicalised and discussion may transition into an intent for violence. However, individual thought may also evolve to the point that a conscious decision is made to engage in physical acts of terrorism. This is recognised within Moghaddam's theory on radicalisation as a transition to the fifth and final floor.[411] This may explain the success of foreign fighter recruitment associated with ISIS's actions in the proposed caliphate.

It is apparent then that membership to religious groups can provide an individual with a variety of rewards including a sense of belongingness, self-esteem fulfilment and in many cases, particularly within the *madrassas,* sustenance and material needs.[412] With regards to Maslow's human motivational model, the provision of physiological and safety needs are defined as lower order needs, those needed to sustain human life.[413] If then membership to a religious organisation acts as the mechanism to satisfy the majority of human drivers, what happens when this group collapses, or the individual becomes dislocated from the membership? The impact of individual displacement from group membership, in particular through immigration (forced or voluntary) carries significant risk with regards to the radicalisation of individuals to terror.

Analysis conducted by Marc Sagemen has identified that those Muslim immigrants residing in the West and disconnected from their family experience high levels of loneliness. This is further compounded when attempts to integrate into a western lifestyle have been unsuccessful resulting in increased levels of marginalisation.[414] In time, it is likely that companionship will again be sought through religion, with Sageman coining the term 'Unfreezing', relating to radicalisation. This new group affiliation may comprise a higher per capita membership of individuals

---

410 Miller, *Terror, Religion and Liberal Thought.* 9.

411 Moghaddam, "The Staircase to Terrorism." 75.

412 McCauley and Moskalenko, *Friction: How Radicalisation Happens to Them and US.* 84.

413 Maslow, *A Theory on Human Motivation.* 5-15.

414 McCauley and Moskalenko, *Friction: How Radicalisation Happens to Them and US.* 84-85.

who feel dejected and victimised from Western society (in the large societies centred on Christian ideals).[415] The risk here relates back to the intentional skewing of messaging through directed communications mediums where this sense of marginalisation is somehow contorted into an ideological conflict associated with an attack on Islam. This unfreezing of potentially radical tendencies is amplified when considering the psychological theory that an identity removed from its homeland will act with more determination when protecting their core values and beliefs if residing in a host country.[416] This is assessed as a significant contributor to lone actor attacks against western targets. An act of hostility from a self-identifying member of ISIS, who could not travel to the caliphate and fight as a 'serving' member of ISIS, can still act in the interest of their group by targeting those individuals perceived to be from the offending group.

Duty, absolution and disdain

Regardless of the strength of group affiliation, sense of displacement and personal grievance, the rational human being is unlikely to engage in violent acts of terrorism unless some final mental inhibitors are overcome. There are two critical by-products formed by groups that exhibit high levels of cohesion which become integral components within the religious radicalisation process. First, those groups that face a common threat (or primary outgroup) are likely to show increased respect for organisational leadership.[417] And secondly, individuals are likely to show an increased idealisation of in-group values, in this case, religious values.[418] Thus, what are abhorrent terrorist acts, become somehow justifiable as they are ordained by the religious leadership or legitimised in the pursuit of retaining the purity of religious values.

Most religions in some form have a notion of a 'just war' which can be interpreted as the need to exercise self-defence or to protect others.[419] Interpretations on Jewish law can be interpreted as the right to 'kill the

---

415 McCauley and Moskalenko, *Friction: How Radicalisation Happens to Them and US.* 84-85.
416 Ercan Citlioglu, "Terrorism Today and Tomorrow: An Analysis and Projection Study," *Homeland Security Organisation in Defence Against Terrorism* 5, no. 1 (2012): 11.
417 McCauley and Moskalenko, *Friction: How Radicalization Happens to Them and US.* 118.
418 McCauley and Moskalenko, *Friction: How Radicalization Happens to Them and US.* 118.
419 Al-Khattar, *Religion and Terrorism: An Interfaith Perspective.* 50.

killer', which has been used to justify the murder of Yitzhak Rabin due to deep-seated religious concerns:

> 'Rabin was going to make peace with the Arab countries even at the expense of Israel's security, so he was perceived as a murderer. According to Jewish law, a murder must be killed if that killing will stop murder. So, according to law, if you see a person about to murder another person, and absolutely the only way you can stop the murder is to kill that person, then you are allowed'.[420]

Christianity also justifies violence in the form of a just war, assuming it is for the greater good and endorsed by the state or government.[421] Although Christianity at large condemns contemporary terrorism, full acceptance of this becomes problematic based on one's interpretation of terror; more specifically state terrorism, being 'terrorism supported by a nation-state'.[422] References within the Judeo-Christian belief system discuss assassinations and even the complete annihilation of enemy nations based on religious alignment.[423] Furthermore, it is difficult to not see the Christian Crusades throughout the Middle Ages as a form of State terror to capture perceived holy lands from the Muslims.[424]

The Quran also justifies the taking of life 'Take not life, which Allah has made sacred, except by way of justice'[425] and furthermore endorses war if a community has been attacked.[426] The most recognisable form of religious consent for enticing an individual to engage in violence, however, relates to the term *Jihad*, meaning to struggle.[427] Within *Jihad* there are two components, *greater Jihad*, associated with the pursuit of spiritual purity and, *lesser Jihad*, relating to defensive warfare.[428] ISIS has managed to weave not only this aspect of religious duty into their

420 Al-Khattar, *Religion and Terrorism: An Interfaith Perspective*. 50-51
421 Al-Khattar, *Religion and Terrorism: An Interfaith Perspective*. 57
422 Jonathan R. White, *Terrorism and Homeland Security* (New York: Thomson Wadsworth, 2006). 211.
423 Martin, *Essentials of Terrorism*. 139
424 Martin, *Essentials of Terrorism*. 140
425 "Koran," n.d. Sura An-am 6:151
426 Saban Ali Duzgun, "Winning Back Religion: Countering the Misuse of Scripture," *Homeland Security Organization in Defence Against Terrorism* 5, no. 15 (2012): 26.
427 Mark Sedgwick, "IS in Syria," in *The New Islamic State: Ideology, Religion and Violent Extremism in the 21st Century*, ed. Jack Covarrubias and Robert J Jnr Pauly (Oxon: Ashgate, 2016), 93–112.
428 Sedgwick, "IS in Syria." 95.

group identity but has also harnessed the power of group cohesion as previously discussed:

> IS has been able to sustain itself and to expand by trumpeting its jihadist ideology to a global audience, placing itself at the nexus of a new Islamic project promising ultimate victory over a lapsed, anti-Muslim world order. The confidence of IS recruits soars when they are told that their mission is blessed by God, that they are the chosen ones, the anointed, waging a war with a preordained outcome…[429]

The point being that the skewed messaging of these principles within DCM and ICM can offer a form of religious absolution. Those with an established personal grievance are now more likely to engage in the actual act of terrorism for two primary reasons. First, engaging in religiously inspired terror acts is endorsed by the groups' leadership, but more so participation in terror action is an expectation of the wider group and central to securing ongoing membership. As such, group affiliation, will not be compromised if they engage in abhorrent violent acts. In all likelihood, an individual's status and prestige (hence individual esteem) would likely increase based on the profile of the act. Secondly, committing the terrorist act is a religious expectation so individual accountability associated with decision making can be deflected toward the guiding scriptures. Also, if killed in the terrorist action (deliberate martyrdom operations or other), entry to a positive afterlife is seemingly assured. Appreciating this pull aspect associated with group expectation and religious authority is critical for understanding how religion enables radicalised progression toward terrorism. Perhaps, more importantly, is that the pull of these components inhibits an individual's ability to engage in any de-radicalisation actions; as their entire identity, social support mechanisms and sense of self-worth is now entirely interwoven into the religious terrorist organisation. One act, however, remains. Killing.

Lieutenant Colonel Dave Grossman in his seminal work 'On Killing' highlights the existence of a powerful and innate human resistance toward killing one's own species and notes that militaries have actively addressed this resistance in order to generate increased levels of

429 Sedgwick, "IS in Syria." 96.

efficiency in combat.[430] He hypothesises that to overcome this inhibition (which is driven from the midbrain) conditioning and desensitisation is required which results in an aspect of dehumanisation with regards to the enemy.[431] Using this theory, any individual who has progressed through a radicalisation process and is prepared to kill another human being will still need to overcome this emotive inhibitor. Religious terrorist organisations have been effective in addressing this concern as highlighted by actions such as suicide attacks, human immolation and mass decapitation. These actions, grotesque as they were, were enacted by someone's son or daughter. The extremist interpretations of religion are assessed as playing a key role in generating this ability to kill humans. What better way to condition yourself to kill a human through the highly visceral act of decapitation, than by viewing the 'subject' as a sub-human, vile creature?

To generate such levels of hate toward another human being requires an extreme level of negative perception to be generated.[432] This can be achieved if descriptive language is used to convey a commonality of evil across the opposing group as it will enhance the dehumanising aspect. Hence why non-Muslins are referred to as infidel, apostate, godless, evil, pigs or dogs.[433] This dehumanising language coupled with the perception that occupation forces are engaged in a holy war not only achieves a degree of dehumanisation it can ultimately lead to a form of demonisation. Thus, the act of killing is seen as purging the evil from earth and is a form of cathartic religious cleansing. This leads to the increased desensitisation from the perspective of the terrorist killer due to a complete revulsion of the individual on multiple levels.[434] If this state of mind is achieved it is highly probably the individual will engage in violent religious inspired acts of terrorism. The radicalised transition from passive observer to active religious terrorist is complete.

---

430 Dave Lt.Col Grossman, *On Killing: The Psychological Cost of Learning to Kill in War and Society*, Revised (New York: Hachette Book Group, 1995). xxxi.

431 Grossman, *On Killing: The Psychological Cost of Learning to Kill in War and Society*. 91-92.

432 McCauley and Moskalenko, *Friction: How Radicalisation Happens to Them and US*. 164

433 Forest, *The Terrorism Lectures*. 242: McCauley and Moskalenko, *Friction: How Radicalization Happens to Them and US*. 168.

434 Robert A Pape, *Dying to Win: The Strategic Logic of Suicide Terrorism* (New York: Random House, 2005). 90.

Conclusions and Concerns

The world today is facing many challenges and one is clearly the threat of religiously inspired terrorism. It would be disingenuous to suggest that religion is the only motivating factor that initiates individual involvement in the radicalisation process. However, it would be equally naïve to suggest that it is not central to individual thought regarding radicalisation and if poorly (or effectively) employed, can act as an enduring influence through the radicalisation process. There are deeply emotive aspects relating to individual identity that shape the issue of religiously inspired terrorism. Often an individual's identity and 'moral compass' associated with life is represented in the commitment one makes to a religion and the wider fraternity of that religion. It defines them and their purpose in life. If the stability of this framework is threatened, or the religion at large is at risk of comprise from an external influence, a retaliatory action is, understandably, likely. The reality today is that actions from one group can easily be perceived by another as an affront to their religious ideals and when coupled with intentionally biased or inflammatory rhetoric continues to divide societies. The power of group loyalty removes the issue of geographic proximity associated with risk and as such the world is experiencing a form of religiously inspired global terrorism.

The challenge for the contemporary counter radicalisation theorist and policymaker is how to address these issues so normalcy is restored, opportunities for religious expression retained and the opportunity for individual and collective de-radicalisation provided. In line with the risks highlighted throughout this paper, it is worthy to note that many counter radicalisation programs appreciate these issues. Singapore's Counter-Terrorism strategy recognises ideological rehabilitation as central to the counter-radicalisation process of recognised terrorists, but also as a pre-emptive action against the radicalisation of future generations.[435] The United Kingdom's Counter-Terrorism Strategy also recognises this need as articulated in the 'Prevent' line of operation where issues such as addressing ideological grievances

---

435 Jolene Jerad, "Idelogical Rehabilitation: A Necessary Component of the Counter-Terrorism Strategy in Singapore," *Homeland Security Organization in Defence Against Terrorism* 5 (2012): 202.

are central to the strategy.[436] And finally, a 2015 Australian Strategic Policy Institute paper on preventing radicalisation recognises the risk religiously divisive language poses to a cohesive Australian Society and recommended policy change.[437]

The risk, however, may be greater than simply establishing the conditions that somehow enable a utopic homogenous society to function where the provision of equitable religious expression is afforded. As highlighted throughout this paper it is assessed that religious terrorism is linked to the issue of group affiliation and is entwined within the field of social-psychology. A society, therefore, that enables freedom of religious practice has by nature established the conditions for multiple group formation were religious ideology is the recognisable differentiator. The risk of religious terrorism will always remain within such a society if this polarisation can be exploited by those with nefarious intent. The world is truly facing a wicked problem if in fact religious tolerance and the opportunity to exercise freedom of religion becomes, in time, recognisable as a root cause for religiously inspired terrorism.

---

436 Maya Sivagnanam and J P I A G Charvat, "CONTEST II - The United Kingdom's Counter-Terrorism Strategy," *Homeland Security Organization in Defence Against Terrorism* 5 (2012): 68-69.

437 Bergin et al., "Gen Y Jihadists: Preventing Radicalisation in Australia." 52-53.

Insurgencies

Essay 8

Insurgency, Iraq 2003 Onwards
(Written 2012)

Introduction

An insurgency, like any conflict, requires certain conditions to be set in order to be effective and achieve operational aims. During this paper the Iraq insurgency post 2003 will be used to demonstrate how three Principle requirements from an insurgent's perspective were employed to set these operational conditions. The paper will focus firstly on how the use of sanctuary and external support contributed to a successful insurgency, secondly why there is the need for effective leadership and a viable recruitment base, and finally how the access to and employment of weaponry contributes to mission success.

Sanctuary and external support

The requirement for insurgents to be afforded sanctuary within the area of operations is not a new concept and is highlighted by Che Guevara:

> 'The guerrilla must possess a highly developed knowledge of the terrain on which he operates, avenues of access and escape, possibilities for rapid manoeuvre, popular support and hiding places'[438]

When considering the above observation, the rise of an insurgent base in the city of Fallujah can be used to demonstrate how the principal of popular support and knowledge of terrain afforded the insurgents sanctuary.

Firstly, the terrain was difficult, more specifically it was complex. This allowed the insurgents the ability to exploit their knowledge of a three-

---

438 Guevara, C *Guerrilla Warfare*. Cassell, London, 1961, p. 113

dimensional urban environment affording them freedom of movement and an ability to identify and target likely avenues of approach. Their knowledge of the terrain afforded them operational sanctuary.

Additionally, and arguably more potent to the US forces, were the complexities associated with the human terrain and host population perceptions. Direct action by US forces on the 28th and 30th of April 2003 resulted in civilian deaths and a significant number of casualties[439]. This action supported the insurgent's propaganda campaign against the US aiding popular support for the insurgency and affording sanctuary.

In addition to this internal support and sanctuary, the occupation by US forces within Iraq acted as a catalyst for an insurgency, and as such support for the insurgency was provided by countries and motivated groups within the region. Due to the grounding as a Ba'athist state, Syria showed support to the Iraqi insurgency[440]. Iranian support with regards to arms and training was more focussed towards the Shia armed groups like the Badr Brigade. Of note is the number of fighters from external countries that volunteered support based on a religious ideology. Evidence has been found of foreign fighters providing support from Saudi Arabia, Libya and Jordan[441]. It was this general disdain for the US occupation within Iraq that led to an ever-increasing leadership and recruitment base.

Leadership and a recruitment base

The Iraqi insurgency consisted of several major organisations, each with differing ideologies, however all committed to the removal of the US and its allies from Iraq[442]. Initially the most influential insurgent group post 2003 was the deposed Sunni Ba'athist party. The de *Ba'athification* process introduced by the US empowered many disenfranchised Iraqi military officers, including not only combat officers, but intelligence officers and strategists to rise against the occupation and develop an insurgent organisation[443]. It is a fair assumption that this initial

439 Mahnken, G, and Keaney, T *War in Iraq: Planning and Execution.* Routledge, London, 2007, p. 164

440 Hashim, A *Iraq's Sunni Insurgency.* Routledge, London, 2009, p. 69

441 DeFronzo, J *The Iraq War.* Westview Press, Boulder CO, 2010, p. 212

442 Hashim, A *Iraq's Sunni Insurgency.* Routledge, London, 2009, p. 17

443 Ricks, T *Fiasco: The American Military Adventure in Iraq.* Penguin Group, 2006, p 165

leadership base had an existing understanding of military strategy, some established logistical channels and ability to train and lead. Evidence also exists that the intelligence officers of the Ba'th party had developed plans to conduct a campaign of guerrilla warfare against the US in the event of Saddam Hussein losing power of Iraq[444].

The recruitment of individuals to join any number of insurgent groups was not difficult. Motivation to become affiliated with an insurgency ranged from Nationalist pride in order to remove the occupiers, through to a deep seated religious positioning based on Islamist views and the opposition to non-Muslim occupation[445]. The Iraq insurgency differed from previous insurgencies in one key aspect of recruitment, that being technology, more specifically the internet. Access to the internet allowed charismatic leaders to passively and actively recruit personnel for the insurgency from both within and external to Iraq[446]. Of note is the recruitment of personnel based purely for Martyrdom operations and how this saw the rise and employment of a new type of weaponry.

The access to and employment of weaponry

Like any defence force the Iraqi Military had a stockpile of conventional weapons and munitions[447]. This was critical to the insurgency both with regards to access, and the development of new tactics. Although suicide bombings and booby traps are not new concepts, the Iraq insurgency saw these employed to a level not seen before in previous insurgencies[448]. A linkage between ex-military members being able to identify and exploit a weakness in conventional forces tactics and an ability to modify munitions can be attributed to this development. With reference to suicide bombings two basic requirements are needed, firstly an individual possessing the motivation to conduct the act and secondly the explosives to deliver the effect. The existing recruitment base in conjunction with the effective leadership and coupled with explosive availability, afforded the Iraqi insurgency both these key requirements.

---

444 Wright, E *War in Iraq: Military Operations, Criticisms, and History.* Six Degrees Books, p 97
445 Ibid, p 99.
446 Forest, J *The Making of a Terrorist: Recruitment, Training and Root Causes, Volume 1: Recruitment.* Praeger Security International, Westport, 2006, p 131.
447 Ricks, T *Fiasco: The American Military Adventure in Iraq.* Penguin Group, 2006, p 191.
448 Forest, J *The Making of a Terrorist: Recruitment, Training and Root Causes, Volume 2: Training.* Praeger Security International, Westport, 2006, p. 155

Separate to the suicide bomber was the rise of the Improvised Explosive Device (IED). The evolution of the IED within Iraq saw the insurgent utilising all means necessary to develop and employ this weaponry including the internet for knowledge development and sharing, utilisation of existing skills sets within the disbanded military, access to conventional munitions and HME and also support from external sanctuaries. The result saw an increase in the complexity of an IED, including the development of multiple means of detonation and delivery. The IED however fell into two main categories, the victim initiated or the command initiated device[449]. These developments afforded the insurgent a high degree of flexibility and freedom of manoeuvre; whilst simultaneously crippling the US's freedom of manoeuvre and having a psychological impact on personnel[450].

Conclusion

The efficiency of the Iraq insurgency cannot be denied. The sanctuary afforded to insurgents by the host population within Iraq in addition to external support can be attributable to the continued success of the insurgency. Additionally, the complexities associated with recognised and tribal factions, provided an almost perfect environment for the employment of charismatic leadership. With a leadership base established, coupled with the perception that the US had launched an unprovoked invasion of Iraq, the recruitment and employment of a dislocated population to fight for an insurgency became inevitable. Finally, with these two conditions met, the Iraq insurgency began to evolve, developing new weaponry in order to provide them with a tactical advantage against a 'superior' conventional force; a conventional force that has and continues to modify its counter-insurgency tactics techniques and procedures based on lessons hard learnt in Iraq post 2003.

449 Ricks, *T Fiasco: The American Military Adventure in Iraq.* Penguin Group, 2006, p 217.
450 Ricks, *T Fiasco: The American Military Adventure in Iraq.* Penguin Group, 2006, p 221.

Insurgency, Pakistan *(Written 2012)*

Introduction

An insurgency takes many forms and has many definitions, ultimately however, it is a political movement driven by a collective with shared motivational ideologies, the purpose of which is generating political instability in order to initiate or prevent change. Often this will result in an insurgent strategy shifting from attempts at political resolution through to the employment of violence as a tactic to generate or leverage public opinion and initiate change. The current insurgency being waged within Pakistan is no exception.

> 'The insurgents' stated aim was to destabilise President General Pervez Musharraf's government, which was seen as hostile to Islam and pro-American'.[451]

To successfully defeat an insurgent movement, the recognised government being targeted must develop a counter strategy that allows the insurgent message to be neutralised. Governmental themes should then be restored and normalcy returned to society. Many theoretical constructs exist in the field of counter insurgency; often however these generic hypotheses fail to recognise the impact that unique non-state players and influence drivers will have. It is these intangible elements that continue to remain problematic for policy makers when strategic theoretical constructs shift toward tactical application and policy implementation.

This paper will focus on three distinct, yet interwoven elements of modern day Pakistan and demonstrate how the combination of these

---

451 Pardesi, M, S 'The Battle for the Soul of Pakistan at Islamabad's Red Mosque', in *Treading on Hallowed Ground: Counterinsurgency Operations in sacred spaces.* Oxford, University Press, New York, 2008 p 88.

elements throughout history have, and continue to, impact on the intensity of the modern-day insurgency being experienced in Pakistan.

First, elements of the Pakistan Military will be reviewed, illustrating issues that arise when a military acts as a pseudo government. The military can also highlight issues associated with ethnicity; in the Pakistan case this is clearly represented by the dynamics associated with personnel of Punjab and Pashtun heritage.

Second, the United States as a non-state actor, has had a complex influence in Pakistan evolution. This will be discussed in two time frames. Initially the support offered to Pakistan during the establishment of a Mujahedeen force to fight the Soviet invasion of Afghanistan from 1978 through to 1992, will be discussed. The enduring legacy of which will then be highlighted with reference to modern day Pakistan and consequently the continued interest afforded by the US.

Finally, the impact of Madrassah culture within Pakistan as an influence driver will be discussed, with specific reference to poverty, and how this impacts on motivational constructs. Furthermore, the inability of government to establish standardised curriculum will be highlighted as a contributing factor to the rise in an insurgent movement.

A potted history

Pakistan as a country was conceptualised. This is largely attributable to the growing influence of Muslim traders during the development of Pakistan as a nation and the perceived need for a Muslim homeland in the Hindu dominated Indian political environment. This resulted in the drive for an Islamic caliphate.[452] This need for 'belongingness', as defined by Maslow, continued until 1930 when the concept of a Muslim state was raised by the political poet Mohammed Iqbal.[453] [454] It is important to emphasise his grounding as a 'Punjabi', whom are still seen as elitist in Pakistan. Support for this concept was further raised in 1940 by the Islamist group Jama'at-i-Islami. Ultimately negotiations between the

---

452 Stephens, I *Pakistan*, Ernest Benn Limited, London, 1963, p 13.
453 Bartol, M, B, Martin, D, C, Tein, M, and Matthews, G, M *Management: A Pacific rim focus*. McGraw, Roseville 1995, p 418.
454 Cohen, S, P *The Idea of Pakistan*. The Brookings Institution, Washington, 2004, pp 5-7.

British Empire, the Hindu National Congress and the Muslim League led to the state of Pakistan being formed on August the 14th 1947.[455]

Governing bodies declared boundaries, people were displaced, ethnicity and religious orientation became a source of violence. Political instability continued post 1947 with the political elite, the military and bureaucrats attempting to establish a stable state. It was in 1956 that the Constituent Assembly approved the first constitution, and the Islamic Republic of Pakistan was born. The first President was a former soldier and his successor following abrogation was a General.[456]

Although this is a crude history of Pakistan it highlights key points, supportive of the argument being raised. The assignment of borders along geographical lines has contributed to poverty, ethnic divisions and deep-seated hatred.[457] This is particularly evident when comparing the fertile country, and subsequently wealthy, Punjabi area, to the mountainous, isolated and arguably inhospitable areas of Baluchistan and what would later become the Federally Administered Tribal Areas (FATA). These borders were made in conjunction with the then ruling British Empire, a western outside influence. The strong Pashtun identity and problems associated with the formation of the Durrani line were yet to materialise.[458] Finally the military and its role as a governing authority makes them an institution more vulnerable to targeting by insurgents.

Pseudo governance, ethnicity and subversion

The military in Pakistan has arguably been the most influential political organisation since independence was declared. Much of this can be attributed to the absence of a functioning civilian led government, as stated by Pervez Musharraf;

> "Sadly, a functioning democracy is exactly what has eluded Pakistan ever since its birth on August 14, 1947. This weakness lies at the root of most of our ills".[459]

---

455 ...7
456 Cohen, S, P *The Idea of Pakistan.* The Brookings Institution, Washington, 2004, pp 5-7
457 Gunaratna, R and Iqbal, K Pakistan: Terrorism ground zero, Reaktion Books, London, 2011 p 21.
458 Gul, I *The most Dangerous Place: Pakistan's lawless frontier*, Penguin Books, London 2010.
459 Musharraf, P *In the Line of Fire: A Memoir*, Simon and Schuster, London, 2006 p

The Pakistan military was founded on the proven British colonial military structure, consequently, due to its existing bureaucratic framework, a leadership base and a functioning subordinate chain, it became a logical organisation to fill this governance void.[460] When General Mohamed Ayub Khan, with support from the military, seized power in October 1958, he brought a stability to Pakistan that was welcomed domestically and by western governments. This can be attributable to his strong political alignment against communism.[461] However, the significant development was the pursuit of land acquisition by senior military officers, predominately Punjabis. The ability to develop business ventures and generate income effectively made the senior echelons of the military independent of the government. They became self-sufficient, powerful and effectively independent of civilian government.

Civilian and Military led governments continued to jostle for power through to July 1977 when General Zia ul-Haq seized power from Zulfikar ali Bhutto, with Bhutto subsequently being hung for conspiracy to murder.[462] Zia's military rule is considered critical to the current insurgency for two reasons. Firstly, it saw the commencement of the 'Islamification' of the military, specifically Sunni Islam, the faith practised by the majority of Pashtuns.[463] Second, his command saw the Inter-Services Intelligence Agency (ISI), with the support of the United States of America, actively unite a number of Sunni organisations to fight the Soviet invasion of Afghanistan.[464]

> 'The CIA assisted the ISI to establish secret schools in the North-West Frontier Province (NWFP) and Baluchistan to teach the Afghan Islamists techniques of guerrilla warfare and urban sabotage'[465]

460 Cohen, S, P *The idea of Pakistan*. The Brookings Institution, Washington, 2004, p 101.
461 Murphy, E and Tamana, A 'State terrorism and the military in Pakistan', in *Contemporary State Terrorism: Theory and Practice,* Jackson, R, Murphy, E and Poynting, S (eds), Routledge, Oxon, 2010, p 53.
462 Hussain, R *Pakistan and the emergence of Islamic militancy in Afghanistan*. Ashgate Publishing Limited, Hampshire, 2005, pp 96-97.
463 Gartenstein-Ross, D 'Religious Militancy in Pakistan's Military and Inter-Services Intelligence Agency' in *The Afghanistan – Pakistan Theatre: Militant Islam, security and stability*, Gartenstein-Ross, D and May, C, D (eds), FDD Press, Washington, 2010, p 31.
464 ... p33.
465 Hussain, R *Pakistan and the emergence of Islamic militancy in Afghanistan*. Ashgate Publishing Limited, Hampshire, 2005, p 116.

The key here is that these organisations evolved into a 'Mujahedeen' or holy warrior force, whose focus was expelling Soviet 'infidels' or non-believers from Afghanistan. Many of these fighters were of Pashtun descent, with shared interests and belonging to communities that lived together regardless of the Duranni line or recognised Pakistan-Afghanistan Border.

The historical linkage between the current insurgency against the civilian lead Pakistan government is clear. First, there is a class division that exists between the predominately senior Punjabi officers and the remaining predominately Pashtun junior officers and other ranks. The primary law enforcement agency within the North-West Frontier Province is the Frontier Corps (FC). Unlike traditional military recruitment, FC personnel are trained and recruited locally. Due to this religious and geopolitical positioning, many of the front-line troops are more closely aligned to Pashtun interests than that of the Army command, based in Punjab[466]. This affiliation to Pashtun nationalism and rejection of the Duranni border and government policy poses a significant threat to Pakistan stability.[467]

Second, many of the military officers developed during the Islam focussed Zia period are now mid to senior officers, trained firstly in insurgent tactics, but more so, sympathetic to and aligned with an insurgency based on an Islamist ideology.

In short the counter insurgent policy devised at the strategic level by government is failing in part due to insubordination, or perhaps more accurately apathy, by military commanders at the operational and tactical level. This fact highlights that tribal affiliation within the military and existing class structures are independent of state control and are having a negative impact on the counter insurgency strategy.

The impact of the United States of America

Although a linkage exists with the military and its perceived negative impact on the current insurgency, it does little to explain why in fact

---

466 Markey, D *Securing Pakistan's Tribal Belt*, Council on Foreign Relations, New York, 2008, p 10.
467 Author not listed, *Afghanistan: India's strategic stakes*. Har-Anand Publications, New Dehli, 2010, p 106.

the current government of the Islamic Republic of Pakistan continues to be targeted by insurgent groups. The explanation to this is linked to the involvement of the United States as a non-state actor in Pakistan's history.

Although involved in Pakistani politics prior to the 1980s, it was the US involvement in the development and mobilisation of a Mujahedeen guerrilla force to fight the Soviet invasion of Afghanistan that continues to impact on the lethality of the current insurgency. It is estimated that the US contributed up to $5 billion between 1980 and 1991 toward the training and arming of a Mujahedeen force.[468]

> 'Perhaps the most significant historical fact in this context is that a part of the American-Pakistan Anti-Soviet campaign involved the joint efforts of both the American Central Intelligence Agency (CIA) and Pakistan's ISI in a recruitment of the most "radical Muslims from around the world to come to fight with the Afghan Mujahedeen[469]

What is significant is the agenda employed to generate recruits; that being not to expel the 'Soviets' from Afghanistan, rather the expulsion of the 'infidel' from Muslim lands. In this case the infidels happened to be Soviet and the land Afghanistan. The recruitment campaign was a brilliant success. Large numbers of ideological fighters, including Arab Islamists, flooded training camps in the NWFP and Baluchistan. Here they were equipped with weaponry and received training in guerrilla warfare, urban sabotage, leadership and planning.[470] This Jihad against the Soviet infidel afforded charismatic leaders the forum in which to influence a recruitment base and progress their ideals.

Osama Bin Laden, the father of 'Al-Qaeda', fought in a number of battles to expel the infidel, and in doing so legitimised Al-Qaeda's ideology and reinforced his place as a proven holy warrior.[471] The actions of a young Osama Bin Laden allowed him to demonstrate not only legitimate

---

468 Haleem, I 'Pakistan, Afghanistan and Central Asia: Recruiting grounds for terrorism' in *Democratic Development and Political Terrorism,* Crotty, W (ed), Northeaster University Press, Boston, 2005, p 124.

469 ...

470 Hussain, R *Pakistan and the emergence of Islamic militancy in Afghanistan*. Ashgate Publishing Limited, Hampshire, 2005, pp 116-117.

471 Bergen, P 'Al Qaeda: Then and Now' in *Al Qaeda Now: Understanding Today's Terrorist,* Greenberg K. J (ed), Cambridge University Press, New York, 2005, p 5.

leadership but also allowed him to develop an aura of charismatic leadership, a critical requirement in the development of collective identity theory.[472][473]

The paradox that exists for the current Pakistan insurgency is that it is a result of the continued involvement of the United States. Following the terrorist attacks against the US on September 11th 2001, the then President of the Pakistan, Musharraf, offered the US complete support to aid in a successful outcome on the war on terror.[474] This is arguably the genesis moment for the modern-day insurgency within Pakistan. The support afforded to the US for the war on terror effectively allowed the Pakistan government to be construed as pro west; thus providing the grounds for an insurgency to commence against the government and the military within Pakistan.[475]

> 'They then perceived western intervention in Afghanistan after 2001 as an extension of the past, with non-Muslims occupying Muslim land. This explains why hard-line Pashtun nationalists and the Islamists are supporting the fight against the US and its allies'[476]

The efforts of the US and coalition forces within Afghanistan forced much of the Al-Qaeda network to seek sanctuary within the FATA of Pakistan. Consequently, the Pakistani Military initiated offensive actions against Al-Qaeda and other militant groups including Hezb-e-Islam and the Haqqani network. This only sought to reinforce the perception that the Pakistan government was pro west which increased support for the insurgency.[477] In addition to this, allowing the US entry into Pakistan air space by manned and unmanned aircraft has proved

---

472 Bartol, M, B, Martin, D, C, Tein, M, and Matthews, G, M *Management: A pacific rim focus*. McGraw, Roseville 1995, p 449.

473 Gupta D, K *Understanding Terroism and Political Violence: The life cycle of birth, growth, transformation, and demise*, Routledge, Oxon, 2008, p 86.

474 Khan, F, H 'The United States, Pakistan and the War on Terrorism: Enduring Allies or Uncertain Partners?' in *Global Terrorism: Genesis, Implications, Remedial and Countermeasures*, (ed unknown), Aziz-ul-Haque, Islmabad, 2006, pp 357-382.

475 Ghosh, T 'Ethnic conflict in Sindh and its impact on Pakistan' in *Ethinc conflict and secessionism in south and southeast Asia*, Ganguly, R and Macduff, I (eds), Sage Publications, New Dehli, 2003, p 122.

476 Gunaratna, R and Iqbal, K *Pakistan: Terrorism ground zero*, Reaktion Books, London, 2011, p 29.

477 ... p 27.

counter-productive, particularly when strikes result in civilian collateral damage.[478]

When compared to principles required from an insurgent's perspective, it is clear that the involvement of the US in the Pakistan political sphere continues to provide the current insurgency with critical requirements to wage a successful insurgency.[479] This includes previous provision and training in weaponry, external support, the development of leadership and a recruitment pool, an organisational structure, knowledge of guerrilla tactics and, perhaps more damning, the grounds for popular support and an ever-increasing motivational purpose to commit terror.

Motivation and the Madrassah

It is clear so far that two non-state influences continue to impact on the current insurgency within Pakistan. Firstly, the Pakistan Military with its ethno-religious divisions is impacting on the legitimacy of government and their ability to effectively employ the military to quell the insurgency. Second, the involvement of the US, if harnessed correctly, provides grounds to justify an insurgency. The question however remains; why is there such a fervent insurgency being waged against a pro Islam government within Pakistan? Ultimately the answer to this question is rooted in theoretical motivational constructs and the mediums in which these are disseminated.

Malsow argues that the human is motivated to action based on the fulfilment of needs, and hypothesised the Hierarchy of Needs theory.[480] The foundation of this theoretical construct is the basic human need to satisfy physiological needs such as food, shelter and human to human stimuli. The Madrassah within Pakistan provided a forum to fill this need;

478 Kronstadt, A, K and Katzman, K 'Islamist Militancy in the Pakistan-Afghanistan Border Region and U.S. Policy' in *Combating Islamic Militancy and Terrorism in Pakistan's Border Region,* Koppel, N, J (ed), Nova Science Publishers Inc, New York, 2010, pp 11-12.

479 Asprey, R, B Jnr ' Guerrilla Warfare', in *Britannica Academic Edition*, viewed on 06 September 2011, < http://www.britannica.com/EBchecked/topic/248353/guerrilla-warfare>

480 Robbins, S, P, Waters-Marsh, T, Cacioppe, R and Millett, B *Organisational Behaviour: Concepts, controversies and applications,* Prentice Hall, Sydney, 1994, pp 242-244.

'Religious madrassah on the other hand, located all over the country have been a regular source of free education, free food, housing and clothing.'[481]

The majority of people enrolled to receive education within the madrassah were children or youth, aged between five and 18 years of age.[482] For many this environment would have afforded them with the greatest stability yet seen in their life, and in doing so, satisfied Maslow's second human need, that being, safety needs and the protection from harm.[483]

The third tier of Maslow's hierarchy is the need for love and belongingness[484]. This need for shared identity and inclusion is not unique to Maslow's hypothesis and can be linked to three main sources of shared identity; one being group formation based on religious positioning.[485] The Pakistan Madrassah are traditionally focussed on providing religious centric education with limited attention to a curricular outside of this realm.[486] Consequently members of the 50,000 plus Madrassah within Pakistan form a natural comradeship and a shared belongingness founded in Islamic commonality, for the most part which is positive.[487]

It is the inability of the Pakistan government to control the curricular within these Madrassah that is contributing to the current insurgency. It is estimated that less than ten percent of Madrassah within Pakistan

---

481 Mahmood, S 'Changing dynamics of centre – provinces relations', in *Margalla Papers 2005: Internal dynamics of Pakistan*, LTCOL Arshad, M (eds), National Defence College, Islamabad, 2005, pp 59-60.

482 Hussain, Z *Frontline Pakistan: The struggle with Militant Islam*, Columbia University Press, New York, 2007, p 78.

483 Bartol, M, B, Martin, D, C, Tein, M, and Matthews, G, M *Management: A pacific rim focus*. McGraw, Roseville 1995, p 418.

484 Robbins, S, P, Waters-Marsh, T, Cacioppe, R and Millett, B *Organisational Behaviour: Concepts, controversies and applications,* Prentice Hall, Sydney, 1994, pp 242-244.

485 Gupta D, K *Understanding Terrorism and Political Violence: The life cycle of birth, growth, transformation, and demise,* Routledge, Oxon, 2008, p 20.

486 Fair, C, C *Urban Battle fields of South Asia: Lessons Learned from Sri Lanka, India and Pakistan,* RAND Corporation, 2004, pp 105-106.

487 Malik, S 'Terrorism and its implications on internal and external security dynamics of Pakistan', in *Margalla Papers 2005: Internal dynamics of Pakistan*, LTCOL Arshad, M (eds), National Defence College, Islamabad, 2005, p 29.

are registered with the government.[488] Consequently a percentage of an estimated student body in excess of 1.5 million are receiving tutorship from a clerical leadership with political and ethno-religious positioning that is inconsistent with governmental strategic objectives.[489] The problem lies in the message:

> 'The education imparted by traditional Madrassah often spawned factional, religious and cultural conflict. It created barriers to modern knowledge, stifled creativity and bred bigotry, thus laying the foundation on which fundamentalism – militant or otherwise – was based.'[490]

The linkage between a percentage of youth indoctrinated in a Jihadist anti-western sentiment and an insurgency against the Pakistan government and military is clear, with the Madrassah culture ultimately providing the fertile environment for the rise of the Taliban.[491] It is likely that members of such a focused group with shared militant ideologies and objectives have a greater sense of self-worth and respect. Effectively the Madrassah has provided the forum for the individual to satisfy esteem needs, Maslow's second highest level of needs fulfilment.[492]

The final component of needs satisfaction is that of 'self-actualisation', effectively the achievement of one's life purpose.[493] This intense level of purpose may explain the increased levels of suicide terror attacks committed in the name of Jihad against Pakistani officials.[494] It is not unrealistic to see why an individual raised and inculcated in a militant Islamist environment would conclude that executing a suicide attack

---

488 Malik, S 'Terrorism and its implications on internal and external security dynamics of Pakistan', in *Margalla Papers 2005: Internal dynamics of Pakistan*, LTCOL Arshad, M (eds), National Defence College, Islamabad, 2005, p 29

489 Hussain, Z *Frontline Pakistan: The struggle with Militant Islam*, Columbia University Press, New York, 2007, p 79.

490 ...ibid

491 Gartenstein-Ross, D 'Religious Militancy in Pakistan's Military and Inter-Services Intelligence Agency' in *The Afghanistan – Pakistan Theatre: Militant Islam, security and stability*, Gartenstein-Ross, D and May, C, D (eds), FDD Press, Washington, 2010, p 33.

492 Robbins, S, P, Waters-Marsh, T, Cacioppe, R and Millett, B *Organisational Behaviour: Concepts, controversies and applications,* Prentice Hall, Sydney, 1994, pp 242-244.

493 Bartol, M, B, Martin, D, C, Tein, M, and Matthews, G, M *Management: A Pacific Rim focus.* McGraw, Roseville 1995, p 418.

494 Malik, S, AIG of Pakistan Police, *Suicide Bombers,* Australian Bomb Data Centre Conference, Sydney, 4th Nov 2011.

against the infidels, the Pakistan government or other, would be the culminating point of existence. And in doing so provide the medium to martyrdom and the transition to the spiritual realm.

Conclusion

Pakistan is a young country; its history however is not. The reality for Pakistan is that ethno-religious positioning continues to undermine the government's ability to maintain and exercise control and therefore allow the population to live in a state of peace. This is clearly evident within the military were the Punjabi-Pashtun divide continues to impact on the successful execution of strategic objectives. This friction point is further exacerbated by the continued influence of the United States.

The overflow, both perceived and real, of US operations in Pakistan territory and the political environment continues to provide extremist leadership with abundant ideological key message themes. Consequently, charismatic leadership within a number of extremist religious organisations continue to wage, and arguably win, the propaganda war with regards to a Jihadist based insurgency.

The continued levels of poverty within Pakistan is seeing high numbers of disaffected youth attracted to Madrassah in order to satisfy basic human needs. In doing so a percentage are exposing themselves to influence from fringe clerical elements with objectives that differ from governmental strategic counter insurgency objectives.

The reality is that through the indoctrination and exploitation of the vulnerable, the insurgent campaign is continuing to develop momentum within Pakistan, with the Madrassah providing a regenerative cycle of recruitment and leadership. In short, the current state of complicity of the Pakistan government with the United States administration appears only to fuel the insurgency not to counter.

PART 2 - WAR

PART 2 - WAR

Grand Strategy

Essay 10

From your readings of Pericles strategy, as it is outlined in Thucydides, what insights do you make about the nature of strategy? *(Written 2017)*

The importance of a considered strategy focused on progressing the interests of a nation state and its' people is barely a new concept. What constitutes strategy (or grand strategy), what determines a successful strategy, and the essence of strategy has been a topic of discussion from the ancient theorist through to the contemporary academic. The intent of this discussion is to draw pertinent insights relating to the nature of strategy; and as such the strategy proposed by Pericles in the interests of Athenian sovereignty will frame the discussion. Ultimately it will be shown a fundamental insight on the nature of strategy is that they, in fact, behave like an organic system. That is, a strategy is not simply struck following careful deliberation and hence successful; but rather strategic concepts are inherently vulnerable, the integrity of which is constantly tested by factors internal and external to the framework.

To situate this thesis, it is necessary to gain a shared understanding of what constitutes a strategy. There has and continues to be much debate on what constitutes a strategy, however, based on the premise that the strategy as proposed by Pericles was in the interest of the survival of Athens, 'Grand Strategy' will be used as a reference. Hal Brands definition provides sufficient context difficult to dispute, "Reduced to its essence, grand strategy is the intellectual architecture that lends structure to foreign policy; it is the logic that helps states navigate a complex and dangerous world."[495] This simplistic definition is central in framing how insights regarding Athenian strategy during the Peloponnesian Wars

---

495 Hal Brands, *What Good Is Grand Strategy? Power and Purpose in American Statecraft from Harry S. Truman to George W. Bush* (London: Cornell University Press, 2016). 10

will be illustrated. It identifies three central components from which strategic insight will be drawn, being the individual, the state and the complexity of a dangerous world. These will then be used to demonstrate how regardless of intent, actions (or inactions) may result in unintended negative consequences up to and including interstate conflict.

Pericles was the central character largely responsible for the strategy adopted by Athens in her defence from the Spartan alliance. Although an orator of repute during the period, it was not his primary focus; rather a tertiary skill developed in part from his (relatively) privileged upbringing and subsequent position as a key commander within the Athenian Military. In short, he was recognised and accepted as an intellectual of the time.[496] His opinion carried gravitas with the governing elite, military fraternity and society at large, the very three subjective institutions as later articulated by Clausewitz when discussing insights on strategy.[497] Understanding the importance of Pericles' ability to influence these subjective institutions is critical to gaining insight on the nature of strategy. Simply put, if these subjective institutions cannot be influenced support will not be forthcoming and any proposed strategy would simply not exist. Hence then if these three subjective institutions are central to strategy, a logical insight relates to the strategic 'architect' and their influence on decision makers when framing an argument in support of a given strategy.

Pericles made the assessment that Athens was superior over the Spartan alliance on several fronts most notably financially and militarily (specifically in the maritime environment). Additionally, he was also deeply patriotic toward Athens believing this level of patriotism extended to the population at large and thus advantageous to Athenian interest.[498] The funeral oration he delivers for the fallen gives insight into the sense of honour he holds, "and then when all her greatness shall break upon you, you must reflect that it was by courage, sense of duty and a keen feeling of honour in action that we were able to win all

---

496 Robert B. Strassler, *Thucydides: A Comprehensive Guide to the Peloponnesian War* (New York: Schuster Inc, 1996). Book 2, Chapter 2.34

497 Antulio J. Echevarria II, "Clausewitz and the Nature of the War on Terror," in *Clausewitz in the Twenty-First Century*, ed. Hew Strachan and Andreas Herberg-Rothe (London: Oxford University Press, n.d.), 4.

498 Strassler, *Thucydides: A Comprehensive Guide to the Peloponnesian War*. Book 1, Chapter 1.141

this...".[499] Consequently, any strategy proposed by him for the defence of Athens held 'her' security in primacy regardless of the potential diplomatic fallout. Additionally, during this speech, he plays on a strong sense of the importance of belonging, as evidenced by the fact that in the event of death, the children of a slain veteran will be raised through state funds. What becomes apparent at this stage through the analysis of Pericles words, is the fact he is emotively committed. He was prepared to sacrifice diplomatic advantage, whereas tact was required to build international relationships, this being a cornerstone required in establishing functional national strategies.[500] Pericles was not being driven simply by military logic, his thoughts were being overly influenced by emotive drivers and with this came risk to the security of Athens.

An appreciation of this remains relevant for decision makers within the strategic echelons of any contemporary military or government. It is critical that the decision maker gains an insight on the individual positioning a given political advisor has with regards to strategy. Knowing this, then identifying their inherent biases and drivers, provides the decision maker enhanced fidelity on which course of action to adopt and whether the strategy proposed is sound. Based in part on his sense of honour and patriotism, Pericles proposed what could be defined as a strategy of deterrence, meaning Athens must accept the inevitability of war through committing resources and commencing preparations.[501] Thus, only through readying for war could Spartan aggression be deterred. On this proposition, he received little debate from those whose vote carried sway. The strategy was adopted.[502]

Understanding this propensity for military action and challenging Pericles may, however, have proven the more prudent course of action. These continued military preparations, likely inadvertently, acted as the catalyst triggering (or at a minimum accelerating) a conflict spiral

---

499 Ibid. Book 2, Chapter 2.43
500 Freedman, "Grand Strategy and Levels" (Canberra: Australian National University, 2017).
501 Greg Cashman and Leonard C Robinson, *An Introduction to the Causes of War: Patterns of Interstate Conflict from World War 1 to Iraq* (Lanham: Rowman and Littlefield Publishers, Inc, n.d.), 15
502 Strassler, *Thucydides: A Comprehensive Guide to the Peloponnesian War.* Book 1, Chapter 1.144

between Athens and Sparta.[503] Although perhaps not a formalised concept of the time, the predictability of enhanced Spartan aggression must surely have been anticipated through a sense of reciprocity.[504] It is these second order or unintended effects that provide insight into the complexities associated with the nature of strategy. In this instance, Pericles, as a key influencer on the subjective institutions, failed in his appreciation of the risks associated with endorsing war. As did those that voted for war, whom at any given time were charged with not only challenging his strategic position but also in time his operational strategy.

Why the recommendation to transition to a war like stance was supported so willingly by the state's decision makers yields as many insights on strategy as did analysing Pericles individual positioning. Pericles was acting in effect as a secretariat of state, his reasoning, when supported, led to the formulation of foreign policy in support of war. But why? At the very basic level, Athens felt convinced they held the advantage on several fronts, notably militarily, as illustrated by Pericles contempt toward Spartan naval ability.[505] This argument was an obvious opening volley for Pericles when proposing war but barely insightful. In contrast, however, the way he played on the decision makers fears for self physically, but also emotionally through the loss of esteem, does prove insightful. One's own esteem is a powerful motivational driver shaping behaviour and is widely identified as a higher order need in several motivational constructs.[506] Pericles argued that submitting to Spartan demands through arbitration on any area in dispute would be conceding defeat; with this submissive action equating no less to the enslavement of Athens. It is apparent then that that decision makers are being influenced by the inherent fear of losing their self-esteem.

When reviewing this decision-making process, little ambiguity existed regarding Spartan intent against Athens. Both Sparta and Athens had

503 Cashman and Robinson, *An Introduction to the Causes of War: Patterns of Interstate Conflict from World War 1 to Iraq*. 14.
504 Cashman and Robinson, *An Introduction to the Causes of War: Patterns of Interstate Conflict from World War 1 to Iraq*. 14.
505 Strassler, *Thucydides: A Comprehensive Guide to the Peloponnesian War*. Book 1, Chapter 1.141
506 Stephen Robbins et al., *Organisation Behaviour: Concepts, Controversies and Applications* (Sydney: Prentice Hall, 1994). 241-243

been in conflict militarily and diplomatically for decades. The relevance of this is important as it gives insight on the disposition of the decision makers when Pericles delivered his speech. Here we see the convergence of any number of contemporary theories relating to potential triggers for war. In this case, Athens superior positioning in the world order was causing tension and ripe for challenge. This notably links to what has been described as Prospect theory were the propensity for war is greatly increased when decision makers believe they are defending the status quo.[507] Additionally, this theory also indicates that decision makers are more inclined to take risks if the potential for failure will result in loss. It is difficult to see a greater motivator for endorsing war when the status quo in question is the inversion of the relationship between master and slave.

The key insight regarding the nature of strategy is the impact of both internal and external influences. Sparta's postulating for war in part due to Athens expanding power was an external influence. However, the group dynamics of those decision makers internally was critical in shaping the national strategy toward war and arguably this decision-making group was functioning at a sub-optimal level. Pericles was a renowned general with a propensity for war; and as such when an influential person pre-disposed to war holds command over government decision makers, the likelihood for conflict is increased.[508] This is further exacerbated when the environment for robust and open debate is denuded, as appears to be the case as evidenced in Book 1 when "The Athenians persuaded of the wisdom of his advice, voted as he desired, and answered the Spartans as he recommended, both on separate points and in general."[509] In this case, it is the internal influence that holds sway and if lacking sufficient unbiased or informed knowledge can result in war.

What is seen through this brief examination of the decision-making group is that if a proposed strategy is not considered in detail with potential second order effects fully appreciated then the impacts on

---

507 Cashman and Robinson, *An Introduction to the Causes of War: Patterns of Interstate Conflict from World War 1 to Iraq.* 7

508 Cashman and Robinson, *An Introduction to the Causes of War: Patterns of Interstate Conflict from World War 1 to Iraq.* 9

509 Strassler, *Thucydides: A Comprehensive Guide to the Peloponnesian War.* Book 1, Chapter 1.145

a nation can be dire. Compare this situation to that of the dynamics and decisions made by the United States government leading up to the invasion of Iraq in 2002. The dominant voices in the room were in favour of war, the remainder through lack of courage, political traction or fear of consequence ultimately abrogated their responsibilities within the decision-making process.[510] The result was war driven by poor intelligence but perhaps more so through ineffective bureaucratic and decision-making process, as it were for Athens.

The examination thus far of Pericles' strategy has provided two key insights relating to the nature of strategy. First, an individual's own perceptions have significant influence toward shaping strategy as evidenced by Pericles' propensity for war. And second, a state's decision-making group may tend toward apathetic decision making if the group lacks sufficient leadership or is motivated by fear. These then are the internal influences involved in strategy design; and as shown when poor decision making has influence the integrity of the strategic system is questionable. What then are the potential external influences and how can they impact on a given strategy once it is struck? In this case, the impact on the third subjective institution as defined by Clausewitz will be examined, that of society at large and the complexities therein.[511]

As discussed, Pericles was, for the most part, a respected individual within Athenian Society. He was leveraged by the government when required to quell public discontent, as illustrated through his funeral oration.[512] What can be deduced when reviewing Pericles' speeches is that he had an innate understanding of the importance of public support. He knew this was important to firstly provide open support for a given strategy and to ensure its continued favour as the ebb and flow of a campaign changed. At what could be described as the operational level, Pericles proposed a strategy that involved the population withdrawing on mass from the greater country region to within the confines of the walls surrounding Athens. The people were to leave their land, collapse housing and relocate livestock. It would be a fair assumption that such a strategy would have met a degree of discontent within the population.

---

510 Thomas E Ricks, *Fiasco, The American Military Adventure in Iraq*, 2006. 46-57
511 Echevarria II, "Clausewitz and the Nature of the War on Terror." 4
512 Strassler, *Thucydides: A Comprehensive Guide to the Peloponnesian War*. Book 2, Chapter 2.41

However, based in part on Pericles' standing, the population acquiesced and withdrew to Athens.[513]

This strategy alone does not provide unique insight regarding the nature of strategy, it does, however, begin to show insight regarding the fragility of strategic concepts if populace support wanes. Although successful in uniting the Athenian people toward his strategy, Pericles understood the risk associated with perceptions of double standards and how these could impact on National unity, potentially unhinging the overall strategy. He foresaw the potential for the Spartan King Archidamus to perhaps spare his estate as the Spartan Armies marched toward Athens. In pre-emption of this he 'gifted' his assets to the public purse.[514] Here the true complexity associated with strategy and foreign policy begins to appear. Simply by anticipating the potential for external influence, Pericles is forced make defensive manoeuvres to mitigate the impact on public support. In theory, this would have ensured the continued support of the populace, however, the enemy's actions are simply one external influence impacting public support. Two additional impacts on popular support are apparent as the campaign continued. One in all reality was predictable and should have been mitigated the other completely unpredictable, reinforcing the thesis that strategies are susceptible to any number of influences.

The mass internal migration of the country's population to Athens predictably impacted those already residing within the city and those who sacrificed their lifestyle to adhere to the strategy. Again, this demonstrates the shortcomings of those who voted in support of Pericles strategy. Had they truly debated and investigated the impacts of his strategy this eventuality would have been anticipated. Measures should have been taken to ensure this migratory movement accommodated the needs of the people, however, the clear majority of those arriving were not adequately housed.[515] This, when coupled with the fact that from within the city walls the population could see their country being desolated, resulted in the validity of Pericles (and thus the strategy) being brought into question:

---

513 Strassler, *Thucydides: A Comprehensive Guide to the Peloponnesian War*. Book 2, Chapter 2.14
514 Strassler, *Thucydides: A Comprehensive Guide to the Peloponnesian War*. Book 2, Chapter 2.13
515 Strassler, *Thucydides: A Comprehensive Guide to the Peloponnesian War*. Book 2, Chapter 2.17

In short, the whole city was in a most excited state. Pericles was the object of general indignation; his previous counsels were totally forgotten; he was abused for not leading out the army which he commanded, and was made responsible for the whole suffering.[516]

Pericles was thus fighting on several fronts, for the real-time defence of Athens but also in the battle for public opinion. He knew the risk if this was to wane.

It is difficult to not draw parallels when reviewing contemporary national strategies and how maintaining public support is an imperative coveted by strategic leadership. The United States government when bogged down in a protracted, bloody and questionable campaign in Vietnam, like Pericles, was required to engage both within the area of operations but also domestically to engender support.[517] Inversely, China's actions with regards to movements into the South China Sea is largely supported by the domestic audience based on the inherent belief the actions are in the security interests of the nation.[518] Any nation challenging these actions is met with rebuke from the Chinese nation at large; which based on the strength of unity within the people, would likely result in military mobilisation if seriously challenged.

However, for Pericles, the greatest threat to public support came via the unpredictability of the plague. When the plague breached the confines of the walls not only was Pericles' leadership further tested but perhaps, more importantly, national unity began to fray. The deep sense of honour that Pericles had leveraged to gain support for war, which in turn united Athens toward the common strategy began to corrode "Perseverance in what men called honour was popular with none".[519] Only when public support had reached a tipping point based on the impacts of war and plague did Pericles intervene publicly. He did so due to his knowledge that victory could be handed to the Spartans if, as it was approaching, Athenian resolve faulted. In Pericles' case, he managed to re-establish public support for his strategy. He achieved this once again by playing

516 Strassler, *Thucydides: A Comprehensive Guide to the Peloponnesian War*. Book 2, Chapter 2.21
517 Nigel Cawthorne, *Vietnam: A War Lost and Won* (London: Arturus Publishing Limited, 2010). 141-165
518 Cj Bouchat, *Dangerous Ground: The Spratly Islands and US Interests and Approaches* (United States Army War College Press, 2013), http://oai.dtic.mil/oai/oai?verb=getRecord&metadataPrefix=html&identifier=ADA591530.
519 Strassler, *Thucydides: A Comprehensive Guide to the Peloponnesian War*. Book 2, Chapter 2.53

off his intelligence as a calculating commander, dismissing the impacts of the plague as an injection from the Gods and reinvigorating a sense of honour. He was ultimately rewarded with outright command for the affairs of the state.

Reviewing Pericles' strategy provides any number of insights relating to the nature of strategy, the fragility of such, however, is most striking. Pericles was intelligent and considered in his approach to strategy development in the interests of Athenian sovereignty. The nature of strategy, however, is that ultimately it is a discussion between parties, be that decision makers, a given population or the enemy. All impart influence either positive or negative and therefore impact on the integrity of the strategy as a system. Those charged with imposing strategy communicate through political posturing and the manoeuvre of forces. Whether through poor due diligence or perhaps simply through bad luck, such posturing may exacerbate the problem. The unpredictability of influences outside of one's control must also be considered. Simply put, strategy design cannot be codified, it is not a science. Hence strategy development must balance redundancy for contingency with reasoned purpose, for in Pericles' case, having not considered one over the other almost unhinged his strategy.

Essay 11

How are the theories of Clausewitz relevant to our understanding of strategy in the early 21st century?
(Written 2017 – exam in 4 hours)

The study of theorists within a given field can provide the contemporary practitioner with many valuable insights, both perils to avoid and opportunities to exploit. The same remains for strategy and those charged to execute the implementation of policy. The purpose of this paper is to review insights drawn from the Prussian theorist, Carl von Clausewitz, and demonstrate how his theories remain relevant to an understanding of strategy within the 21st Century. The underlying hypothesis being that a knowledge of these remains of benefit for not only those engaged with the execution of contemporary warfare but also more widely regarding national strategy.

Prior to defining this relevance, it is necessary to contextualise strategy and therefore Clausewitz's views, as although he engaged in thought on the execution of war at the tactical level his implications are far more reaching and of benefit at the strategic or grand level. Hal Brands definition provides context regarding Grand Strategy being "Grand strategy is the intellectual architecture that lends structure to foreign policy; it is the logic that helps states navigate a complex and dangerous world."[520] To achieve this Grand Strategic view, all the elements at a nation's disposal be it diplomatic, military or economic are leveraged toward achieving the goal.[521] A diplomatic strategy may exist, as would be leverage by a Nations Foreign Minister, an economic policy would

520 Hal Brands, *What Good Is Grand Strategy? Power and Purpose in American Statecraft from Harry S. Truman to George W. Bush* (London: Cornell University Press, 2016). 10
521 James D. Clayton, "American Japanese Strategies in the Pacific War," in *Makers of Modern Strategy from Machiavelli to the Nuclear Age*, ed. Peter Paret (Princeton University Press, 1971), 703–32.

exist with a view to maximise gross domestic product output and, importantly when reviewing Clausewitz, a military strategy would exist.

When reviewing warfare, Clausewitz distilled the act of war to its most basic level and therefore regardless of the scale of conflict, he saw the intent as being to impose one's will on another through the application of force; and for Clausewitz this was more likely to be achieved through the application of violence, hence military strategy. Although he appreciated that war and conflict is driven by either hostile intent or hostile feelings he sought to fully develop this primordial aspect of man into a larger strategic framework. He had a firm grasp on the subordination of the Military (consequently the military strategy) to policy and therefore the government,[522] and he also understood that engaging in war was a deeply emotive activity. He clearly understood the human impact on war and therefore strategy. Although a somewhat crude distillation of Strategy, Grand Strategy and Clausewitz it is necessary in framing arguably the most relevant insight regrading strategy from Clausewitz; as it relates not simply to military strategy in the execution of warfare, but on a more holistic level with insights and implications at the Grand Strategic level. These insights into the nature of war resulted in Clausewitz attempting to contextualise his theories and in doing he has identified three subjective institutions of fundamental relevance to the contemporary strategists in the 21st Century being the Government, the People and the Military.[523]

Understanding the base level driver of hostile feeling contributing to war can be of relevance to the contemporary strategist in several ways, most notably through self-awareness. If a country or even small group is aware of how their actions may be perceived by another the outcome can be anticipated, and if deemed necessary, intended action modified. If, as example, a Nations Grand strategy involves the build-up of military forces in an area, it is foreseeable that this action could be viewed as potentially hostile by other Nations within that area, which can easily

---

522 Antulio J. Echevarria II, "Clausewitz and the Nature of the War on Terror," in *Clausewitz in the Twenty-First Century*, ed. Hew Strachan and Andreas Herberg-Rothe (London: Oxford University Press, 2007), 197–218.

523 Thomas G. Mahnken, "Strategy Theory," in *Strategy in the Contemporary World: An Introduction to Strategic Studies*, ed. John Baylis et al. (Oxford University Press, 2007), 66–81.

lead to conflict through the perception of threat.[524] This basic insight from Clausewitz regarding the fact that hostile feelings and hostile intent can be sources for conflict can then act in a preventative role for the contemporary strategic practitioner. Although this understanding is beneficial in attempting to negate war through an understanding of the emotive aspects of conflict, Clausewitz theories are arguably more effective when hostilities have commenced and this is achieved by ways of leveraging the three subjective institutions as previously highlighted being the military, government and the people.

Clausewitz's theoretical construct was heavily founded on the premise that war was simply the execution of politics through violent means with the military being subordinate to policy. How then is this of relevance for the contemporary practitioner that may be waging war against an ideological force? The answer lies in a deeper understanding of the influence of the people and what drives the hostilities. Importantly at this stage it is necessary to understand that the influence of people is expanded to include not simply the country's populace were the conflict is occurring (hence forth referred to as the host populace) but extends to the populace that provides the military force (referred to as the supporting populace). Additionally, it is important to appreciate that the 'contemporary strategic practitioner' can mean a member within the profession of arms ranging in rank, therefore position, along the strategic spectrum from the tactical, to the operational to the strategic.

Within the operational task spectrum recognised by the Australian Defence Force irregular war or insurgencies are a recognised form of conflict being a consistent and arguably growth area of conflict within the early 21st Century.[525] In conjunction with this, an exponential growth in theorists have emerged who attempt to provide the guidelines on how to defeat an insurgency. One common theme however that presents with regards to counter insurgency warfare is the importance of the people, a critical component identified by Clausewitz. Kilcullen identifies the need to know the people as paramount within his 28 articles for successful counter-insurgency (COIN)[526] and interestingly here is an obvious overlap to Mao's

524 Greg Cashman and Leonard C Robinson, *An Introduction to the Causes of War: Patterns of Interstate Conflict from World War 1 to Iraq* (Lanham: Rowman and Littlefield Publishers, Inc, 2007). 5

525 LWD 3-0-3 Land Operations

526 David Kilcullen, *Counter Insurgency* (Carlton North: Scribe Publications, 2010). 16

'eight points for attention' in Revolutionary War that are heavily influenced by respect for the population.[527] The point being that within COIN warfare the importance of effective support from the host population is integral to success. An insurgency or revolution is founded on several needs including popular support and protection from the population. It logically flows then that if those attempting to counter the insurgent disregard this subjective institution as identified by Clausewitz, support will likely flow to the insurgent making tactical, let alone strategic success problematic. An understanding of this remains highly relevant to military strategist within the 21st Century and arguably not fully appreciated.

Although this illustrates the importance of populace support with regards to military strategy, the importance of the people is equally relevant for the contemporary strategic practitioner with regards to Grand Strategy. Perhaps the obvious example with regards to contemporary (relative) warfare and the impact the populace can have relates to the Vietnam War and the continuity of involvement by western forces. It is arguably at this level where an appreciation on the importance of the populace is most significant for the contemporary strategist. The Vietnam War and the involvement of both US and Australian military forces was highly divisive, leading to open displays of hostility by the supporting populace toward the governments directing military involvement. This example demonstrates how the influence of one institution, the populace, shapes the decision of another, the government, which subsequently impacts on the third institution, being the military. With regards to Clausewitz's theories the relevance to the contemporary strategist of the 21st Century revolves around this interplay between the people, the government and the military which remains extant. In the case of Vietnam, the political objective as endorsed by government, in turn executed via military strategy, was questionable from the viewpoint of the supporting populace. Both grand and military strategy was in question. Clausewitz had an acute understanding on the importance of a united population and recognised that national enthusiasm was a key strength regarding strategy,[528] with Vietnam demonstrating how the people component as defined by Clausewitz's can unhinge strategy.

---

527 Mao, "Slected Works of Mao Tse-Tung," *Foriegn Languages Press* II, no. May 1938 (1967): 1–26.

528 Hew Strachan, *Carl von Clausewitz's On War* (Vancouver: Douglas and McIntyre, 2008). 125

It would appear perhaps that those within the senior echelons of the contemporary defence force (both advisor, staff and commander) have developed a greater appreciation of this aspect of Clausewitz's theories. Based on a Public Relations strategy founded on the 'War on Terror' message, military involvement in Afghanistan by the Australian Defence Force enjoyed broad levels of endorsement from the population; consequently, the military enjoyed support, often fiscally from government. Although the political object remained somewhat ambiguous the subjective institutions were united and the strategy, albeit questionable, endured.

Thus far the review of Clausewitz's theory has demonstrated his relevance to the contemporary strategists largely through an appreciation of one of his trinities being the government, people and the military. His intimation being, and as should be appreciated by the contemporary strategist, that if leveraged correctly, strategic success will follow. Clausewitz, however, had witnessed the realities of war, he noted that it was based on violence and hatred, he understood the subordinate relationship between the military to policy; and in rounding out another of his trinity constructs, appreciated the play of chance.[529] Understanding and appreciating this enduring aspect of war remains critical for the contemporary strategist to consider, or perhaps simply acknowledge, during strategic planning. Within the contemporary operating environment of the 21st Century this element as identified by Clausewitz is often overlooked and has an overly negative impact of strategies when introduced.

As previously discussed conflicts of the 21st Century have thus far been largely short of major combat, more simply framed as irregular warfare. Such conflicts are increasingly being contested amongst the people and within urban centres, a trend that is only likely to continue. Consequently, much of contemporary warfare is being driven by the 'need' for a near perfect intelligence picture, primarily with a view to reduce collateral damage. This in turn links back to the previous components of this paper, as collateral damage very much undermines popular support and hence the cascading effect of influence relating to continued involvement follows. However, and as recognised by Clausewitz, this is a fallacy with

---

529 Mahnken, "Strategy Theory." 72

the only situation a commander can know is his own, and arguably this is not complete.[530]

What contemporary militaries are thus currently experiencing is the influence of this search for the perfect intelligence picture when developing strategies. Those charged with devising Grand Strategy are fully aware of the negative impacts of collateral damage, consequently military strategy development within the 21st Century is increasingly bound by restrictions based on collateral estimates. They are often overly restrictive and predictable resulting in a lack of flexibility on the ground.[531] Clearly the enemy has influence and will seek to shape opposing commanders. Rather than fearing this imperfect knowledge of the situation, contemporary commanders should in fact acknowledge this enduring principle and develop plans with inherent flexibility that recognise the play of chance within war. Additionally, personnel need sufficient psychological development to accept this reality and the inherent risk of war and the role chance plays. Perhaps the most obvious example of this relates to the contemporary use of Improvised Explosive Devices and the psychological impact this has on forces engaged in wars of the 21st Century. No technological advancement has thus removed this risk from the battlefield and military strategies at the tactical through to the strategic are influenced by this element of chance.

Clausewitz was a deep thinker who, having been exposed the land wars of the 1800s sought to contextualise the reasons for war and the constituent components therein. His theoretical hypothesis as outlined within 'On war' remains open for debate and even interpretation. However, this paper has argued that many of his theories remain of relevance to the contemporary strategists within the 21st Century. His observations on the interplay between the people, the government and the military remain extant. Arguably today with the increase of communication mediums the ability of the population to influence government is largely more so than when he wrote on war. This is almost exponentially so if the populace questions the political object and can drive the support or not of strategy, thus his assertion that the military is subordinate to the government rings true. The other key area of relevance relates to

530 Carl Von Clausewitz, *On War*, ed. Michael Howard and Peter Paret, *English*, Indexed (Princeton: Princeton University Press, 1976). 84
531 Colonel Chris Smith, Land Forum 2016

the fact that regardless of technological advances a perfect intelligence picture cannot exist and the role of chance within contemporary war and strategy development remains. Currently this component of Clausewitz's theories is under appreciated by the strategists of the 21st Century; arguably this is being driven by the desire to remove doubt and mitigate the ugliness of collateral damage at the Grand Strategic level. Nonetheless, chance remains, and the desire to remove it is having a detrimental effect at the military strategic level for the strategist of the early 21st Century.

Essay 12

'The German historian, Carl von Clausewitz, stated: 'No one starts a war - or rather, no one in his senses ought to do so - without first being clear in his mind what he intends to achieve by that war and how he intends to conduct it'. Explain this assertion. *(Written 2017 - exam in 4 hours)*

The German historian Car von Clausewitz was correct in stating that 'no one should start a war, no one in his senses ought to do so - without first being clear in his mind what he intends to achieve by war and how he intends to conduct it', yet wars (and minor conflicts) have and continue to be waged throughout the globe. The purpose of this essay, by way of analysing Adolf Hitler and the actions of Germany during the Second World War, will be to describe two components. Firstly, a reason for quantifying why in fact the German nation empowered by Hitler embarked on war, and secondly to demonstrate how after some initial successes this campaign ultimately failed.

In gaining an understanding of the issues associated with Hitler and the Second World War it is important not simply to view them in isolation. Hitler of course fought in the First World War and felt the humiliation of defeat, which can be drawn from his writings in 'Mein Kampf'. First published in 1925, this publication highlights a sense of purpose and details his intent for the future of Germany.[532] Additionally, the writings within this publication begin to show clear insight into not only his anti-Semitic standpoint but also his concern for Marxist theory. In short he viewed the Jewish race and others as inferior to the 'Aryan' Nation whom he had assessed as racially superior. When linking back to the source of this question being Clausewitz, he also states that men are

---

532 Liddell Hart, *Strategy*, Second Rev (London: First Meridian Printing, 1991). 207

motivated toward war based on two motives being hostile feeling and hostile intent.[533] Clearly Adolf Hitler possessed both, and through the empowerment driven by broad political support, the catalyst for war was set.

Therefore in explaining Clausewitz's' assertion we begin to see several linkages that supports the assertion. First, a key contributor to triggering war is a leader's own personality, psychological makeup, beliefs and perceptions of the world; and inversely an additional contributor can also be an individual's misperception on the world and reality.[534]

> Just as an individual's personality predisposes him to response in a certain situation in certain ways, so do his images and belief systems. The important point here is that national decision makers do not act on reality, they act on their perceptions of reality, and sometimes these are seriously distorted.[535]

On reviewing Hitler's psychological makeup and beliefs the intent for war, which Clausewitz articulates as necessary to initiate war, becomes clear. Hitler's objective for initiating the Second World War, although somewhat driven by a need for power transition, was not simply a land grabbing exercise. He was driven by an inherent desire to drive a demographic revolution that would result in a Global shift seeing Germany, and 'her' people as dominant.[536] Now whether Hitler was 'in his senses' as defined by Clausewitz is dependent on one's view of history, however the fact remains he had a clear view on what he wished to achieved during the war, and to a point, an understanding on how he was to achieve it.

Once the popular support had been achieved domestically Hitler then sought to leverage this unity of effort in justifying what was a clear political objective being the annihilation of Poland and its people.[537]

533 Antulio J. Echevarria II, "Clausewitz and the Nature of the War on Terror," in *Clausewitz in the Twenty-First Century*, ed. Hew Strachan and Andreas Herberg-Rothe (London: Oxford University Press, 2007), 197–218.
534 Greg Cashman and Leonard C Robinson, *An Introduction to the Causes of War: Patterns of Interstate Conflict from World War 1 to Iraq* (Lanham: Rowman and Littlefield Publishers, Inc, 2007). 4-5
535 Ibid. 5
536 Roger Chickering, Dennis Showalter, and Hans van de Ven, eds., *The Cambridge History of War*, Vol IV (Cambridge: Cambridge University Press, 2012). 583
537 Ibid. 583

At this stage Hitler's grasp on Grand Strategic levers becomes clear. He identifies the risk of fighting in isolation and firstly identifies a shared interest in Poland between Germany and the Soviet Union. He then seeks to leverage this to his benefit. He avoids the potential for diplomatic resolution by withdrawing key political advisors from allied countries. Consequently, when the Soviet-German agreement is made and Germany initiates its invasion plan under the ruse of Polish infringements, the country falls with relative ease. Although it would appear at this stage that Hitler's actions were achieving his intended war aims it begins to glean insight into a relationship that later shifts toward Germany's detriment. It can be seen therefore that the Poland Invasion was successful in achieving Hitler's initial war strategy of securing Poland and placating Russia, however it naturally stimulated strength with an increasing alliance.

Due in part on their insistence that the allies would protect Poland, they were now forced to act. However, buoyed by success Hitler switched his focus toward France. This was done not simply to shore up his western defences but also to stimulate action, or perhaps more accurately, shape allied movements to his benefit. In short he was successful. France ultimately fell based in part on the application of new military tactics fostered and developed by a military culture that was pre-disposed to adaptation. Secondly the allied forces were weakened due to successful air attacks on an over extended allied line within Belgium.[538] At this stage of the Second World War it is difficult to fault Hitler's Grand Strategy and the military strategy being employed to support his policy. He had managed to secure key land areas integral to security, through diplomacy he had managed to negate the impact of the Russian forces to his north and for the most part operational planning employing massed mechanised force was forcing opposition capitulation with relative ease. However, history demonstrates that Hitler was defeated, but through what means and what was the trigger that caused this spectacular reversal of success? Ultimately it will be shown, like in the decision to initiate the war, the spiral from an apparent victorious position to that of the defeated, was driven in large part by leadership.

Until this stage of the conflict the importance of a united approach had been working to Germany's benefit. However, this component critical

---

538 Hart, *Strategy*. 216-217

for any successful strategy now shifts to other stakeholders, not only through the formation of an enhanced alliance, but also the resilience of the people. All these components then combine to create a united effect that ultimately unhinges Hitler's Grand Strategy. The British Empire at the time, although vast, was also somewhat insecure. She had seen the rapid success of the German war machine and importantly (largely due to Churchill) recognised her own vulnerability if control of the Mediterranean Sea line of communication was lost. Had Hitler perhaps held a greater appreciation of this sense of vulnerability and sue for a peace of sorts, Britain and thus the Allied forces, may have accepted German success to this point of the war in Europe. However, Hitler through poor judgement or misguided advice sought to bring the war to the British mainland.

Germany sought to defeat Britain through the employment of Airpower prior to switching focus toward Russia. However, to secure the mainland, control of the air needed to be secured.[539] In this regard Hitler miscalculated in several areas. First he misunderstood the advances Britain had made with regards to not only aviation technology, but also pilot proficiency. Hence the British held the advantage. Secondly, and perhaps more importantly, he undervalued the resolved of the British people. The air theorist of the interwar period clearly had an impact on Germany strategy of the time and when defeated in Air combat the military strategy switched to targeting population centres. The air theorist Douhet identified the potential for airpower to be employed as a tool to effectively bypass ground forces and employ strategic bombardment. The rationale being that by targeting critical centres, notably the population, it would force the early capitulation of an enemy's strategic command. In short his concept involved the employment of massed bombardment on population centres which would completely demoralise the civilian morale rendering them ineffective as resource tool. Inversely it would make them a highly effective tool of leverage to influence a government to yield to an aggressor demands.[540]

Although this military strategy had some effect on destroying civilian centres and damaging infrastructure it was largely counterproductive.

---

539 Chickering, Showalter, and van de Ven, *The Cambridge History of War*. 594
540 Giulio Douhet, "The Command of the Air," in *Roots of Strategy: Book 4*, ed. David Jablonsky (Mechanicsburg: Stackpole Books, 1999), 263–408.

First it acted as a source of propaganda, leveraged internally by the British with a view to consolidate the resolve of the British public toward the war. This it achieved. Simply put the bombing campaign only strengthened the political objective Churchill was projecting and had also increased the capacity for this country to source an increasingly motivated human resource pool for the war, with human resource pools another crucial component that Hitler failed to appreciate

Although initially co-operating with Russia for the invasion of Poland, Hitler simply saw this as means to an end for his ultimate push into Russia, which arguably led to the defeat of German Strategy. The Invasion commenced on the 22nd June 1941 and enjoyed early initial success, again appearing to justify Hitler's decision to invade, however he underestimated the effect it would have on strengthening the Alliance, which again would be compounded in future months with the Bombing of Pearl Harbor.[541] Although to a degree it may have been anticipated, the consequence of the invasion of Russia was the catalyst for galvanising the relationships of what would be known as the big three being Britain, Russia and the United States, all of which offered differing capabilities that in time would mutually support a co-ordinated approach to defeating Germany. The United States, still at this time relatively isolated from the conflict, saw the opportunity to provide increased material support to Russia to support their defence whilst still continuing to profit from the war.

However, on December 7th 1941, and without Hitler's knowledge, the Japanese bombed Pearl Harbor and with that action the entire dynamic of World War two changed for Hitler. Germany was already heavily engaged in Russia and although successful in part the push was being blunted not only through the limitations imposed by geographic layout but also through the sheer scale of man power that Russia could draw from, albeit under equipped. With the actions of Pearl Harbor however, America was now fully committed and in a position where it could support the resourcing and sustainment of both Russia and Britain. This was the beginning of the decline for the German grand strategic plan that arguably commenced a predictable path from this date onwards.

Hitler was now being forced to fight a combined and focused alliance. The United States due in part from her geographical isolation was free to

541 Hart, *Strategy*. 242

engage in the production of military equipment of an industrial scale not yet seen in human history. This when combined with powers legislated through the Lend-Lease agreement resulted in massed military material being provided to Russia, that had the human resource pool to draw from which largely compensated for deficiencies in military capacity.

It would be unfair to suggest that Germany did not have other opportunities for victory from 1942 onwards, but rather through the consolidation of the Alliance it became increasingly problematic. Britain was in a perilous position and sought the total support from the United States in order to support her strategy, largely shaped within the Mediterranean and Europe. Through declaring war on the United States, Hitler provided Churchill with what he needed to support his political strategy. This resulted in a European strategy although problematic at times resulted in a 'Germany First' strategy.[542] Ultimately this led to a plan resulting in German forces being drawn south into the Mediterranean area of operations being Churchill's intent. Simultaneously due to Hitler's ideological desire Germany remained heavily committed to the Russian Front, which by now was heavily resourced by both materiel from the United States and manning internally.

Clausewitz is accurate in his intimation that in the pursuit of war one must have a clear understanding on the ends sought and the methods to achieve it. Hitler during World War II was clearly motivated by ideological aspects of where he saw large elements of European society as inferior to the German race. He had a clear vision on the end state, which as history shows he sought to achieve not only militarily but also through massed genocide. His actions show insight into another aspect of Clausewitz's statement being that one should only wage war if of sound mind, which for Hitler was clearly not the case. Had Hitler been better advised and more focused on his original political objective of the defeat of the Polish people, World War II may have culminated far earlier. However, due to aspects only known to him, he over-reached and in doing so galvanised a united Alliance that with their combined strengths saw him defeated.

542 C Parker, Robert, A, *Struggle for Survival: The History of the Second World War* (Oxford and New York: Oxford University Press, 1990). 115-130

Leadership

'How did aspects of the individual, the organisation and/or society impact on the leadership of your historical figures?' *(Written 2017)*

Introduction

The effectiveness of a leader can be judged on their ability to achieve outcomes which align with higher organisational objectives. To achieve this, it is important for leaders within a given organisation to develop a cultural environment that influences individuals to achieve these objectives willingly.[543] This component of leadership is assessed as central to the effectiveness of the two paired leaders being discussed, Air Marshall Arthur Harris of the United Kingdom's Bomber Command and General Curtis LeMay of the United States Airforce.[544] Both these individuals were heavily involved in the development of sizeable air commands and the subsequent application of strategic bombardment during World War II.[545] This period will form the focal area for discussion and centre on the commander subordinate relationship. It will be argued that Harris and Lemay were transformational leaders, who employed elements now recognised within the social identity leadership construct to achieve organisational change. Specifically, their expertise allowed them to

---

543 Jack Wood et al., *Organisational Behaviour: An Asia-Pacific Perspective* (Milton: John Wiley and Sons, Inc, 1998). 500.

544 For ease of reading the United States Airforce has been used for General LeMay; however during World War Two, military aviation capability was referred to by the US as the United States Army Air Corps with the USAF becoming a separate branch of the military in 1947; Walter Oleksy, *Military Leaders of World War II* (New York: Facts On File Inc, 1994). 13.

545 Spence T. Tucker, ed., *500 Great Military Leaders* (Santa Barbara: ABC-CLIO, n.d.). 430-431; Sebastian Cox, "Sir Arthur Harris and the Air Ministry," in *Airpower Leadership and Practice*, ed. Peter W. Gray and Sebastian Cox (Shrivenham: Joint Doctrine and Concepts Centre, 2002), 210–26.

become prototypical group members, which enabled the development of group cohesion within their command. Furthermore, their ability to act as identity entrepreneurs and craft a unique sense of unit identity was directly attributable to effective performance.[546]

When considering the effectiveness of these commanders, aspects relating to them as individuals and how this correlated with high levels of followership within their organisations will form the basis for discussion. Two critical elements relating to their professional and personal development became central tenets to effective command. Both had relatively dislocated upbringings and consequently had an inherent sense of the importance of (or desire for) social belonging.[547] Secondly, they both possessed a high work ethic, the result of which was proficiency within the field of aviation.[548] Consequently, before assuming leadership positions, they both held high levels of expert power. This aspect of them as individuals contributed to the formation of referent power within their commands.[549] Because of these two primary factors, both commanders appeared naturally inclined to develop an organisation where individuals strove to achieve high levels of performance for the betterment of the group. They achieved change by employing the complementary effects of elements found within the social identity and transformational leadership constructs.

Formative Impacts

By definition 'formative' years have a lasting impact on individuals.[550] For Harris and LeMay their formative years were to become central to the development of a command style that contributed to high levels of

---

546 V. Knippenberg, Daan and Naomi Ellemers, "Social Identity and Group Performance: Identification as the Key to Group-Oriented Effort," in *Social Identity at Work: Developing Theory for Organizational Practice*, ed. Alexander S. Haslam et al. (New York: Psychology Press, 2003), 29–42.

547 Abraham Maslow, *A Theory on Human Motivation*, 1943rd ed. (Mansfield Centre: Martino Publishing, 2014). 14.

548 Williamson Murray, "Curtis E. Lemay: Airman Extraordinary," in *Air Commanders*, ed. John A Olsen (Dulles: Potomac Books, 2013), 132–43; Cox, "Sir Arthur Harris and the Air Ministry." 210-26.

549 Kathryn M Bartol et al., *Management: A Pacific Rim Focus* (North Melbourne: McGraw-Hill Book Company Australia Pty Limited, 1995). 448-452.

550 Arthur Delbridge and Bernard J, eds., *The Macquarie Concise Dictionary*, 2nd ed. (Sydney: The Macquarie Library Pty Ltd, 1988). 375.

followership. LeMay had a dislocated upbringing. He was the eldest of seven children, the son of working class parents and due to his father's inability to retain full-time employment, had several moves as a child.[551] His mother balanced the disciplinarian aspects of his father, acting as an initial role model instilling a sense of honesty, integrity and drive into LeMay.[552] This formative period had several lasting impacts on LeMay. Firstly, he developed a high degree of responsibility, appreciating the reality that hard work was an integral component of life.[553] While still a child he often had to act as the 'bread-winner' for the family, learning to put the needs of the team before the individual.[554] Secondly, this lack of stability had an adverse impact on his ability to establish stable social groups. His childhood was devoid of a sense of belonging beyond the family unit, with this being of questionable benefit due to the violence inflicted on him by his father.[555]

Militaries can act as mediums that satisfy an individual's need to belong as the cultural norms and practices inherent within such institutions provide people with a sense of social identity.[556] In addition to the stable employment and opportunities the military offered, it is likely that LeMay was drawn to the military because of this sense of belonging. This belongingness concept became an aspect he later strove to develop within his command, as typified through the post mission briefings he instituted where all personnel were free to critique the mission and even the commander's role in it.[557]

Arthur Harris was dislocated from his family during his formative years, driven primarily by choice and the relative privilege afforded by his family's social status. Harris was the younger of three brothers, and due to financial limitations, his education at Allhallows was less prestigious than that of his brothers who attended Eton and Sherborne.[558] Although removed from his family during this period,

551 Warren Kozak, *Curtis LeMay: Strategist and Tactician* (Washington D.C.: Regnery History, 2009). 4-5.

552 Murray, "Curtis E. Lemay: Airman Extraordinary." 132-133.

553 Murray, "Curtis E. Lemay: Airman Extraordinary." 132-133.

554 Kozak, *Curtis LeMay: Strategist and Tactician.* 4-5.

555 Kozak, *Curtis LeMay: Strategist and Tactician.* 3.

556 Boas Shamir et al., "Leadership and Social Identification in Military Units: Direct and Indirect Relationships," *Journal of Applied Social Psychology* 20, no. 3 (2000): 612–40.

557 Barrett Tillman, *LeMay* (New York: Palgrave Macmillan, 2007). 31.

558 Henry Probert, *Bomber Harris: His Life and Times* (London: Greenhill Books., 2006). 23.

the institutional aspects of a boarding school likely provided Harris with an insight into how organisations can provide a sense of belonging to individuals. Like LeMay, Harris, would later successfully cultivate this within his command.[559] There was an expectation that the younger Harris would follow a traditional career into the civil or military service. However, exposure to Rhodesia and the concept of a nation that rewarded ability, rather than class, saw him leave school and pursue opportunities there.[560]

Harris also accepted the need for hard work, and over a six-year period spent in Rhodesia, he managed to forge his own identity and would ultimately self-identify as Rhodesian as opposed to British.[561] With the outbreak of World War I, Harris initially served with the 1st Rhodesian Regiment in German West Africa, however with victory in this theatre he returned to the United Kingdom seeking continuance with the military.[562] He found service within the Royal Flying Corp (RFC) after unsuccessful attempts to join the Cavalry and the Royal Artillery.[563] It is difficult to confirm if class status played a part in this decision, but due to the relative infancy of air-power in this period, service in the RFC would likely be seen as inferior to that of the Royal Artillery or Cavalry. That aspect aside, the greatest legacy that this period had on Harris was witnessing the loss of life associated with attrition warfare due to the actions on the Western Front.[564] This had a significant impact on him regarding the risks associated with a stalemated conflict: the need to gain a decisive victory through whatever means necessary became central in his approach to warfare.[565] This exposure and his consequent resolve to seek decisive victory through strategic bombardment would be an ongoing friction relating to the use of Bomber Command during the Second World War.

---

559 Charles Messenger, *"Bomber" Harris and the Strategic Bombing Offensive, 1939-1945* (London: Arms and Armour Press, 1984). 203-205.

560 Martin Middlebrook, "Marshal of the Royal Air Force: Sir Arthur Harris," in *The Warlords: Military Commanders of the Twentieth Century*, ed. Michael Carver (London: Weidenfeld and Nicolson, 1976), 317–33.

561 Middlebrook, "Marshal of the Royal Air Force: Sir Arthur Harris." 317.

562 Henry Probert, *High Commanders of the Royal Air Force* (London: The Air Historical Branch, 1991). 27.

563 Probert, *Bomber Harris: His Life and Times*. 35-36.

564 Middlebrook, "Marshal of the Royal Air Force: Sir Arthur Harris." 317-33.

565 Middlebrook, "Marshal of the Royal Air Force: Sir Arthur Harris." 317-33.

When reviewing the early lives of both Harris and LeMay, several traits become apparent that can influence organisational effectiveness. Firstly, they both possessed (developed through necessity) a high work ethic, with the expectation being then that individuals within their organisations would react positively to hard work. Both members can, therefore, be defined as 'Theory Y' individuals with regard to Douglas McGregor's motivational construct that is they like work, are creative and will seek responsibility.[566] Conversely, 'Theory X' individuals, those who dislike service, are lazy, and need coercion to perform were removed from the organisations they commanded.[567] Therefore, based simply on the idea of a high work ethic, one can surmise that both Harris and LeMay sought to develop organisations where individuals strove to represent the distinctive characteristics of the group (in this case a high work ethic). Developing such a culture can contribute to the formation of organisational identity as individuals will seek to adopt the organisational norms and goals.[568]

Another aspect is their appreciation of the inherent human drive to seek out social interaction or belongingness, and how this contributes to individual and organisational health.[569] In time, they both created organisations that had high levels of group identity, with personnel identifying as a collective self, rather than an individual. This is a contributor to elevated levels of organisational output (in this case highly stressful bombing runs) and is an example of how group cohesion became central to operational success.[570]

Power and influence

Sir Arthur Harris took command of Bomber Command on 23rd February 1942, and General Curtis LeMay command of the 305th Bomber group

566 Alexander S. Haslam, *Psychology in Organisations: The Social Identity Approach* (London: SAGE Publications Ltd, 2004). 61-63; Stephen Robbins et al., *Organisation Behaviour: Concepts, Controversies and Applications* (Sydney: Prentice Hall, 1994). 249.

567 Haslam, *Psychology in Organisations: The Social Identity Approach*.61-63; Robbins et al., *Organisation Behaviour: Concepts, Controversies and Applications*. 249.

568 Knippenberg, Daan and Ellemers, "Social Identity and Group Performance: Identification as the Key to Group-Oriented Effort." 32; Haslam, *Psychology in Organisations: The Social Identity Approach*. 68-71.

569 Joseph P. Forgas, *Interpersonal Behaviour: The Psychology of Social Interaction* (Sydney: Pergamon Press, 1989). 301-307.

570 Knippenberg, Daan and Ellemers, "Social Identity and Group Performance: Identification as the Key to Group-Oriented Effort." 29-34.

in March of 1942. In doing so, they both inherited largely dysfunctional organisations, the utility of which remained misunderstood or under-appreciated by the other services.[571] Nonetheless, they were both charged with the responsibility of increasing organisational efficiency and hence improving combat effectiveness against Germany (and later Japan for LeMay).[572] To achieve this, the leader must influence the individual (and subsequently groups) to achieve the organisational goals. Influence and power are tools with which to achieve this.[573] Simply by virtue of their rank and position within a military organisation, both Harris and LeMay possessed legitimate and coercive sources of power which could be used to generate compliance.[574] They did, in fact, employ these sources of power both within a positive reward context and also a coercive punishment role.[575] Examples of reward can be highlighted through the provision of additional leave for high performance and a relaxed approach to liquor consumption following stressful operations.[576]

Conversely, both commanders, when recognising an individual as being a poor organisational fit (or theory X inclined), enacted their command authority and removed these types of personnel from their command. LeMay identified individuals within his command as residing in one of two groups, 'the good ones', and the 'no goods'.[577] Upon recognising a 'no good', meaning an individual not committed to the command vision or lacking a high work ethic, he actively removed them from his command.[578] Similarly, Harris sought to balance the skill sets within the Air Ministry by 'cleansing the Augean Stable' so that the talented individuals were not lost in a sea of mediocrity.[579] Both Harris and LeMay appeared to sense that individuals with a poor work ethic were detrimental to group morale. Their removal demonstrates an ability to appreciate how employee identity and group cohesion

---

571 Correlli Barnett, *The Lords of War: From Lincoln to Churchill, Supreme Command 1861-1945* (South Yorkshire: The Praetorian Press, 2012) 188; Oleksy, *Military Leaders of World War II.* 120

572 Tillman, *LeMay.* 23-25; John Gingell, "'Bomber' Harris - The Commander and The Man," *RUSI Journal* 130(2), no. June (1985): 65–66.

573 Robbins et al., *Organisation Behaviour: Concepts, Controversies and Applications.* 521.

574 Bartol et al., *Management: A Pacific Rim Focus.* 449.

575 Robbins et al., *Organisation Behaviour: Concepts, Controversies and Applications.* 523.

576 Messenger, *"Bomber" Harris and the Strategic Bombing Offensive, 1939-1945.* 67.

577 Kozak, *Curtis LeMay: Strategist and Tactician.* 116.

578 Kozak, *Curtis LeMay: Strategist and Tactician.* 116-118.

579 Messenger, *"Bomber" Harris and the Strategic Bombing Offensive, 1939-1945.* 44.

aided operational effectiveness.[580] As such, they sought to develop an organisation of 'like' individuals as this would likely be of benefit.[581] Ultimately, however, both appeared to appreciate the limitations of this transactional approach to leadership.[582] Rather, on review, it appears they appreciated the individual needs of personnel, recognising how if leveraged correctly, it could provide additional support for their organisational vision.[583]

Aviation is a complex profession, not simply because of the skills necessary for flight, but because of the logistics and science required to support the entire enterprise. It can be of organisational benefit if a commander can demonstrate competency in the field. LeMay was involved in the advancement of aviation concepts during the interwar period, including critical supporting concepts such as over sea and night navigation.[584] He broadened his skill sets becoming a pilot on multiple airframes including the B-17 heavy bomber. Additionally, he served as an operations officer, an intelligence officer and when the opportunity presented, he developed his knowledge relating to bomb sight effectiveness.[585] For Harris the situation was similar, not only had he seen operational service and received decorations for his service throughout World War I, but during the interwar period, he actively pursued the field's development. He served in various staff and command roles within and external to the United Kingdom, engaged in the strategic discussion on airpower theory and even postulated the relevance of subordinating an Airforce to the Army.[586] Therefore, when assuming their respective commands, it was a result of proficiency within the field and hence suitability for the role. For both Harris and LeMay their ability to demonstrate high levels of expert power across multiple areas within aviation became critical to their command.

---

580 Forgas, *Interpersonal Behaviour: The Psychology of Social Interaction.* 273.
581 Rolf Van Dick and Rudolf Kerschreiter, "The Social Identity Approach to Effective Leadership: An Overview and Some Ideas on Cross-Cultural Generalizability," *Front. Bus. Res. China* 10, no. 3 (2016): 363–84.
582 Bernard Bass, "From Transactional to Transformational Leadership: Learning to Share the Vision," *Organizational Dynamics* 18, no. 3 (1990): 19–31.
583 Bass, "From Transactional to Transformational Leadership: Learning to Share the Vision." 19-31.
584 Oleksy, *Military Leaders of World War II.* 119.
585 Tillman, *LeMay.* 18.
586 Middlebrook, "Marshal of the Royal Air Force: Sir Arthur Harris." 317-33.

Expert power is a highly effective tool of influence, particularly within technologically orientated fields where individuals depend on the leader's ability to employ their expertise for the betterment of those concerned.[587] For LeMay, the recognition by higher command of his expert capabilities came in the form of rapid promotion.[588] However, for his subordinates, he displayed it in the form of professional mastery at both the macro and micro level. His aviation knowledge allowed him to solve a variety of problems, be it issues with frost accumulation at altitude affecting the bomb sights and hence denuding accuracy, or through the implementation of new flight formations that enhanced crew survivability by mitigating enemy anti-air defensive capabilities.[589]

Similarly, for Harris, he appreciated that the relative ineffectiveness of bombardment prior to his tenure could impact on the very survivability of the Air Force.[590] Consequently, he developed the concept of the 'Thousand Bomber' raid, which was to become his vision acting as the concept to generate high levels of organisational identification within Bomber Command.[591] This untested concept related air craft numbers, coupled with increased bomb density, to improved effectiveness and increased crew survivability.[592] He developed this concept based on his understanding of anti-air capabilities and how to overwhelm German defences, but also through specific knowledge relating to the complementary effects of high explosive and incendiary munitions.[593] Implementing change, however, was not without question or rebuke from subordinates or superior command. In the end, the concepts were supported (based on their expertise), and for LeMay at least, he would often quell discontent within his command by flying lead on missions that implemented a new tactic or procedure.[594]

Based on their ability to employ expertise for the betterment of the group, another more valuable source of influence began to develop,

---

587 Robbins et al., *Organisation Behaviour: Concepts, Controversies and Applications*. 524-525.
588 Oleksy, *Military Leaders of World War II*. 120; Tillman, *LeMay*. 24.
589 Tillman, *LeMay*. 42-43; Murray, "Curtis E. Lemay: Airman Extraordinary." 139-140.
590 Cox, "Sir Arthur Harris and the Air Ministry." 212-216.
591 Arthur Harris, *Bomber Offensive* (London: Collins, 1947). 109; Haslam, *Psychology in Organisations: The Social Identity Approach*. 75.
592 Cox, "Sir Arthur Harris and the Air Ministry." 216.
593 Harris, *Bomber Offensive*. 112.
594 Murray, "Curtis E. Lemay: Airman Extraordinary." 140; Kozak, *Curtis LeMay: Strategist and Tactician*. 111.

being admiration, or more specifically, referent power.[595] This expert driven influence became central to their command, as not only did it drive admiration, it allowed both commanders to become prototypic representatives of the organisation.[596] Therefore not only did they belong, but they exemplified what "belonging" to this group meant.[597] Although subordinates referred to Harris and LeMay as 'Butch' (short for butcher) or 'old iron ass' respectively, they somehow managed to overlook their commander's personality shortfalls and held them in great admiration.[598] This is primarily attributable to subordinates' recognition of their commander's expertise and an appreciation of how procedural shifts or tough training was centred on supporting the interest and advancement of the group (being their survival).[599]

The multiple facets of motivation

Motivation differs from leadership in the context that motivation is 'a set of processes that arouse, direct and maintain human behaviour toward attaining a goal'.[600] It is the tool that enables leadership and has clear linkages to social identity theory, as Haslam states:

> social identity theory is actually founded on motivational assumptions in arguing that intergroup behaviour is partly motivated by the esteem-related need to achieve or maintain a positive social identity.[601]

Ultimately both commanders being discussed, employed aspects of several known motivational constructs, which aided the formation of a collective identity. Firstly, this paper has already indicated that through

---

595 Forgas, *Interpersonal Behaviour: The Psychology of Social Interaction*. 216; Bartol et al., *Management: A Pacific Rim Focus*. 449.

596 Haslam, *Psychology in Organisations: The Social Identity Approach*. 45-58; Forgas, *Interpersonal Behaviour: The Psychology of Social Interaction*. 216-217.

597 Stephen D. Reicher, Alexander S. Haslam, and Michael J. Platow, "The New Psychology of Leadership," *Scientific American Mind*, no. August/September (2007): 26.

598 Robin Neillands, "Facts and Myths About Bomber Harris," *RUSI Journal* 146(2), no. April (2001): 69–73; Murray, "Curtis E. Lemay: Airman Extraordinary." 138.

599 Kozak, *Curtis LeMay: Strategist and Tactician*. 77; Niklas K Steffens et al., "Leadership as Social Identity Management : Introducing the Identity Leadership Inventory (ILI) to Assess and Validate a Four-Dimensional Model," *The Leadership Quarterly* 25, no. 5 (2014): 1001–24.

600 Robbins et al., *Organisation Behaviour: Concepts, Controversies and Applications*. 241-243.

601 Haslam, *Psychology in Organisations: The Social Identity Approach*. 67.

an appreciation of the human need to seek out belongingness or social affiliation, both commanders strove to establish group cohesion within their commands.[602] It would seem they appreciated this concept as now addressed by several motivational theories founded on needs acquisition.[603] Secondly, they recognised the negative influence an individual with a poor work ethic could have on group cohesion, thus sought to forge a group identity centred on professionalism.[604] They simply removed the 'no goods' as defined by LeMay, or 'Theory X' individuals as articulated by McGregor in his motivational construct.[605] Finally, and based on their expertise within the field of aviation, they both actively strove to improve aspects of personnel living conditions that they could influence. This was evident in basic attempts by both commanders to improve living conditions, food quality, provide cold weather clothing, develop an appropriate leave policy or recognise high levels of achievement.[606] By improving these 'motivator factors', personnel, according to Herzberg's two-factor motivational construct, would be more inclined to achieve the organisational objectives.[607] These efforts continued to elevate the admiration levels personnel held for their commanders, leading to an increase in commitment to the group. The ability for Harris and LeMay to appreciate the importance of group identity, cultivate admiration through expertise and develop motivation, became central to achieving organisational change.

Mutually supporting concepts

The discussion thus far has centred on those aspects of the individual commander that allowed them to establish the baseline elements of admiration, group cohesion and motivation within their commands. Having achieved this, they were both well placed to execute their vision and transform their commands. Transformational leadership can be an effective leadership style and is dependent on a leader's ability to:

---

602 Wood et al., *Organisational Behaviour: An Asia-Pacific Perspective.* 169-176.
603 Haslam, *Psychology in Organisations: The Social Identity Approach.* 60-65.
604 Haslam, *Psychology in Organisations: The Social Identity Approach.* 68-71.
605 Kozak, *Curtis LeMay: Strategist and Tactician.* 116; Haslam, *Psychology in Organisations: The Social Identity Approach.* 60-65.
606 Kozak, *Curtis LeMay: Strategist and Tactician.* 92-94; Messenger, *"Bomber" Harris and the Strategic Bombing Offensive, 1939-1945.* 203.
607 Haslam, *Psychology in Organisations: The Social Identity Approach.* 62-63.

broaden and elevate the interests of their employees, when they generate awareness and acceptance of the purposes and mission of the group and when they stir their employees to look beyond their own self-interest for the good of the group.[608]

To achieve this, a transformational leader should seek to leverage the 'Four I's' inherent within the transformational leadership model, being idealised influence, inspirational motivation, individualised consideration and intellectual stimulation.[609] Harris and LeMay did, in fact, employ these. However, they appeared to balance this model heavily with the concepts of identity management now recognisable within the social identity theory of leadership.[610] Specifically, it was their ability as leaders to act as champions for their respective command which resulted in the advancement of organisational identity through acts of representation and reflection, which then allowed organisational goals to eventuate.[611]

With regard to idealised influence, meaning establishing a sense of vision and purpose for the group, Harris achieved this via his advocacy for the thousand-bomber plan. This concept represented a radical change to the principles of strategic bombardment being employed at the time and carried strategic risk due to the volume of aircraft required.[612] He was of the belief that high-volume bombardment was the most efficient way to undermine German morale and thus impact military effectiveness.[613] In doing so, he garnered support from the civilian leadership ensuring additional airframes would be provided.[614] Therefore, what we begin to see are aspects of concepts now recognisable in the transformational and social identity leadership theories. The support for this idea ultimately provided Bomber Command with a unique identity. The thousand-

---

608 Bass, "From Transactional to Transformational Leadership: Learning to Share the Vision." 21.

609 Peter Northhouse, *Leadership Theory and Practice* (London: SAGE Publications Ltd, 1997). 157.

610 Niklas K Steffens et al., "Leadership as Social Identity Management : Introducing the Identity Leadership Inventory (ILI) to Assess and Validate a Four-Dimensional Model," *The Leadership Quarterly* 25, no. 5 (2014): 1001–24.

611 Matthew J. Slater, Andrew L. Evans, and Martin J. Turner, "Implementing a Social Identity Approach for Effective Change Management," *Journal of Change Management* 16, no. 1 (2016): 18–37.

612 Harris, *Bomber Offensive*. 109.

613 Messenger, *"Bomber" Harris and the Strategic Bombing Offensive, 1939-1945*. 63.

614 Messenger, *"Bomber" Harris and the Strategic Bombing Offensive, 1939-1945*. 74-78.

bomber concept, founded on Harris's expertise, saw him acting as a change agent with regards to transformational leadership. However, it also saw him acting as an identity entrepreneur for Bomber Command, as he was crafting a sense of 'us' for the organisation. This group cohesion was further strengthened with air-crew openly supporting the operations as they now felt like their effort had a purpose and a clear aim.[615]

Similarly, within the European theatre, LeMay developed his own vision. To date, the effectiveness of precision bomb tactics employed by the US Air Force had been questionable at best.[616] Like Harris, LeMay leveraged his knowledge and expertise within aviation (and artillery) to seek a solution. This resulted in the development of the 'straight run' approach doctrine.[617] Although initially unpopular with the air-crew, the effectiveness of the new doctrine was to solidify the identity of the 305th Bomb Group within the Eighth Air Force. In the pre-mission briefing for the first mission employing the doctrine, the logic of the concept was openly questioned by subordinates within the group.[618] Rather than disciplining this member publicly, he countered the concern from air-crew by stressing that the concept would result in an operational effect on Germany, and again, he would fly lead.[619] This had several significant impacts regarding the identity of the 305th. First, it confirmed Lemay's organisational prototypicality, an integral element within the social identity leadership construct.[620] Second, due to the potential for enhanced effectiveness and combat survival, it had the potential to advance the individual identity of the 305th Bomb Group.[621] LeMay was 'doing it for us'. This appealed to the wider group membership, as effectiveness had to that point been poor; if this new doctrine were successful, it would provide meaning and enhance the sense of unity identity.[622] This is a critical aspect to appreciate, as success

615 Steffens et al., "Leadership as Social Identity Management : Introducing the Identity Leadership Inventory (ILI) to Assess and Validate a Four-Dimensional Model." 1004.
616 Kozak, *Curtis LeMay: Strategist and Tactician.* 94-95.
617 Kozak, *Curtis LeMay: Strategist and Tactician.* 95-107.
618 Kozak, *Curtis LeMay: Strategist and Tactician.* 105.
619 Kozak, *Curtis LeMay: Strategist and Tactician.* 105-106.
620 Alexander S. Haslam, Stephen D. Reicher, and Michael J. Platow, *The New Psychology of Leadership: Identity, Influence and Power,* 2009. 78-90.
621 Steffens et al., "Leadership as Social Identity Management : Introducing the Identity Leadership Inventory (ILI) to Assess and Validate a Four-Dimensional Model." 1003.
622 Steffens et al., "Leadership as Social Identity Management : Introducing the Identity Leadership Inventory (ILI) to Assess and Validate a Four-Dimensional Model." 1004.

provided personnel with a sense of purpose: their efforts now mattered in the grander scheme of the war.[623]

So, like Harris, LeMay, implemented change by elevating the interest of the group and is thus recognisable as a leader who leveraged the transformational construct.[624] However, in achieving this, his leadership techniques extended beyond concern simply for the individual. He leveraged the importance of group affiliation (a need he appreciated from his formative years), and thus he also acted as an identity entrepreneur which led to higher levels of performance.[625] For both commanders their ability to identify alternate methods to achieve the mission being asked of their command demonstrates two additional aspects found within social identity theory. Firstly, not only did they represent the organisation to external stakeholders, but they also reflected on the concerns of group membership and demonstrated an interest in cultivating a unique group identity.[626] In contemporary theoretical terms, Harris and LeMay addressed fundamental aspects as now considered inherent within social identity leadership theory.[627] This enabled both Harris and LeMay to implement their transformational vision with less friction than traditionally associated with change management as the collective group supported the concepts.

Both commanders' appreciation of the importance of human motivation has already been discussed, however within the transformational leadership model the ability to provide inspirational motivation is central to effectiveness. To achieve this, the leader must 'communicate high expectations to followers, inspiring them through motivation to

---

623 Steffens et al., "Leadership as Social Identity Management : Introducing the Identity Leadership Inventory (ILI) to Assess and Validate a Four-Dimensional Model." 1004-1005.

624 Bass, "From Transactional to Transformational Leadership: Learning to Share the Vision." 21.

625 Steffens et al., "Leadership as Social Identity Management : Introducing the Identity Leadership Inventory (ILI) to Assess and Validate a Four-Dimensional Model." 1004; Van Dick and Kerschreiter, "The Social Identity Approach to Effective Leadership: An Overview and Some Ideas on Cross-Cultural Generalizability." 364-365.

626 Slater, Evans, and Turner, "Implementing a Social Identity Approach for Effective Change Management."

627 Van Dick and Kerschreiter, "The Social Identity Approach to Effective Leadership: An Overview and Some Ideas on Cross-Cultural Generalizability." 363-384.

become committed to and be a part of the shared vision".[628] The most obvious example of this was LeMay and his ability to support missions by flying lead. Harris, although not flying and being largely disconnected from his subordinate elements, was also able to generate high levels of motivation within the group. Perhaps the most obvious example of this relates to his sombre assessment on crew survivability within Bomber Command where on one occasion he conferred the reality that surviving their tenure held a likelihood of one in three.[629] Therefore, to achieve continued air-crew support for missions, not only did he leverage his charisma and rhetorical ability (skills required of transformational leaders) but he seemed to leverage the strength of group salience now present within Bomber Command.[630]

The personnel within both Bomber Command and the 305th Bomb Group were completing tasks that carried extraordinary risk. Their missions required the synchronisation of multiple teams to execute tasks under highly stressful and perilous circumstances: suggesting that a well-delivered speech is sufficient motivation alone is implausible. Rather, in hindsight, their command efforts related aspects of idealised influence within transformational leadership and identity entrepreneurship within the social identity construct, which when combined established high levels of collective group identification.[631] The ability to achieve deindividuation is identifiable as a contributor that enables a shift in decision making from the interest of the individual alone, toward the interests of the collective group.[632] As such, the ability to inculcate a sense of inspirational motivation could arguably be more a result of those with 'membership' to Bomber Command or the 305th Bomb Group seeking to achieve the collective group goal. This had simply become the normalised individual expectation.[633] This demonstrates how Harris and LeMay

628 Northhouse, *Leadership Theory and Practice*. 135-136.

629 Probert, *Bomber Harris: His Life and Times*. 199-200.

630 Wood et al., *Organisational Behaviour: An Asia-Pacific Perspective*. 519-521.

631 Bass, "From Transactional to Transformational Leadership: Learning to Share the Vision." 19-31; Steffens et al., "Leadership as Social Identity Management: Introducing the Identity Leadership Inventory (ILI) to Assess and Validate a Four-Dimensional Model." 1001-24.

632 Forgas, *Interpersonal Behaviour: The Psychology of Social Interaction*. 300-310.

633 Knippenberg, Daan and Ellemers, "Social Identity and Group Performance: Identification as the Key to Group-Oriented Effort." 31-41.

achieved organisation change and mission support through the application of aspects recognisable within the transformational and social identity leadership constructs.

The third component within the transformational leadership model is the concept of individualised consideration, where the leader pays close attention to the needs of individuals and establishes a supportive environment.[634] This paper has already intimated that based on their appreciation of the demands placed on air-crew, both commanders sought to improve the immediate working conditions of members within the command. Furthermore, they extended this concern toward efforts to improve tactics that increased crew survivability.[635] However, both commanders were largely dislocated from the wider membership of their commands due to the geographical placement of their forces and a perceived need to maintain an element of command separation.[636] This, however, did not have an adverse impact on the respect subordinates held for their commanders.

To achieve this individualised consideration, both commanders had an ability to identify talent and thus developed a loyal and dedicated inner command circle. It was within this context that direct mentorship occurred.[637] There are examples of both commanders making attempts to improve morale based on the individual needs of key personnel. LeMay, on one occasion, organised a dinner for himself, another pilot and both their wives in an attempt to maintain morale.[638] For Harris, on one occasion, he openly supported a subordinate command decision to cancel a well-progressed mission. The decision was made in isolation due to a communication disconnect, but was ultimately backed by Harris based on the confidence he had in his staff.[639] For both commanders, the adherence to this aspect of individualised consideration came in the form of identity advancement as articulated within social identity

634 Bass, "From Transactional to Transformational Leadership: Learning to Share the Vision." 21.
635 Craig Scarlett, "Sir Arthur 'Bomber' Harris: An Effective Leader in Command?," *Geddes Papers*, 2004, 33–41.
636 Kozak, *Curtis LeMay: Strategist and Tactician.* 80; Messenger, *"Bomber" Harris and the Strategic Bombing Offensive, 1939-1945.* 54.
637 Kozak, *Curtis LeMay: Strategist and Tactician.* 78-79.
638 Kozak, *Curtis LeMay: Strategist and Tactician.* 87.
639 Probert, *Bomber Harris: His Life and Times.* 153.

leadership theory.[640] Therefore, Harris and LeMay's actions to fight for the advancement, and subsequently protect the interests of the individual, was achieved through ongoing efforts to nurture the collective group identity of their commands.

Two examples have already been highlighted that demonstrated how Harris and LeMay achieved identity advancement, being the 'thousand-bomber' concept and LeMay's 'straight run' doctrine. Two other examples further emphasise their appreciation of the interests of the group and how this complements the organisation. For Harris, this related to the proposed development of a 'Pathfinder' group, a *corps d'elite* used to identify targets.[641] Harris and his immediate staff were opposed to this concept as proposed by the Air Ministry, as it would have resulted in the removal of personnel from established groups and 'likely lead to a good deal of trouble and might be thoroughly bad for morale'.[642] In the Pacific theatre, LeMay sought to increase bomb load capacity of the B-29 bomber by removing the defensive guns and gunners. The tactical concept was successful, and when coupled with low altitude incendiary bombing, efficiently destroyed large urban centres within Japan.[643] However, it also had an additional unintended consequence:

> Two days after Tokyo, LeMay had to deal with an unusual protest from the crews. The gunners who sat out the Tokyo raid were upset that they had been left behind, and the crews demanded to be reunited.[644]

Albeit with an impact on payload capacity, LeMay acquiesced to this request, reinstating the gunners to the group. This was not by chance, but rather implemented through an appreciation on the need for individuals to feel connected to the team and how this leads to higher outcomes for the individual and group. This is an element widely accepted as integral to the social identity approach to leadership, and

---

640 Steffens et al., "Leadership as Social Identity Management : Introducing the Identity Leadership Inventory (ILI) to Assess and Validate a Four-Dimensional Model." 1001-1024.
641 Harris, *Bomber Offensive*. 128-129.
642 Harris, *Bomber Offensive*. 128-129.
643 Kozak, *Curtis LeMay: Strategist and Tactician*. 217-238.
644 Kozak, *Curtis LeMay: Strategist and Tactician*. 237.

although not employing the concepts in their current guise, LeMay clearly appreciated this aspect of leadership.[645]

The above examples demonstrate how components within both the leadership constructs being discussed complement each other. When issues with new concepts were raised, both Harris and LeMay reflected on the interest and concerns of the group and amended decisions as required. This reflection process is seen as an integral component of social identity leadership and is one that both commanders employed for the betterment of their commands.[646] Upon appreciating how the concepts could be detrimental for advancing the identity of their commands, they sought a resolution that would ensure group salience was protected.[647] For Harris, this came in the form of raising a capability internally as opposed to a unique force and for LeMay, he simply reversed his decision.[648] By addressing these group concerns, the potential to degrade cohesiveness and identity was removed. Both commanders paid close attention to the needs of the individuals within their command, establishing a supportive environment as defined by transformational leadership.[649] However, it was achieved by protecting the collective identity of their commands and ensuring that group-oriented effort remained.[650]

The final component of transformational leadership relates to the concept of intellectual stimulation, where leaders are 'willing and able to show their employees new ways of looking at old problems, to teach them to see difficulties as problems to be solved and to emphasise rational solutions'.[651] This paper has already highlighted several occasions

---

645 Van Dick and Kerschreiter, "The Social Identity Approach to Effective Leadership: An Overview and Some Ideas on Cross-Cultural Generalizability." 367.

646 Slater, Evans, and Turner, "Implementing a Social Identity Approach for Effective Change Management." 25.

647 Van Dick and Kerschreiter, "The Social Identity Approach to Effective Leadership: An Overview and Some Ideas on Cross-Cultural Generalizability." 373.

648 Harris, *Bomber Offensive*. 128-129; Kozak, *Curtis LeMay: Strategist and Tactician*. 237.

649 Bass, "From Transactional to Transformational Leadership: Learning to Share the Vision." 21;

650 Knippenberg, Daan and Ellemers, "Social Identity and Group Performance: Identification as the Key to Group-Oriented Effort." 31-38; Steffens et al., "Leadership as Social Identity Management : Introducing the Identity Leadership Inventory (ILI) to Assess and Validate a Four-Dimensional Model." 1003-1004.

651 Bass, "From Transactional to Transformational Leadership: Learning to Share the Vision." 21.

where the commanders being discussed employed their expertise to initiate change. However, there were several times when bottom-up concepts were supported and introduced. On both occasions, these aided the command not simply through increased effectiveness, but more importantly by solidifying collective identity through the concept of identity advancement. For Harris and the UK Bomber command, the most powerful example of this was 'Operation Chastise' or the Dam Buster Raids as they are more colloquially known.[652] These raids executed in 1943 employed an entirely unique approach and have been defined as the greatest epic in the annals of RAF Bomber Command due to the technical ingenuity, imagination and courage involved.[653] For LeMay, perhaps the most practical example of this relates to an approach to command, rather than an individual event. Early in his command, he implemented the concept of the 'closed-door briefing' where personnel could freely raise not only concerns, but also opportunities for increased efficiency.[654] LeMay understood that although at times this may challenge the traditional command-subordinate relationship, it was critical in ensuring an effectiveness edge against the threat.[655] If a logical recommendation were made, then LeMay would amend policy and implement change.[656]

These changes, when implemented, were driven by an appreciation from both commanders on the need to maintain an operational advantage. However, wittingly or not, their ability to engage with the group, reflect on their concerns (or recommendations), then effect change, further strengthened the existing group salience and advanced the sense of collective unit identity. This aspect of command is central to leadership effectiveness. It is difficult therefore to not recognise the concept of intellectual stimulation as found within the transformational construct.[657] However, perhaps it was the weight it offered when viewed against the social identity construct that was more beneficial, as it was this aspect of their leadership style that greatly enhanced followership

---

652 Messenger, *"Bomber" Harris and the Strategic Bombing Offensive, 1939-1945*. 118.
653 Messenger, *"Bomber" Harris and the Strategic Bombing Offensive, 1939-1945*. 118-119.
654 Kozak, *Curtis LeMay: Strategist and Tactician*. 232-232.
655 Tillman, *LeMay*. 30-31.
656 Tillman, *LeMay*. 31.
657 Bass, "From Transactional to Transformational Leadership: Learning to Share the Vision." 21-22.

and organisational effectiveness.[658] Social identity theory is founded on several principles, including that of realisation which involves 'achieving group goals and creating a world for the group that reflects its identity'.[659] By establishing opportunities for the group to offer 'their' ideas and execute unique concepts, the leader can create an environment where membership to the group holds additional meaning.[660] The efforts of Harris and LeMay to positively engage their subordinates did, in fact, provide them the opportunity to realise the achievement of group goals.[661] Personnel felt that they mattered, and risking their lives for the team by actively supporting the organisational vision was worthy of their commitment.

Conclusion

For the commanders being discussed, Air Marshall Arthur Harris and General Curtis LeMay, there was a lack of information regarding leadership concepts in comparison to which the contemporary commander can now draw. They did what felt 'right' based on their experiences and observations. This paper has argued that their background instilled in them a sense of the importance of social belonging and group affiliation. This then became integral to their command style as they strove to implement this within their commands. Further, they would seek out subordinate opinion and make amendments as required. This highlighted the complementary effect of how elements now recognisable within transformational leadership aided those discussed within the social identity construct. One can weigh Harris and LeMay against almost any leadership (and by association motivational) construct and see elements of that theory. They were charismatic in their own way, they were coercive, they wielded expertise, they transformed their organisations, they generated high levels of motivation and they most

---

658 Bass, "From Transactional to Transformational Leadership: Learning to Share the Vision." 21.

659 Haslam, Reicher, and Platow, *The New Psychology of Leadership: Identity, Influence and Power*. 206.

660 Steffens et al., "Leadership as Social Identity Management : Introducing the Identity Leadership Inventory (ILI) to Assess and Validate a Four-Dimensional Model." 1004-1005.

661 Steffens et al., "Leadership as Social Identity Management : Introducing the Identity Leadership Inventory (ILI) to Assess and Validate a Four-Dimensional Model." 1003-1004.

definitely developed a unique organisational identity. The strength of this organisational identity is arguably the most important outcome of their approach to leadership. The demands and risks being asked of air-crew predicated a need of subordinating the interest of one's self, to that of the team. Without this, neither Bomber Command, nor the 305th Bomber Group, would have functioned to the standard required. Harris and LeMay achieved this through an approach to leadership that created significant levels of group identity. This allowed them to lead massive air formations and in the process, execute arguably abhorrent missions that one may not have considered sane, unless acting through a sense of collective self, as opposed to a singular individual.

Australian Strategic Policy

Essay 14

'How has Australia's evolving relationship with South-East Asia influenced Australian defence strategy? Is there an alignment between Australia's current defence strategy and its relationships today with your selected region? *(Written 2017)*

Introduction

Since the release of 'Australian Defence' in 1976, another six Defence White Papers (DWP) have been published that seek to articulate Australia's rationale for the strategic employment of military capabilities. Throughout these publications, however, one region has remained a dominant source of commentary, with the thematic reference to this area remaining largely consistent; it warrants due strategic consideration.[662] The 1976 DWP refers to South-East Asia as a 'region of abiding importance to Australia, ' and four decades later the DWP of 2016 states that 'Australia has deep strategic security and economic interests in South-East Asia.[663] The reality of geographic positioning, linked with adversarial analysis, predicates that conventional military action against mainland Australia will require secure avenues of approach, with these

---

662 No Author, *Defence White Paper: Australian Defence* (Canberra: Australian Government Publishing Services, 1976). 6-8; No Author, *Defence White Paper: The Defence of Australia* (Canberra: Australian Government Publishing Services, 1987). 6-16; No Author, *Defence White Paper: Defending Australia* (Canberra: Australian Government Publishing Services, 1994). 86-90; No Author, *Defence White Paper: Defence 2000 Our Future Defence Force* (Canberra: Defence Publishing Service, 2000). 19-21; No Author, *Defence White Paper: Defending Australia in the Asia Pacific Century, Force 2030* (Canberra: Defence Publishing Service, 2009). 34-35; No Author, *Defence White Paper: 2013* (Canberra: Defence Publishing Service, 2013). 11-12; No Author, *Defence White Paper: 2016* (Canberra: Defence Publishing Service, 2016). 56-59.

663 ' Author, *Defence White Paper: Australian Defence*. 1; Author, *Defence White Paper: 2016*. 56.

likely being through the northern archipelagic region.[664] This is a long-held belief consistent throughout all DWP and in large part attributable to the contemporary force and logistical laydown of Australia's military capabilities.[665] If South-East Asia is the global region that has centred Australia's strategic focus for close to half a century, then Indonesia in particular, acts as the litmus in which to gauge success.

The relationship between Australia and Indonesia has long been problematic and perhaps it is best to refer to Susilo Bambang Yudhoyono who articulates that 'there was a lot of baggage between Jakarta and Canberra'.[666] This baggage can be traced to the period immediately before the release of Australia's first DWP when the then Whitlam Labor government gave implicit support for what became the forcible Indonesian annexation of Portuguese Timor.[667] The response from the Australian government immediately following the actions of December 1975, coupled with the vitriolic reaction from the Australian public became the catalyst for what remains a tenuous and strained relationship between both countries. It is likely that public scepticism and deep seeded cultural differences will continue to hamper the development of a more holistic relationship between both countries.[668] Consequently, when public perceptions trigger diplomatic action on a given issue, and it fails, military intervention is the result. This was clearly the case during the 1999 Australian led military intervention to support East Timor. South-East Asia and Indonesia continues to shape Australia's current defence strategy; however, at times it appears more akin to a devolutionary relationship. This paper

---

664 Paul Dibb, *Review of Australia's Defence Capabilities: Report to the Minister for Defence by Mr. Paul Dibb* (Canberra: Australian Government Publishing Services, 1986) 4; Author, *Defence White Paper: 2016.* 56.

665 Author, *Defence White Paper: The Defence of Australia.* 51-52.

666 Sastrohandoyo Wiryono, "An Indonesian View: Indonesia, Australia and the Region," in *Different Societies, Shared Futures: Australia and the Region,* ed. John Monfries (Singapore: Institute of Southeast Asian Studies, 2006), 11–19; https://www.aspistrategist.org.au/australias-strategic-outlook-the-view-from-indonesia

667 John Birmingham, "Appeasing Jakarta: Australia's Complicity in the East Timor Tragedy," *Quarterly Essay,* no. 2 (2001): 7–90; Paul M Monk, "Secret Intelligence And Escape Clauses : Australia and the Indonesian Annexation of East Timor 1963-76," *Critical Asian Studies* 33:2 (2001): 181–208.

668 Brendan Taylor, "Introduction," in *Australia as an Asia-Pacific Regional Power: Friendships in Flux?* ed. Brendan Taylor (New York and London: Routledge, 2007), 26; Wiryono, "An Indonesian View: Indonesia, Australia, and the Region." 11.

will reflect on Australia's formalised approach to Indonesia through the lens of Australia's Defence White Papers and juxtapose this against the reality of the broader societal relationship when considering the varying, often counterproductive impacts, of stakeholders. In short, the relationship remains strained due to shifting political approaches and public sentiment within both countries which impacts negatively on the alignment of defence strategies.

The Elephant in the Room

It is hard to contextualise Australia's evolving relationship with South-East Asia and Indonesia without addressing what is now Timor Leste, but once also known as Portuguese Timor or East Timor. From an Australian perspective, looking north, the Indonesian drift across the archipelago into Portuguese Timor in 1975 (and West Papua) seems to reinforce the strategic belief that Australia is vulnerable to encroachment via the archipelago chain. The fact that the position within the Department of Foreign Affairs leading up to the Indonesian invasion of Portuguese Timor was that 'Indonesian annexation of Timor makes geopolitical sense' and it effectively had government support is irrelevant.[669] The subsequent invasion intimated to the wider community that Australia was vulnerable to its north, and when coupled with the ensuing violence, susceptible to the Indonesian military.[670] Noting the period, it is evident, that a fear of the 'domino effect' remained within the wider Australian populace.[671]

The other perspective, looking south-east from Indonesia, could rightly be viewed as a betrayal, albeit betrayal teetering on a 25-year hung fuse.[672] The diplomatic correspondence and political liaisons occurring in the period leading up to the Indonesian annexation in 1975 seemed clear from this perspective; "Our southern neighbour supports our annexation of Portuguese Timor." In fact at the Townsville meeting's held in 1975, Prime Minister Whitlam conveyed to President Suharto that 'he would side with

---

669 Monk, "Secret Intelligence And Escape Clauses : Australia and the Indonesian Annexation of East Timor 1963-76." 187.
670 Birmingham, "Appeasing Jakarta: Australia's Complicity in the East Timor Tragedy." 30.
671 Gary R. Hess, *Vietnam: Explaining America's Lost War* (Malden: Wiley Blackwell, 2015). 28.
672 Birmingham, "Appeasing Jakarta: Australia's Complicity in the East Timor Tragedy." 10.

Suharto rather than insist on self-determination with the Timorese'.[673] Furthermore, and as highlighted in 2000 when the National Archives released diplomatic cables relating to Portuguese Timor, Indonesia was providing the Australian government with details of its covert and overt military plans.[674] The point here is that 'Australia' supported Indonesian annexation of Portuguese Timor in 1975; however in 1999 when their administration of the region had become unpalatable, Australia employed the use of force to expel Indonesia from East Timor.

Although the previous two paragraphs are a crude dalliance into 25 years of complex state relations, it is important to appreciate as it gets to the heart of the question under consideration. It is difficult to view Australia's evolving relationship with Indonesia and the associated strategic defence implications and not be drawn towards the subjective institutions of the Civil Authority, Military, and People as defined by Clausewitz.[675] It is ultimately the interplay between these subjective institutions on both sides of the Arafura Sea that continues to retard the 'evolution' of Indonesian-Australian relations. The incidents surrounding East Timor exemplify the disconnect between public policy formation and execution on the one hand and public opinion on the other.[676] Until these align, frictions will remain, and for Indonesia, she can rightly consider Australia as a 'friend who had turned on her'.[677]

Slow and steady

When delving deeper into the contemporary relationships and their influence on current defence strategy, it is logical to commence first with the government as they develop the policy to guide a military.[678] The northern archipelago region has been viewed as an area of strategic interest by both sides of politics as highlighted throughout various

673 ' Monk, "Secret Intelligence And Escape Clauses : Australia and the Indonesian Annexation of East Timor 1963-76." 203.

674 Monk, "Secret Intelligence And Escape Clauses : Australia and the Indonesian Annexation of East Timor 1963-76." 203: https://recordsearch.naa.gov.au/SearchNRetrieve/Interface/ViewImage.aspx?B=4151579

675 Carl Von Clausewitz, *Carl von Clausewitz: On War*, ed. Michael Howard and Peter Paret, *On War* (New Yotk, 1976). 89.

676 Birmingham, "Appeasing Jakarta: Australia's Complicity in the East Timor Tragedy." 10.

677 Birmingham, "Appeasing Jakarta: Australia's Complicity in the East Timor Tragedy." 10.

678 Clausewitz, *Carl von Clausewitz: On War*. 607.

DWP. Therefore, the Australian Government has sought to implement policies that would engender positive relations in these areas. A proven method to develop this is by leveraging what have been referred to as the eight tools of diplomacy, ranging from co-operation on one end to the use of force on the other.[679] Australia has a long history of lending diplomatic support to Indonesia including supporting their desire for independence from the Dutch following the World War II.[680] Another proven method to enhance relations is through the implementation of Defence Cooperation Programs (DCP). As early as 1968 the Australia government sought to employ this diplomatic tool by establishing a formalised DCP with Indonesia, second only in scale to that of Papua New Guinea.[681] However, political decisions continue to impact negatively on the relationship between Indonesia and Australia.

When viewing the government's involvement in Indonesia, the polarities of the two major Australian political parties (being the conservative Liberal Party and the left of centre Labor Party) become apparent. In particular, the Whitlam Labor government in power from 1972-75 was an influential driver in advancing the Indonesian-Australian relationship.[682] Richard Woolcott, Australia's representative within Indonesia, championed the advancement of the Indonesian-Australian relationship based on his overt belief that having strong ties with South-East Asia and Indonesia would be beneficial to Australian strategic interests.[683] His commitment to this can be traced back as early as 1967 when he drafted a speech for the sitting Prime-Minister stating 'a basic tenet of our national policy is to live in friendship and understanding with our Asian neighbours'.[684] The resultant and potential unintended consequence is at times both he and Whitlam have borne the burden of being inferred to as the implicit supporters of the Indonesian violence associated with the annexation of Portuguese Timor in 1975.[685]

---

679 Richard Woolcott, "Pathways of Modern Diplomacy," *Australian Journal of International Affairs* 51 (1997): 103–8.

680 Allan Gyngell, "Australia-Indonesia," in *Australia as an Asia-Pacific Regional Power: Friendships in Flux?* ed. Brendan Taylor (London and New York: Routledge, 2007), 97.

681 Gyngell, "Australia-Indonesia." 100.

682 Gyngell, "Australia-Indonesia." 99.

683 Richard Woolcott, "Reflections on Diplomacy: Australia's Role in an Ever-Changing World," *The Sydney Papers* Summer (2003): 108–20.

684 "House of Representatives Official Hansard," *No Author* April, no. 15 (1967): 1139–1209.

685 Birmingham, "Appeasing Jakarta: Australia's Complicity in the East Timor Tragedy." 29.

Since this time there have been varying levels of political engagement and equally varying levels of success. Following the annexation (and on change of government following Prime Minister Whitlam's sacking) the Liberal Fraser Government, although effectively supporting the concept of Indonesian Annexation, engaged in 'double talk' and only recognised Indonesian annexation of East Timor in 1979.[686] The Indonesian Government may rightly question Australia's sincerity toward fostering positive relations at the time, as although a DCP with Australia existed, the 1976 White Paper clearly states 'we now have one significant alliance-the ANZUS Treaty, with New Zealand and the US'.[687] This imbalance toward Indonesian engagement is further compounded when overlayed with an open commitment by Australia for ongoing involvement with the Five Powers Defence Agreement (FPDA).[688] This of course included the potentiality of stationing Royal Australian Airforce (RAAF) assets in Malaysia.[689] One cannot help but see how Australia's words seem poorly aligned to actions and rightly, from an Indonesian perspective, appear disingenuous.

Relations did not alter radically throughout the late 1970s and early 1980s. Under the Hawke government from 1983-91 political engagement positively dropped, although not to the detriment of amicable relations and defence co-operation.[690] One significant policy shift did occur in this period having the potential to improve Indonesian-Australian relations. This relates to the Dibb Review in which it is articulated that:

> Our important neighbour, Indonesia, has neither the motive nor the capability to threaten Australia with substantial military assault. Its principle security concerns are internal stability and threats from the north.[691]

From an Australian strategic and defence perspective, it signalled the need to shift strategy from protection from Indonesia, but rather toward

686 Monk, "Secret Intelligence And Escape Clauses : Australia and the Indonesian Annexation of East Timor 1963-76." 203.
687 Author, *Defence White Paper: Australian Defence.* 2.
688 Author, *Defence White Paper: Australian Defence.* 7.
689 Author, *Defence White Paper: Australian Defence.* 7.
690 Allan Gyngell, "Ambition : The Emerging Foreign Policy of the Rudd Government," *Lowy Institute*, no. December (2008). 100.
691 Dibb, *Review of Australia's Defence Capabilities: Report to the Minister for Defence by Mr. Paul Dibb.* 33.

the provision of support (be it diplomatic or military) to support the internal stability of Indonesia. Unfortunately, it must be said, if viewed from an Indonesian perspective it also implies an inability to maintain internal security and hence 'govern'. It acts as a backhanded insult on government and military capacity further degrading trust.

Coming off the back of the Dibb review the change of leadership within the Labor Party to Paul Keating indicated a renewed era that sought to establish positive relationships with Indonesia. It is assessed that Richard Woolcott, now Secretary for the Department of Foreign Affairs and Trade (DFAT), was influential in shaping Keating in this respect. Woolcott's vision of having Australia actively included within South-East Asia was a natural fit to Keating's who states 'in the growing political liberalisation of Asia we're not an aberration, but a natural fit'.[692] His first international engagement as Prime Minister was to meet with President Suharto in Indonesia. He also openly questioned why Australia did not have a formalised security relationship with Indonesia beyond DCP and one more akin to existing relationships such as the ANZUS and FPDA agreements.[693] It is not surprising that a political shift toward Asia would see a change in Defence strategic alignment.

First, there was a new DWP released, and the intent was clear 'We will continue to give our highest priority in regional defence approach to the pursuit of interests with the countries of South-East Asia' and later 'Our defence relationship with Indonesia is our most important in the region'.[694] Perhaps under this new leadership mutual beneficial inter-state relations would ensue? Keating vigorously pursued his desire to strengthen the Indonesian-Australian strategic alliance which culminated with the formalisation of shared security concepts under the 'Agreement on Maintaining Security' in 1996.[695] Although the agreement was short, it was articulate seeking to deepen the relationship through co-operation on common security interests.[696] Finally, it seemed, that with senior political leadership relations solidified, the flow onto military

---

692 http://www.keating.org.au/persistent/catalogue_files/products/19920407australiaand asia.pdf

693 Gyngell, "Australia-Indonesia." 101.

694 Author, *Defence White Paper: Defending Australia*. 86-87.

695 Alan Dupont, "The Australian-Indonesia Security Agreement," *The Australian Quarterly* 68, no. 2 (1996): 49–62.

696 Dupont, "The Australian-Indonesia Security Agreement." 49-61

and wider country relations was improving. Funding was flowing, DCP was active, bilateral defence structures were in place with functional Defence committees operational. Defence strategy was finally aligned to the relationship. Then in 1999 came the strategic shift which would negate close to 30 years of relationship building, fracturing established trusts that mostly remain damaged across the political, military and wider populace of both countries.

The Great Betrayal

The transition for Australia from the Keating Labor government to the Howard Liberal government occurred in the usual relatively benign Australian way, the most significant impost to the population being the loss of a Saturday in March of 1996. However, during his tenure, Australia's perspective on regional and global security was to undergo two tectonic shifts. First, driven in large part by increasing levels of constituent pressure regarding East Timor and the Indonesian actions therein, Howard wrote to Indonesian President Habibie, suggesting the concept of East Timorese autonomy.[697] It was, as history shows, a catastrophic strategic own goal, which led to Indonesia ceasing the Agreement on Maintaining Security established by Keating and Suharto.[698] The resultant conflict spiral within East Timor triggered military intervention via the Australian led International Forces East Timor (INTERFET). INTERFET actually seized East Timor from Indonesian control, an act that remains a source of friction for multiple stakeholders on both sides of the Arafura Sea.

From the average Australian perspective (and driven in large part by an increasing media flow) the atrocities being inflicted against the Timorese seemed to reinforce long-held public sentiment about the violence and practices inherent within the Indonesian Military, particularly the notorious Battalion 745, known as the 'Brave ones'.[699] Additionally, the tactics, techniques, and procedures, if they can be referred to as such, were an affront to serving Australian military members, further straining an already tenuous understanding of one another.

---

697 Gyngell, "Australia-Indonesia." 105.
698 Gyngell, "Australia-Indonesia." 105.
699 Birmingham, "Appeasing Jakarta: Australia's Complicity in the East Timor Tragedy." 13.

From an Indonesian perspective, it was, as has been suggested an unwelcomed, unwarranted interference and act of betrayal. Furthermore, when the media professed the 'triumphant' actions of INTERFET (read Australia), Indonesian nationalists viewed this as an act of humiliation, responding in kind through attacks on the Australian Embassy in Jakarta.[700] In short, relations within and across the spectrum of the three Clausewitzian subjective institutions of government, military, and population were fractured. Funding channels towards DCP were cut, joint military exercises were cancelled and military exchanges reduced.[701] There were, interestingly, pockets within both militaries that sensed this was simply another diplomatic storm to weather and in time military co-operation would again be cordial.[702]

Shared Interests and Enduring Frictions

The second tectonic shift to occur during Howard's tenure as Prime Minister related to an increasing global trend of terrorism, exemplified by the September 2001 attacks on New York.[703] For Howard (who was in the United States at the time) it triggered an apparent shift in defence orientation back towards support to the United States of America; a drift from the not insignificant attempts of regional engagement achieved under the Keating government.[704] It also led to the employment of expeditionary military forces to secure Australia's interests, with this intent exemplified through Howard's comments relating to the right to 'pre-emptive strike'.[705] The reality was that such an overt shift by the Australian government relating to alliances and the method in which

700 Gyngell, "Australia-Indonesia." 106.
701 Gyngell, "Australia-Indonesia." 107.
702 Gyngell, "Australia-Indonesia." 107.
703 Lance Collins and Warren Reed, *Plunging Point: Intelligence Failures, Cover-Ups and Consequences* (Sydney: HarperCollins Publishers, 2005). 3-26.
704 Richard Woolcott, "Foreign Policy Priorities for the Howard Government's Fourth Term : Australia, Asia, and America in the Post-11th September World Fourth Term : Australia, Asia, and America," *Australian Journal of International Affairs* 59, no. June (2005): 141–52.
705 Woolcott, "Foreign Policy Priorities for the Howard Government's Fourth Term : Australia, Asia, and America in the Post-11th September World Fourth Term : Australia, Asia, and America." 143.

to achieve strategic defence outcomes was to have consequences.[706] For many countries within South-East Asia, Indonesia included, Australia now seemed less independent. Australia's approach to defence strategy was seen simply as enforcing the United States policy within our region.[707] Australia had become puppets, at best 'deputy sheriff' and the relationship was most definitely misaligned.[708]

More disturbingly, many of our regional defence partners including the Indonesian President, Foreign Minister and Defence Minister were of the belief that the actions of the Howard government stimulated recruiting interest for those susceptible to Islamic terrorism within the region.[709] Australia then had acted with limited consultation or due consideration of what would be mostly predictable second order effects. Howard's decision had effectively undermined an objective contained within the 2000 DWP being the need for a stable Indo-Pacific region. [710] He had effectively provided the stimulus that would deliver a destabilising effect to South-East Asian countries, specifically Indonesia. As it turns out our South-East Asian partner's fears were correct, and thus, the relationship suffered. First came the Bali Bombings in 2002 killing 202 people including 88 Australian's, then a direct car bomb attack on the Australian Embassy in 2004.[711] It would be a fair assessment that Australia's relationship with Indonesia was not in a good place. These events became the mediums in which to feed distrust between the Indonesian and Australian populations which were largely rooted in cultural differences and religious misunderstanding.[712]

---

706 Woolcott, "Foreign Policy Priorities for the Howard Government's Fourth Term : Australia, Asia, and America in the Post-11th September World Fourth Term : Australia, Asia, and America." 143.

707 Woolcott, "Foreign Policy Priorities for the Howard Government's Fourth Term : Australia, Asia, and America in the Post-11th September World Fourth Term : Australia, Asia, and America." 144.

708 Woolcott, "Foreign Policy Priorities for the Howard Government ' S Fourth Term : Australia, Asia and America in the Post-11th September World Fourth Term : Australia, Asia and America." 144.

709 Woolcott, "Foreign Policy Priorities for the Howard Government ' S Fourth Term : Australia, Asia and America in the Post-11th September World Fourth Term : Australia, Asia and America." 144.

710 Author, *Defence White Paper: Defence 2000 Our Future Defence Force.* 19.

711 Gyngell, "Australia-Indonesia." 107.

712 Woolcott, "Foreign Policy Priorities for the Howard Government's Fourth Term : Australia, Asia, and America in the Post-11th September World Fourth Term : Australia, Asia, and America." 144.

Perhaps through the recognition of this strategic own goal and post the 2002 bombings, the Howard Government sought to correct this error by increasing defence co-operation. This was heavily focused towards support for counter-terrorism training.[713] Funding support increased with a memorandum of understanding relating to counter-terrorism signed in 2002 which extended through to the establishment of the Jakarta Centre for Law Enforcement Cooperation in 2004.[714] Attempts to re-establish positive relations were being made at both the governmental and military level. However, relations in the wider community remained strained.

The greatest thawing of this relationship inhibitor came via the tragedy that was the 2004 tsunami which killed more than 130,000 Indonesians. Australia responded as should be expected of a regional friend. Prime Minister Howard was the first international leader to offer support to Indonesia setting a new global standard in humanitarian funding.[715] The military provided humanitarian support (a proven tool for developing positive diplomatic relations), and the population was generous in their fiscal support to those effected providing over $42 million in donations.[716] Relations, and in particular security agreements, appeared aligned, culminating in the signing of the Framework for Security Co-operation in 2006.[717] This agreement sought to expand bilateral co-operation and notably contained a non-aggression pact.[718]

From 2006 through until today, Australian Defence policy continued to focus on the proven pillar of DCP enabling effective relations which will support the provision of a stable Indo-Pacific region.[719] Regardless of the effectiveness of this political and military engagement, enduring frictions relating to cultural differences remain. In 2006 positive sentiment within both the Australian and Indonesian population to the other sat at or around 50 per cent.[720] This friction is acerbated within

713 Gyngell, "Australia-Indonesia." 108.

714 Gyngell, "Australia-Indonesia." 108.

715 http://www.theage.com.au/news/Asia-tsunami/PM-pledges-1bn-in-aid/2005/01/06/1104832185285.html

716 https://www.care.org.au/boxing-day-tsunami/; Gyngell, "Australia-Indonesia." 109.

717 Gyngell, "Australia-Indonesia." 108.

718 http://www.austlii.edu.au/au/other/dfat/treaties/2008/3.html

719 Author, *Defence White Paper: Defending Australia in the Asia Pacific Century, Force 2030.* 96-97; Author, *Defence White Paper: 2013.* 25; Author, *Defence White Paper: 2016.* 56-57.

720 Gyngell, "Ambition : The Emerging Foreign Policy of the Rudd Government." 111.

the wider community and diplomatic fraternity when considering other divisive issues, notably Indonesia's right to enforce their rule of law relating to drugs (and conversely Australian apathy toward the Indonesian rule of law).[721] When overlaid with differences and decisions at the strategic level, the relationship is further tested. One only need to scan the open source media to appreciate the variable's placing strain on Indonesian-Australian strategic relations be that the 2011 ban on the live cattle trade to Indonesia, illegal fishing or both countries approach to people smuggling.[722] These issues continue to test the evolving relationship and hence the alignment of defence strategies between both countries. Furthermore, when defence exchanges go awry like they did recently resulting in the cessation of military exchanges, the alignment of defence policy and the 'evolving' relationship is rightly questionable.[723]

Conclusion

This essay has assessed the alignment of contemporary Australian defence strategy and its relationship with South-East Asia with emphasis on Indonesia given it remains of vital interest.[724] It is a relationship, it must be said, built on questionable foundations that are challenged across all spectrums including the diplomatic, wider population and the military. If it were to be viewed as a 'relationship' it would be one were one party checks the others text messages when the opportunity presented; which Australia effectively did in 2009.[725] There is close alignment relating to counter-terrorism with a heavy Australian commitment. This it must be acknowledged is driven through the self-interested ideal of achieving

---

721 Richard Tanter, "Shared Problems, Shared Interests: Reframing Australia-Indonesia Security Relations," in *Knowing Indonesia: Intersections of Self, Discipline and Nation*, ed. Jemma Purdey (Melbourne: Monash University Press, 2012), 1–38; http://www.theaustralian.com.au/national-affairs/bali-9-execution-australia-reacts-to-the-deaths-of-chan-and-sukumaran/news-story/b00abc0aa2bb1704046e42b532ea8d4c

722 Tanter, "Shared Problems, Shared Interests: Reframing Australia-Indonesia Security Relations."1-38; http://www.smh.com.au/national/ban-on-live-cattle-trade-to-indonesia-20110607-1frdg.html

723 http://www.sbs.com.au/news/article/2017/01/04/adf-investigating-teaching-materials-after-indonesia-suspends-military-ties

724 No Author, *Defence White Paper* (Canberra, 2016). 59.

725 http://www.abc.net.au/news/2013-11-18/australia-spied-on-indonesian-president,-leaked-documents-reveal/5098860

strategic defence via stability within the region.[726] However, in doing so, the nagging fear remains that if Australia were to be threatened by conventional land invasion, it would likely come via the northern archipelagic approach. Australia's current defensive posture, including force dispositions in the North, remains committed to this (albeit unlikely) potentiality. Consequently, the relationship remains tenuous. Australia's current primary defence objective of being able to 'deter, deny and defeat any attempt by a hostile country or non-state actor to attack, threaten or coerce Australia', implies, wittingly or not, that we must be postured to defend the northern approaches. Indonesia, as Australia's nearest significant military 'ally', may rightly question if this potentiality extends toward them and as such our defence policy is poorly aligned to fostering a genuinely positive relationship with Indonesia and South-East Asia at large.

---

726 Author, *Defence White Paper: 2016.* 59.

Essay 15

What are the key factors to be considered for Australia's strategic and defence policies in relation to tensions on the South China Sea. *(Written 2017 – exam in 4 hours)*

Introduction

The role of a government in establishing strategy and associated defence policy has been an ongoing discussion between the military and civil authority for generations. Clausewitz rightly recognised that it is the government's role to develop strategy and policy, then the military's role to implement.[727] The reality is, little today has changed. Since 1976 the Australian Government has released several Defence White Papers (DWP) that define the key factors to be considered when developing strategic and defence policy. When looking to the future, the shifting geopolitical landscape adds additional complexity worthy of consideration. Currently, the world, including Australia's near region, is experiencing high levels of instability driven by state and non-state power struggles, global terrorism and an increase in mass human migration. The risks associated with this uncertainty is perhaps typified by the Global Doomsday clock, a metric used for determining global demise through man-made effects, predominately a nuclear catastrophe. Currently, it sits at two and half minutes to midnight, topped only by the nuclear risk posed to the world in the 1950s.[728]

One of the most significant causes of friction relates to tension within the South China Sea, an area stretching from Singapore and the Strait

---

727 Carl Von Clausewitz, *Carl von Clausewitz: On War*, ed. Michael Howard and Peter Paret, *On War* (New Yotk, 1976). 607
728 "It Is Two and Half Minutes to Midnight," *Science and Security Board: Bulletin of the Atomic Scientists*, no. Jan (2017): 1–16.

of Malacca through to the Strait of Taiwan and incorporating areas around Vietnam, Borneo, the Philippines, the Spratly islands and many other contested regions.[729] The tension is being caused primarily by China's military infrastructure build up, but also stimulated by competing territorial claims by several countries. Given this instability, the Australian Government must identify the key factors that will shape Australia's strategic and Defence policies into the future. The underlying interests will likely align to existing defence documents; the Australian government should remain committed to providing a secure and resilient country with secure northern approaches, providing a secure nearer region, specifically South-East Asia and enabling a stable Indo-Pacific that functions in accordance with the 'recognised' rules-based order.[730] Therein lies the rub for Australia. To achieve these strategic security objectives, Australia has long aligned itself with powerful partners forming alliances, most notably with the United States through the Australian New Zealand United States (ANZUS) alliance.[731] This alliance remains integral to Australia's national security. It's is highly questionable if Australia could achieve any reputable defence from a near-peer military if this alliance failed. This is founded on Australia's ongoing need for materiel and intelligence support.[732]

This paper will argue that the key factors that must be considered for Australian strategic and defence policy formation will be driven by four elements recognised as being integral to the formation of a national grand strategy; these being, context, capabilities, constraints, and coherence.[733] These, it is assessed, will shape Australian strategic and defence policy formation toward the tensions within the South China Sea. However, due to competing military and economic dependencies from the two major belligerents, Australia remains vulnerable to coercion.

---

729 Raul Pedrozo, "China versus Vietnam: An Analysis of the Competing Claims in the South China Sea," *CNA Analysis and Solutions* August (2014): 1–142.

730 No Author, *Defence White Paper* (Canberra, 2016). 68.

731 Michael Wesley, "Australia ' S Grand Strategy and the 2016 Defence White Paper," *Security Challenges* 12, no. 1 (2016): 19–30; Michael J. Green et al., "The ANZUS Alliance in an Ascending Asia," *The Centre of Gravity Series*, no. July (2015): 1–31.

732 Green et al., "The ANZUS Alliance in an Ascending Asia."; No Author, *Defence White Paper: 2016* (Canberra: Defence Publishing Service, 2016). 30-31.

733 Wesley, "Australia's Grand Strategy and the 2016 Defence White Paper." 21-23

Context

'Context' is what guides a nation's decision makers when formulating policy and is the ability to develop a 'nuanced and intuitive understanding of the evolving circumstances that affect national interests.[734] For Australia, this has remained relatively consistent for the last 40 years and as such the key factors in policy formation have centred on geographical positioning and the establishment of key alliances. The reality at this point in time is that Australia is bound to US interests with the nation's policy at times viewed simply as 'Australian strategic policy has always been a derivative of the grand strategy of its great power ally.[735] This traditional alliance between Australia and the US has for a long period served Australian defence policy well. The negative impacts to existing or evolving relationships Australia has (or desires) with other states has been relatively limited. However, the context with which Australia views the world is rapidly shifting, forcing strategists and policymakers to reassess how Australia reacts to global tensions including within the South China Sea. The primary reason for this shifting contextual perspective is the economic rise of China coupled with the apparent demise of the United States regional dominance within Asia and the Pacific.[736] With these shifting geopolitical structures comes the reality that Australia may need to question its current defence policy relating to the South China Sea or risk legitimacy within its immediate geographical span of influence.

In an increasingly connected world economy, the economic rise of several states is shaping Australia toward a problematic strategic position. It is China's economic rise over the last two decades that sees it currently postured as one of the most important global economies.[737] Australia has mostly benefited from this rise, and it must be said, it is a relationship on which the country is heavily dependent. As of 2016 Australian exports to China was representative of 28 per cent of all exports (with the US only 6%).[738] However, Australia is also heavily dependent on trade exports to Japan, India, and members of the Association of South-East

---

734 ' Wesley, "Australia's Grand Strategy and the 2016 Defence White Paper." 21.

735 ' Wesley, "Australia's Grand Strategy and the 2016 Defence White Paper." 20.

736 Wesley, "Australia's Grand Strategy and the 2016 Defence White Paper." 25.

737 Vinit Ranjan and Gaurav Agrawal, "FDI Inflow Determinants in BRIC Countries: A Panel Data Analysis," *International Business Research* 4, no. OCT (2011): 1–9.

738 Mark Thomson, "Lecture: Trade, Investment, and Strategy" (Canberra, 2017).

Asian Nations (ASEAN) some of which are in disagreement with China regarding territorial claims within the South China Sea.[739] To date, Australia has been able to balance this economic relationship with China (and wider South-East Asia) with its US military dependency relatively well. The question that must be asked is what happens to strategic and defence policy if (or when) Australia is forced to make a firm decision on where their true alliance lies? Will these ease tensions within the South China Sea or further exacerbate frictions?

Capabilities and Constraints

The second element to be discussed regarding the formation of defence strategy and policy relates to 'capabilities' which extend beyond simply the application of military force to achieve strategic interests.[740] Richard Woolcott, a renowned Australian diplomat, recognises eight tools of diplomacy ranging from the use or threat of force at one extreme through to trade embargoes, financial pressure, and co-operation at the other.[741] Achieving national security and defence policies extends beyond simply the application of military force. Increasingly then, achieving national strategic interests is dependent on the harmonious exchange between countries on several fronts. The DIME (Diplomatic, Informational, Military and Economic) paradigm is an effective lens in which to contextualise the factors that Australia must balance when formulating policy to address the tensions in the South China Sea.[742]

Although, currently, the risk of economic coercion by China against Australia is perceived to be relatively low, it remains a factor that cannot be discounted. Economic pressure is a proven method of influence and one that China has forced on nation states in the past.[743] The shared economic investment between China and Australia has, to date, been beneficial. Australia has benefited financially through the export of iron

---

739 Pedrozo, "China versus Vietnam: An Analysis of the Competing Claims in the South China Sea."

740 Wesley, "Australia's Grand Strategy and the 2016 Defence White Paper."

741 Richard Woolcott, "Pathways of Modern Diplomacy," *Australian Journal of International Affairs* 51 (1997): 103–8.

742 Franklin D. Kramer, Larry Wentz, and Stuart Starr, "I-Power: The Information Revolution and Stability Operations," *Defence Horizon* 55, no. Feb (2007): 1–8.

743 Woolcott, "Pathways of Modern Diplomacy." 103-108; Thomson, "Lecture: Trade, Investment, and Strategy."

ore and coal. These resources, in turn, have allowed China to continue its national development objectives, likely empowering China to pursue interests within the South China Sea. The strategic and therefore policy risk for Australia relates to how this relationship overlaps with the competing military interests of the United States. The current expansion of military bases within the South China Sea is viewed as a global security risk, mainly from the US. It is highly likely that the products developed from Australia's exports of ore and coal have directly or indirectly enabled this strategic development. There exists then a misalignment between Australia's strategic economic policy and Australia's strategic military policy which is a key factor that must be considered:

> Our commercial activities have and continue to play a central role in facilitating the rise of the single greatest challenge to American Power since the Second World War – meaning that our economic interests are directly undermining our strategic interests in continuing uncontested regional unipolarity.[744]

When coupled with strategic blunders such as the port of Darwin sale and the seemingly endless security breaches within the wider Australian Defence environment, the US, our major ally, may rightly question if this alliance indeed remains at the 'core' for Australian Defence planning.[745]

If the US were to press Australia on the issue forcing a policy shift by the Australian government, it is not unrealistic that China could decrease their Foreign Domestic Imports (FDI) of Australian products; as has been shown with their actions against Norway.[746] When contrasting this against the economic realities associated with Australia's need for trade relations with China, it is clear that current Australian policies relating to influencing the tensions within the South China Sea are problematic. Simply put, the economic interest of the country are misaligned to the broader military strategies of major, recognised, allies. Until this is more effectively balanced, it will remain a key factor to be considered when developing defence policies.

---

744 Wesley, "Australia's Grand Strategy and the 2016 Defence White Paper." 29
745 Peter et al. Jennings, "Chinese Investment in the Port of Darwin: A Strategic Risk for Australia?," *Strategic Insights* 101, no. Dec (2015): 1–20;.Author, *Defence White Paper: 2016.* 121; Green et al., "The ANZUS Alliance in an Ascending Asia." http://www.abc.net.au/news/2017-10-11/hacker-stole-data-from-defence-subcontractor/9040906
746 Thomson, "Lecture: Trade, Investment, and Strategy."

To date, this remains a somewhat benign reality accepted by all. However, Australia has effectively manoeuvred itself into a position where 'both' global powers can influence Australian decision makers, and by association shape the future of Australia through diplomatic tools and leverage. This 'constraint' or vulnerability of the state is driven by the interconnectedness of states and the tools on which they can draw on to coerce a state.[747] If China disagreed with Australian policy toward the management of tensions in the South China Sea, then trade relations and foreign investment could be restricted or even cease. This would have an immediate and profound effect on Australia at large. For the US, if dissatisfied with Australian policy relating to the South China Sea, military co-operation and intelligence sharing could be reduced impacting on Australian sovereign security. This problematic position relating to the US, China and by association the South China Sea, although largely dismissed when Australian strategic and defence policy is formulated, is in time, likely to act as a key decision point that Australia will be forced to make.

Coherence?

The final element to be discussed relating to the formation of strategic and defence policy is the concept of 'coherence', being the integration of sources of national influence including governmental institutions and industry.[748] This may, in truth, be the primary factor that influences Australian policy toward the tensions within the South China Sea. Without any consistent governmental position regarding these tensions, Australia is simply drifting along with the wider US policy. Disturbingly the current DWP fails to appreciate the shift in regional unipolarity which has been recognised as the primary factor likely to shape Australia's strategic environment (and by association policy) into the future.[749] Coherence at an Australian governmental level is problematic on seemingly simplistic tasks, therefore when devising defence strategy centred on the volatility within the South China Sea the ability to achieve any true coherence is questionable. This is being driven due to competing interests and alternate world views of the

---

747 Wesley, "Australia's Grand Strategy and the 2016 Defence White Paper." 22
748 Wesley, "Australia's Grand Strategy and the 2016 Defence White Paper." 22
749 Wesley, "Australia's Grand Strategy and the 2016 Defence White Paper." 27.

major political parties; primarily it must be stated, based on differences in the previously discussed factors relating to alliances and economic management. Wesley rightly articulates:

> Bringing coherence to these elements is arguably beyond the capabilities of the Australian political system. It would mean confronting the bifurcation between our strategic and economic interests.[750]

The 2016 DWP was unique in the sense that for the first time it brought together the disparate elements and approaches required to achieve the strategic vision through the partner document, the 2016 Integrated Investment Program. The Integrated Investment Program acts as the tool to transform strategic 'intent' into reality and includes capability programs to achieve Australian Defence Interests, notably a stable Indo-Pacific which incorporates the South China Sea.[751] It represents a recognition of the shortfalls associated with the coherence related to capability acquisition, development and delivery into service of critical capabilities required to achieve defence strategy. It focuses on the development across six primary areas integral to defence capability out to and beyond 2030.[752] The effectiveness of this policy and its role in addressing the tensions within the South China Sea are yet to be seen; with success or other likely not to be evident until many of the projects reach maturity (potentially beyond 2030).

In addition to the recognition of a lack of coherence within the capability and acquisition stream, the other strikingly apparent tone within the Integrated Investment Program is the ongoing commitment to alignment with the United States. Many of the platforms scheduled for introduction and enhancement are US capabilities including the C-17A (air-lift) and F-35 Joint Strike Fighter Aircraft and the M1A1 Main Battle tank.[753] Again when coupled with the need for Australia to leverage intelligence and technology capabilities (including munitions) that reside within the US, our strategic alignment seems clear. Australia defence policy relating to South China Sea tensions would appear to

---

750 Wesley, "Australia's Grand Strategy and the 2016 Defence White Paper." 29.

751 No Author, *The Integrated Investment Program* (Canberra: Australian Government Publishing Services, 2016). Author, *Defence White Paper: 2016.* 70

752 Author, *The Integrated Investment Program.* 13

753 Author, *The Integrated Investment Program.* 93-105

correlate into the following statement, 'we will leverage our existing alliance with the United States Military and Defence industry and contribute military capabilities to coalition operations that enable a stable Indo-Pacific regions and a rules-based global order.' This seems obvious and logical enough. However, the issue relates to perspective and one's definition of a 'rules-based global order'. The true friction for Australia will be when the major world powers disagree to such a point on this issue that it forces Australia to decide one way or another regarding an approach to the tensions in the South China Sea.

Conclusion

When assessing the key factors relating to tensions in the South China Sea, contemporary policy makers must view the problem holistically when developing Australian strategic and defence policy. Although Australia's defence force is small in comparison to the two major belligerents involved being the US and China, we are still very much in the fight. By engaging in global trade Australia has enabled the rise of China, which although amicable in diplomatic circles, must undoubtedly cause friction within United States military circles. Based on the DWP and 2016 Integrated Investment Program Australia has clearly chosen to remain aligned with the US, any other consideration outside of this is a fallacy. Australia's military combat capability would simply cease to function without the inputs and alignment of this defence relationship. The somewhat taboo question that remains for Australian and strategic defence policy makers is which way will Australia 'jump' when genuinely pressured, east or west? Australia's competing factors of economic dependence on the one hand and military dependency on the other are the primary factors that Australia has been effectively balancing when it comes to tensions within the South China Sea. However, the reality is in time Australia will be forced to decide on military or economic interests with the South China Sea tension likely being the catalyst that forces the nation's hand. Simply put, will Australia be 'King maker' or remain a contented 'Deputy Sheriff'?

World War I

Essay 16

'The First World War was prolonged by the inability of the Entente/Allies to establish a unified coalition command until 1918' *(Written 2017)*

Introduction

The review of historical events has long been employed as a tool of leverage providing the contemporary practitioner with insights from which to enact positive change. Much energy from within the academic fraternity and those within the profession of arms has been invested in sourcing a resolution of sorts regarding the execution and duration of World War I. There are obvious indicators suggesting the war was prolonged through inefficiencies within the Entente and Allied Coalition, and in truth, it is difficult to look past this issue. However, simply laying blame on those charged with establishing the necessary cohesion between these disparate groups would be disingenuous to the circumstances of the time. This paper will appraise the statement that the First World War was prolonged through inefficiency, specifically that the Entente and Allied coalition failed to establish a unified coalition command until 1918. In doing so, however, World War I will not be viewed in pure isolation as gaining an appreciation of the period provides valuable insight on key areas, all of which in their way act as inhibitors to the establishment of a unified coalition command.

World War I, as with others since, provides a snapshot into a window of time where the character of war evolved at a pace difficult to comprehend.[754] The demands of this war drove technological advances

---

754 Niall J A. Barr, "The Elusive Victory: The BEF and the Operational Level of War, September 1918," in *War in the Age of Technology: Myriad Faces of Modern Armed Conflict*, ed. Geoffrey Jensen and Andrew Wiest (New York and London: New York University Press, 2001), 211–38.

across multiple domains including the land, sea and air, thus altering the character of war as it was then recognised.[755] Consequently, those charged with executing war on the people's behalf, notably the government and military, experienced what would now be recognised as a degree of cognitive dissonance.[756] The tempo of changes in warfare retarded one's ability to form cohesive thought relating to campaign design. The results, understandably, were often problematic with this breeding conflict in an organisation behavioural sense. These conflicts occurred not only at an inter-state level, but additionally and perhaps with greater detriment, internally between the established civil and military institutions of individual countries. It will be shown that it was these tempo induced conflicts, which were the principle impediment to the timely formation of a unified coalition command. The duration of the war was prolonged, as tactics could only be executed efficiently once supported by a united Entente grand strategy that enabled the integration of theatre level operational actions. This did not occur until during 1918.

Character(s) in Crisis

> When all is said that can be said, the men on foot remain the greatest thing in war: they are the vertebrae in the spine of battle, and without them, the other arms are as trunkless limbs. The black guns may spit at each other, and the glittering squadrons crash together, but it is the volley firing at five hundred yards that beggars treasuries and alters maps.[757]

The statement above is important as it provides insight into the psyche of military strategists in the period leading up to World War I. Their logic at that point in time was relatively sound. Contemporary military history, founded in Napoleonic style conflict was being used as the guiding premise for decision making relating to military operations.[758] The writings of

---

755 Matthew Hughes and Matthew Seligmann, "People and the Tides of History: Does Personality Matter in the First World War?," in *Leadership in Conflict 1914-1918*, ed. Matthew Hughes and Matthew Seligmann (South Yorkshire: Leo Cooper, 2000), 1–37.

756 Stephen Robbins et al., *Organisation Behaviour: Concepts, Controversies and Applications* (Sydney: Prentice Hall, 1994). 212-214

757 Norreys Connell, *How Soldiers Fight: An Attempt to Depict for the Popular Understanding the Waging of War and the Soldiers Share in It.* (London: James Bowden, 1899). 169

758 Unknown, *Field Service Regulations: Part 1* (London: Harrison and Sons, 1901). 126

Clausewitz (increasingly recognised within the Military education fraternity) espoused the primacy of offensive action over defensive.[759] As did the works of Jomini, whose maxims on military operations were heavily skewed toward the offence; with one central tenet being the need to mass one's forces toward a decisive point.[760] This propensity of thought toward the offensive was prevalent not only within Entente countries but also within the German military.[761] The result saw the birth of what has become known as the 'cult of the offensive' a cult increasingly nurtured by both Entente and Central Power commanders and largely to blame for the horrors during the early years of the war.[762]

In addition to this issue, the duration of the war (not yet recognised as the first global conflict) was not seen as cause for concern requiring commitment from any elements other than a countries military force.[763] Why then would decision makers of the period consider themselves misguided? History is providing sound context for the execution of war, and the increasingly professionalised military establishment is yielding effective results. What the above does contextualise is the disposition of these influential personnel involved in decision-making at the war's inception and how these alternate views led to friction.

These frictions can be traced to the initial stages of the war and how visions of a perceived end state, character, duration and strategy differed across and within various civil and military institutions. As example, Kitchener, as Secretary of State at the onset of war had a largely different view on the possible nature of the conflict to that of popular opinion including his principle Generals, notably Haig.[764] Kitchener rightly envisioned

759 Sir John Smyth, *Leadership in Battle* (London: David and Charles (Holdings) Limited, 1975). 26
760 Antoine Henri de Jomini, *The Art of War*, E-Book (Rockville: Arc Manor, 2007). 49-52
761 Eric Brose, *The Kaiser's Army: The Politics of Military Technology in Germany during the Machine Age, 1870-1918* (New York: Oxford University Press, 2001). 87
762 Eugenia C Kiesling, "Resting Comfortably on Its Laurels: The Army of Interwar France," in *The Challenge of Change: Military Institutions and New Realities 1918-1941*, ed. Harold R Winton and David R Mets (Lincoln: University of Nebraska Press, 2000), 1–28.
763 Norman Stone, *World War One: A Short History*, Second (New York: Perseus Books Group, 2009). 35-37
764 David French, "The Strategy of Unlimted Warfare? Kitchener, Robertson and Haig," in *Great War, Total War: Combat and Mobilisation on the Western Front, 1914-1918*, ed. Roger Chickering and Stig Forster (Washington D.C.: Cambridge University Press, 2000), 281–95.

the War would be a prolonged affair.[765] Consequently, he focused on a holistic campaign employing strategic levers other than simply force. He saw utility in applying naval force to establish economic advantage, or perhaps more accurately, impose disadvantage. Additionally, he was reticent to commit British forces *en masse* to the European mainland, a task he viewed as being a Franco-Russian responsibility.[766]

More insightful, however, and potentially founded on his prior experience with strategy development, was, in fact, his grasp on grand strategic levers.[767] He was of the belief that an internal populace revolt was the most effective means through which the then current German political establishment could be destroyed.[768] This concept on analysis was well considered and as war progressed the importance of national morale became a consideration relating to success or otherwise for both Entente and Central forces. Kitchener effectively sought the political reform of Germany (not simply the defeat of her military), through the application of alternate power sources to influence the less obvious path to victory.[769] His grand strategy was founded on targeting the German populace to lobby government (hence military) with a view to pursuing a course of action in a direction favourable to British ends. Clausewitzian logic is obvious.[770]

In contrast, however, General Haig, a recognised military practitioner with combat experience against the 'Boche', opposed elements of Kitchener's logic.[771] Initially, he was of the belief that defeating Germany could only be achieved through the destruction of her military, the second of the three subjective institutions as recognised by Clausewitz.[772] Further, Haig questioned the strategic abilities of his immediate superior, General French, who incidentally had a somewhat strained relationship with his

---

765 Smyth, *Leadership in Battle*. 19
766 French, "The Strategy of Unlimted Warfare? Kitchener, Robertson and Haig." 281–95
767 Hal Brands, *What Good Is Grand Strategy? Power and Purpose in American Statecraft from Harry S. Truman to George W. Bush* (London: Cornell University Press, 2016). 9-24
768 French, "The Strategy of Unlimted Warfare? Kitchener, Robertson and Haig." 281–95
769 French, "The Strategy of Unlimted Warfare? Kitchener, Robertson and Haig." 281–95
770 Peter Paret, "Clausewitz," in *Makers of Modern Strategy from Machiavelli to the Nuclear Age Edition*, ed. Peter Paret (Princeton: Princeton University Press, 1986), 182–213.
771 French, "The Strategy of Unlimted Warfare? Kitchener, Robertson and Haig." 281–95
772 Antulio J. Echevarria II, "Clausewitz and the Nature of the War on Terror," in *Clausewitz in the Twenty-First Century*, ed. Hew Strachan and Andreas Herberg-Rothe (London: Oxford University Press, 2007), 197–218.

civil master, Kitchener.[773] What this demonstrates is the dichotomy of thought existing simply within one Entente country. Haig was the product of a general staff training continuum founded in late 1800's knowledge and a proven member of the profession of arms.[774] 'Lord' Kitchener however, and likely due to his societal position, had a finer appreciation on the interplay between the military, populace and government (including Royal).[775] As such, a military-centric strategy is logical when viewed through a militarist lens, whereas the proposal for applying other levers of power is plausible when viewed through a behaviourist's lens.[776] Nonetheless, conflict existed between British military commanders and the civil authority. Such conflicts also extended to the civil authority alone with Kitchener on occasion having to leverage his political skill simply to garner support in his favour over Churchill, the then Home Secretary.[777] The issue becoming apparent is how divergent thought across the civil-military, military-military and civil-civil institutions of a given country has a negative impact on the formation of a united command. This in turn impacts on the ability to develop a cohesive coalition Grand Strategy; with the resultant being a cascading negative influence that hinders effective theatre operational planning. Tactical failure executed on small parcels of earth is the end state.

As previously indicated, the world in general, including the military, was in a state of change leading up to the First World War. Logically this extended beyond Britain to the wider geopolitical environment including countries required to form the Entente and Allied coalition. If a single country can have alternate views on the execution of war and strategy development, it is a reasonable hypothesis that inefficiency will compound when multiple states are needed for a coalition. In the case of World War I, more than thirty countries each with their own political and military agendas were required to form an effective coalition.[778] Given that the scale of such a coalition had not yet been seen in human

---

773 John Terraine, *Ordeal of Victory* (Philadelphia: J.B. Lippincott Company, 1963). 80

774 Smyth, *Leadership in Battle*. 19-22

775 French, "The Strategy of Unlimted Warfare? Kitchener, Robertson and Haig." 281–95

776 Kathryn M Bartol et al., *Management: A Pacific Rim Focus* (North Melbourne: McGraw-Hill Book Company Australia Pty Limited, 1995). 54-58

777 Paul Guinn, *British Strategy and Politics 1914-1918* (Oxford: Oxford University Press, 1965). 35

778 Jehuda L. Wallach, *Uneasy Coalition: The Entente Experience in World War 1* (Westport: Greenwood Press, 1993). 3

history, it is understandable that the formation of a harmonious group was problematic. However, these opposite views ultimately confused campaign direction and impacted morale, the very element Kitchener sought to exploit in the Central Powers.[779]

These inter-state impediments occurred from the outset, most notably with friction between France and Britain. At times the formation of amicable relationships was indeed feigned, driven in large part by solitary interests, not necessarily the defeat of the Central Powers.[780] This is typified from the onset as illustrated through the ongoing insistence of the French to retain forces whose sole focus would be to defend Paris. This agenda they continued to push regardless of whether it ran contrary to a wider more effective military strategy.[781] Clearly then, the opportunity for success presents itself in an environment where your opponent lacks a unified political objective, has a disparate command and a fractured strategy.

Exploitation

> Like organisms, according to Boyd, armed forces compete, learn, evolve survive or not. Military doctrine and strategic theory are also seen in this evolution theoretical light. The ones that work survive and will be retained.[782]

It would be a false representation of history to portray the German Military in an all flattering light devoid of the discord experienced within the Entente. They also experienced friction at a military-military level before and early in the war. At a strategic level, the Germans sought war with multiple countries including the British, Belgians and French, yet their Navy failed to appreciate the sophistication of British sea lines of communication.[783] These disconnects also extended to the tactical level

---

779 Matthew Hughes, "General Allenby and the Palestine Campaign, 1917–18," *Journal of Strategic Studies* 19, no. February 2013 (1996): 59–88.

780 Wallach, *Uneasy Coalition: The Entente Experience in World War 1*. 3-19

781 Wallach, *Uneasy Coalition: The Entente Experience in World War 1*. 3-19

782 Frans P B Osinga, *Science, Strategy and War: The Strategic Theory of John Boyd* (New York: Routledge, 2007). 124

783 Wilhelm Diest, "Strategy and Unlimited Warfare in Germany: Moltke, Falkenhayn and Ludendorff," in *Great War, Total War: Combat and Mobilisation on the Western Front, 1914-1918*, ed. Roger Chickering and Stig Forster (Washington D.C.: Cambridge University Press, 2000), 265–79.

including ongoing debate relating to mission command, the decisive battle and what lessons should be drawn from the Russo-Japanese War.[784] There was no grand strategy, and they, too, were blinded by the offence with their vision increasingly canalised toward the tactical.[785]

For the Germans, this discord ultimately manifests itself in the form of confidence decay as shown by the removal from command of Moltke (Junior) and others during the early stages of the war.[786] However, for the German military, the process for strategy endorsement of military campaign direction varied to that of the Entente. The German military in contrast to senior partners within the Entente experienced less influence from the civil authority as this bureaucratic layer had effectively been removed. Germany at the time had a Supreme War Lord, the Kaiser, and two Chiefs of General Staffs one each for the Navy and Army.[787] In theory, the Chiefs received their guidance from the Kaiser and were thus subordinate in a Clausewitzian sense. However, in reality, the Chiefs enjoyed freedom of action simply having to seek endorsement from the Kaiser after the fact on proposed strategies.[788] It could be argued that this clarity of purpose afforded the Central Powers efficiencies when mobilising forces for action, regardless of the success or otherwise of the campaigns in 1914. Effectively the Germans capitalised on the disunity within the Entente coalition and hence initiated war on their terms. However, as history shows, the potential impacts of reduced manning to the Schiefflen plan, although discussed, was not fully appreciated.[789]

The German military based in part on intrinsic pride founded on a militaristic lineage had seemed to develop a culture more predisposed to learning and adaptation. Following the attrition campaigns of the Somme, the German Army High Command, *die Oberste Heeresleitung* (OHL) recognised that the character of the war was evolving. Hence change was directed when the realisation struck that offensive action

---

784 Diest, "Strategy and Unlimited Warfare in Germany: Moltke, Falkenhayn and Ludendorff." 268

785 Diest, "Strategy and Unlimited Warfare in Germany: Moltke, Falkenhayn and Ludendorff." 268

786 Philip Neame, *German Strategy in the Great War* (London: Edward Arnold and Co). 2

787 Neame, *German Strategy in the Great War.* 2

788 Russell Barnes, "Armistice" (United Kingdom: Historical Documentaries, 2008).

789 Gunther E. Rothenberg, "Moltke, Schlieffen, and the Doctrine of Strategic Envelopment," in *Makers of Modern Strategy from Machiavelli to the Nuclear Age*, ed. Peter Paret (Princeton: Princeton University Press, 1986), 296–325.

was being blunted through integrated defence networks supported by advancements in military technology.[790] Perception of need was identified, solution sought and corrective action implemented.[791] The logical example of this is the application of evolved tactics, notably 'Storm Trooper' actions employing manoeuvre warfare as it would be defined today.[792] This extended to include elements of Mission Command, suitable for the dislocated command required for dispersed forces on the contemporary battlefield. The developing tactics were complete and involved a devolution of command authority to lower-ranking personnel, empowering soldiers and local commanders to execute quick decisions and capitalise on local success.[793] They were, however, singular in focus lacking operational cohesion. The point is not necessarily that the German military was better than the Entente before 1918; all were struggling to comprehend the evolving character of war, the impact of technology and the logistical demands of an increasingly complex military system. Rather (initially at least) it seems the German military and strategists therein had merely found more cognitive 'space', leveraging this more efficiently at the tactical level than the Entente. Boyd is correct in his assertions that organisational agility and adaptability is integral to success.[794]

Prior to 1918, the Entente forces from the tactical through to grand strategic were experiencing multiple forms of dislocation, with these often being self-imposed.[795] Simply put the German military was triaging an organism in flux more efficiently than the Entente. Consequently, they were somewhat free from the effects a unified Entente and Allied coalition should have been imposing and hence

790 Timothy T Lupfer, "The Dynamics of Doctrine: The Changes in German Tactical Doctrine During the First World War," *Leavenworth Papers*, vol. 4 (Fort Leavenworth, 1981). 4-16

791 Lupfer, "The Dynamics of Doctrine: The Changes in German Tactical Doctrine During the First World War." 4-16

792 John English, "The Operational Art: Development in the Theories of War," in *The Operational Art: Developments in the Theories of War*, ed. BJC McKercher and Michael A Hennessy (Westport, 1996), 8–29.

793 Michael S Neiberg, "World War 1," in *The Cambridge History of War: Volume IV*, ed. Roger Chickering, Dennis Showalter, and Hans van de Ven (Cambridge: Cambridge University Press, 2012), 315–43.

794 Osinga, *Science, Strategy and War: The Strategic Theory of John Boyd.* 87-127

795 Robert Leonhard, *The Art of Maneuver: Maneuver-Warfare Theory and the Airland Battle* (Novato: Presido Press, 1991). 66-70

enacted change at a more dynamic rate. This in part is attributable to the freedom of action afforded by the Kaiser to the military. Thus, initially, their efficiencies, coupled with a propensity for innovation had proven superior to the Entente establishment; whose decision-making cycle had been compromised through a form of decision paralysis.[796] Friction, indecision and inefficiencies reigned within the Entente. A holistic appreciation of the complexity of the system they found themselves within remained elusive.[797] It's hard to question how this inability to evolve and adapt at an organisational level from an Entente and Allied perspective did not prolong the War.

Trigger

> Once the policy objectives have been chosen, strategy is the function that delivers the theory of victory. If the theory is inappropriate, then policy must fail, and soldiers will die to no worthwhile purpose.[798]

The transition to a unified Entente coalition, and hence an advantageous position from an organisational efficiency position, did not just occur with a one-off decision. It was driven by necessity. The period of 1914 through 1917 saw the ongoing evolution of military campaign execution within both the Entente and Central powers. This was driven in large part by technological advances and the associated effects of attrition warfare; as illustrated through the tactical failures and loss of life experienced at the Somme and Verdun.[799] However, it was the scale of loss that became the trigger for action as the direct and indirect consequences were undermining the war effort. First, there was the immediate impact of a reduction in effective manoeuvre elements at the operational level and then indirectly the scale of loss placed stress on the recruitment system. This issue with regards to recruiting personnel and delivering effectively trained personnel to the fronts was recognised by key leadership; as at times they accepted questionable figures relating to losses with a view of

796 Osinga, *Science, Strategy and War: The Strategic Theory of John Boyd*. 87-127

797 John D Sterman, *Business Dynamics: Systems Thinking and Modelling for a Complex World, Management* (Boston: Irwin McGraw-Hill, 2000). 5

798 Colin S Gray, *Fighting Talk: Forty Maxims on War, Peace and Strategy* (Lincoln: Potomac Books, 2009). 54

799 Liddell Hart, *History of the First World War*, Revised (London: Redwood Burn Limited, 1973). 423

negating the loss of public opinion.[800] The loss of life however ultimately became unpalatable for government and the wider populations within Entente nations forcing action. However, in reality, it was the inability to provide trained personnel in the required time frames caused by attrition warfare that was becoming the real strategic risk triggering action.

The 'Third Battle of Ypres' at Passchendaele could arguably be the tipping point that forced civil intervention based on concern for military direction. Following this operational failure, the working relationship between Haig and Lloyd George had devolved to the point where the later doubted the integrity (and likely military ability) of the former.[801] Driven in part by concern associated with the loss of popular support, the government was forced to initiate change. At this stage, Lloyd George makes the critical leadership decision to drive change through the establishment of an inter-allied body whose focus would be strategy development from a holistic position.[802] This saw the formation of the Supreme War Council at Versailles in November 1917, forcing commanders and leaders within the Entente to recognise their shortfalls and seek unity of purpose.[803] This switch to a unified coalition command ultimately occurred at two levels. Firstly, leadership within the civil authority driven principally by Lloyd George, allowed efficiencies to be found with regards to the strategic level of leadership. And secondly at an operational level with the formation of an active war council.

Military unity culminated during the Entente command conference on 24 July 1918, with Foch being appointed *Generalissimo* of Entente forces.[804] It is important to note that this authority of command was still limited to a degree as the commanders in chief of both Britain and America retained the right of refusal affording government appeal if they opposed strategies proposed by Foch.[805] However, Foch was not selected simply due to his strategic foresight. Arguably of more importance, was the ability to disseminate his ideas and engender support from multiple

---

800 Robin Prior and Trevor Wilson, *The Somme* (London: Yale University Press, 2005). 308

801 Smyth, *Leadership in Battle*. 135-149

802 Smyth, *Leadership in Battle*. 143

803 Tasker H Bliss, "The Evolution of Unified Command," *Foreign Affairs1* 1, no. 2 (1922): 1–30.

804 Bliss, "The Evolution of Unified Command." 1-30

805 Anthony J Rice, "Command and Control: The Essence of Coalition Warfare," *Parameters* 27, 1, no. Spring (1997): 152–67.

personalities within the Entente, including that of Haig.[806] Foch identified that victory would not come through a decisive action, the prize was not Berlin. He understood that the German military had transformed into an organisation that consisted of two elements; firstly, the effectively trained 'Storm Trooper' element and secondly the inferior defensive holding forces.[807] He identified this as a targetable vulnerability with this providing further insight into the operational foresight of Foch. However, it wasn't simply his ability to orientate toward the changing character of war and apply effective leadership that yielded success; there was an element of chance in his timing.

As previously discussed the Central Powers appeared to have adapted with increased efficiency at the tactical level to the Entente. However, the Entente, specifically Britain had a greater appreciation of the complexities associated with logistical supply on a global scale. This likely stems from their place in the world at the time, having built the British Empire by leveraging an efficient Maritime infrastructure.[808] By acknowledging that the character of war as previously recognised had changed, the Entente seemed more predisposed to reorientate their thinking toward what is now recognised as a grand strategic solution.[809] Victory did not occur simply because Foch was effective. Rather he arrived at a time when the German military system was in decay thanks to a unified Entente and Allied command employing a holistic global strategy to defeat the German Military indirectly. Today this approach would easily be recognised as the application of systems thinking and business dynamics with the intent to fracture the German logistical supply system.[810] When this opportunity became fully appreciated, and the Grand Strategy endorsed, real coalition unity of command began to appear. This occurred by leveraging the effects the blockade was delivering by reducing military effectiveness through critical resource denial and the continued benefit of mobilising the German populace for revolt (as originally envisioned by Kitchener).

---

806 William Philpott, "Marshal Ferdinand Foch and Allied Victory," in *Leadership in Conflict 1914-1918*, ed. Matthew Hughes and Matthew Seligmann (South Yorkshire: Leo Cooper, 2000), 38–53.

807 Philpott, "Marshal Ferdinand Foch and Allied Victory."

808 PJ Marshall, "1783-1870: An Expanding Empire," in *British Empire*, ed. Marshall PJ (Cambridge: Cambridge University Press, 1996), 24–51.

809 Brands, *What Good Is Grand Strategy? Power and Purpose in American Statecraft from Harry S. Truman to George W. Bush*.

810 Sterman, *Business Dynamics: Systems Thinking and Modelling for a Complex World*.

This combined with Fochs' operational strategy and his ability to lead a unified coalition command is what afforded victory. This culmination of effects did not occur until late 1918.

Collapse

Unity of command between the Allied and Entente forces enabled a co-ordinated approach to the allocation of resources to sustain their war effort, but more so it was effective with the effects it imposed on the Central Powers. The effectiveness of the prolonged Naval Blockade, although not purely a decisive action, cannot be denied in its contribution to Allied success. Clarity of thought in relation to leadership is a central premise on which the blockade and associated effects must be measured, not simply resource denial. It is here where the effectiveness of the Allied strategy begins to truly appear, as do the inefficiencies within the Central Power's approach to the 'management' of war.

German leadership recognised the blockade was having an adverse impact on theirs and other Central Power economies. This in addition to the mass casualties experienced during the campaigns of March through July of 1918 was impacting military morale and the combination of these effects was delivering a destabilising effect to social order.[811] The manifestation of this social decay is perhaps most effectively illustrated through the formation of the Spartacus League, an extreme wing of the Independent German Social Democratic Party who advocated revolution.[812] No doubt, had Kitchener still been alive, conversations between himself and Haig would have differed somewhat to those at wars commencement. The further effects of a breakdown of social order came via industrial action with up to one million workers initiating strike action in January of 1918.[813] In addition to military intervention and forced conscription, programs were introduced in an attempt to restore normalcy including industrialised public rationing and a national shipbuilding program.[814] These, however, were largely unsuccessful with public

---

811 Barnes, "Armistice."

812 William Philpott, "Germany's Last Cards," in *Attrition: Fighting the First World War* (New York: Overlook Press, 2014), 301–22.

813 Philpott, "Germany's Last Cards." 301-322

814 Philpott, "Germany's Last Cards." 301-322

discontent remaining an overt presence. This when coupled with the inflow of American forces to the operational area further reduced morale to the German forces and civilian populace. It is only when understanding this connectivity, can the Allied strategies influence on the collapse of the Central Powers be truly appreciated. It wasn't simply the blockade or Fochs' operational leadership; it was how these combined effects drove poor decision making in the opponent.

In a classic Clausewitzian sense the German Military driven in large part by a perceived need to quell populace discord, decided 1918 was the window in which to pursue the 'battle of annihilation'.[815] They were being driven by a self-imposed time pressure.[816] This in hindsight was not operationally sustainable from a logistical perspective, but more importantly, it was not achievable from a grand strategic perspective due to immaturity of thought. Although perhaps holding the advantage initially with regards to clarity of thought, the German military was now being out manoeuvred physically and mentally by a unified coalition command. From a manoeuvrist perspective, they had become dislocated.[817] As previously indicated (from an advantageous perspective) the influence of the civilian sphere on German military planning was less than that experienced by the Entente military. This occurred in part by natural design due to the monarchist nature of Germany. However, it was also forced by a perceived need for control by key military commanders notably Ludendorff.[818] However, it appears that with the evolution of war's character toward a totalitarian form, this degree of military freedom becomes an impediment to successful execution.[819]

> Germany lacked a forum in which strategic issues could be comprehensively deliberated – an institution such as the cabinets in Paris and London, the joint council of ministers in Austria-Hungary, the British Imperial Defence, or the French *conseil*

815 Roger Chickering, Dennis Showalter, and Hans van de Ven, eds., The Cambridge History of War, Vol IV (Cambridge: Cambridge University Press, 2012). 315-316

816 Diest, "Strategy and Unlimited Warfare in Germany: Moltke, Falkenhayn and Ludendorff." 265-279

817 Leonhard, *The Art of Maneuver: Maneuver-Warfare Theory and the Airland Battle*. 61-77

818 Chickering, Showalter, and van de Ven, *The Cambridge History of War*. 315-316

819 Hew Strachan, *Carl von Clausewitz's On War* (Vancouver: Douglas and McIntyre, 2008). 19-20

superieur de la guerre. Wilhelm II was personally incapable of exercising the necessary co-ordinating influence.[820]

In 1918 Germany remained overly focused on the 'decisive battle' and as illustrated Ludendorff lacked the strategic mechanism and guidance to link his operational plans.[821] The success of operations in 1918 was often inflated by the German high command, and with this, the divide between perception and military reality generated further conflict within the military-military domain.[822] The Germans continued to remain overly focused on fighting the battle as opposed to managing the war effort; a concept now fully appreciated and being executed by a unified Entente and Allied coalition. One may rightly question whether German leadership at the time, specifically Ludendorff was out of his depth.[823] However, it would be a more accurate assertion that Ludendorff experienced cognitive overload due to the forced necessity to manage actions from the tactical through to grand strategic.[824] At the time Ludendorff identifies this issue of inefficiency at a holistic level (and the associated pressure of co-ordinating it) as a matter that may lead to defeat; it ultimately becomes an issue he discusses post-war as a contributing factor in failure.[825] The other was the disproportionate internal focus toward the domestic population's concerns or the 'stab in the back' as it has been coined.[826] However, in reality, both were being cultivated by the Entente Grand Strategy and nurtured to fruition through the absence of a focused bureaucratic layer of German government. It was this that ultimately brought about the downfall of the German Empire in 1918. Tactical efficiency is moot if under-resourced or lacking purpose within a larger offensive system. Victory at the tactical level is easy to identify; however, it is subordinate to multiple layers and must be enabled for victory. Given that the German military industrialisation had not progressed on the same trajectory as the Entente, their ability to maintain mobile

820 Diest, "Strategy and Unlimited Warfare in Germany: Moltke, Falkenhayn and Ludendorff." 265-279
821 Barnes, "Armistice."
822 Barr, "The Elusive Victory: The BEF and the Operational Level of War, September 1918." 211-238
823 Chickering, Showalter, and van de Ven, *The Cambridge History of War.* 315-316
824 Barnes, "Armistice."
825 Strachan, *Carl von Clausewitz's On War.* 19-20
826 Strachan, *Carl von Clausewitz's On War.* 19

combined arms campaigning suffered.[827] This tactical action at the time remained their only source of hope. However, the impacts of the blockade took hold on the battlefield simply through a lack of mobility assets be they horse or mechanised, or the inability to match Entente munition production. In reality, their fate was sealed through a lack of strategic foresight.[828]

Consequently, they reverted to traditional methods of warfare. Storm Trooper actions although effective at the tactical level, ultimately led to failure at the operational level as the conventional forces did not appreciate the logistical requirements of modern warfare.[829] Nor were they sufficiently trained or commanded to defend against a co-ordinated Entente coalition. Foch was becoming increasingly efficient and calculated in his execution of the operational art.[830] When in a defensive posture he identified the utility of affording initial success to the principle force only to destroy the secondary forces when they became over-extended.[831] In the offence when actions became suitable for flowing manoeuvre warfare he achieved success by engaging then disengaging forces on multiple fronts to force a command dilemma on his opponent; he would then employ the Grand Reserve to destroy inferior forces.[832] Although not recognising the theories as such, Foch achieved operational success by dislocating German operational command while simultaneously levering Boyd's concepts relating to decision superiority at the tactical.[833]

Conclusion

World War I left a legacy on society the impacts of which continue to be experienced today. The effects of the conflict, including

---

827 Jean Dr Bou, "The German Spring Offensives, and the Western Front" (Canberra: Australian National University, 2017).

828 Diest, "Strategy and Unlimited Warfare in Germany: Moltke, Falkenhayn and Ludendorff." 265–279

829 Bou, "The German Spring Offensives, and the Western Front."

830 Michael A Hennessy and BJC McKercher, "Introduction," in *The Operational Art: Developments in the Theories of War*, ed. BJC McKercher and Michael A Hennessy (Westport: Praeger, 1996), 1–6.

831 Bou, "The German Spring Offensives, and the Western Front."

832 Barnes, "Armistice."

833 Osinga, *Science, Strategy and War: The Strategic Theory of John Boyd.* 87-127

restructuring the geopolitical environment, continue to shape contemporary conflict most notably in the area that would once have been recognised as the Ottoman Empire. However, World War I should most importantly be identified as a period that initiated significant changes to the character of war on multiple levels, even arguably creating the operational level. The intensity of the conflict forged learning and adaptation within several fields; with technological advancements too numerous to mention. However, they led to the development of combined arms theory and subsequently the industrialisation of militaries. It was, however, this industrialisation of war that drove the greatest change, as those charged with managing the logistical demands needed for victory realised the totalitarian nature of modern warfare. The character of war had changed, and with it brought new demands.

With regard to the Entente, and in no small part other than simply the British style of governance, these changes were more readily recognised and their approach to warfare accordingly modified. In short, the Entente codified the inter-relatedness of resource supply and demand within an increasingly interconnect global environment. This extended beyond mission critical supplies through to the simple needs of a given populace. It was the birth of global 'Grand Strategy' and the concept of 'Total War'. The effects the blockade had on Germany did contribute to Entente success. However, if this economic strategy had been employed in conjunction with a holistic military strategy earlier, victory may have occurred before 1918. Kitchener, perhaps if enabled by Haig in 1914, may have built an operational line of effort leveraging what is now known as information operational effects; as the decay in German social order did support the military results.

Ultimately, however, Foch demonstrated the ability to distil operational lessons learnt as the campaign shifted from 1914-1918 and employed this knowledge through to the execution of warfare at the operational level. World War I was more than a conflict between military forces or even grand strategists. It was ultimately a battle of the mind that saw decision makers fight to orientate themselves within an adaptive system, then execute actions before their adversary. This evolutionary challenge was persistent in nature occurring at the tactical to grand strategic level, occurring within the civil and military institutions of all nations involved. For the Entente and Allies, decision superiority was successful; however, the full effects were not experienced until the closing stages of 1918. Did the Entente's inability to form a united coalition until 1918 prolong the war? I would argue yes, with the millions of war dead supporting my assertion.

'Choose two campaigns and examine how the environment affected the way the belligerents conducted their campaigns. How did the environment lead to different approaches to fighting the campaigns and what caused similarities regardless of the environment?'

(Written 2017 - exam in 4 hours)

Introduction

The period between the commencement of World War I and the conclusion of World War II saw an evolution in military capability and thought the foundations of which remain extant regarding contemporary operations. Today a land force would consider at their peril executing a military operation unless it was combined in nature; and with a level of Air support on which to draw from. Furthermore, military operations are now inherently joint requiring detailed synchronisation at arguably a new level created in this period, being the operational level. By way of in depth investigation this paper will examine the influence the environment had on two belligerents and their execution of military campaigns. To identify environmentally driven implications and draw similarities, two separate campaigns will be examined. First, the British as part of the Entente on the Western Front in World War I will be reviewed and then the United States during the Central Pacific Campaigns in World War II will be viewed to identify different approaches and similarities. However, to frame the response accurately it is necessary to contextualise how the 'environment' will be viewed. There is the instinctive response that this examination will focus purely on elements of the natural environment, in a military sense, the operating environment. Although discussion will focus on this aspect, what is arguably of greater impact is the social or cultural environment that exists, as the aggregate sum of these can also exert influence.[834] It will be shown that when a military has established a cultural environment predisposed and supportive of innovation, then they are in a more advantageous position to adapt to the limitations imposed by the operational environment that one that is not.

Britain and the Western Front

The military actions of World War I, perhaps like no other since, have been reviewed and analysed in search of answers to justify the scale of loss suffered. However, initially at least, it would seem it was the cultural environment present within the senior echelons of the British Military that was largely to blame. Prior to World War I most militaries, including the British, had become overly focused on the primacy of the offensive with regards to attaining military success; in essence a military bias existed.[835] This was evident in existing doctrinal publications that espoused the knowledge of prewar theorists such as Clausewitz and Jomini and to British detriment, wholeheartedly endorsed by General Haig, the Commander in Chief of the British Expeditionary Force. In addition to this self-imposed bias, conflict existed between General Haig and the Civil authority, Lord Kitchener, with this creating a command environment that was far from harmonious with friction ever present.[836] In time this would contribute to the reinforcement of failures experienced within the operational environment, as effectively, Haig through a misguided sense of esteem was too proud to adapt to the exigencies being imposed by the operating environment.

The attritional warfare executed in the initial years is largely what World War I is remembered for. However, the reality is this was being driven by restrictions imposed by the operating environment at a

---

834 https://www.google.com.au/webhp?sourceid=chrome-instant&ion=1&espv=2&ie=UTF-8#q=environment+define&*

835 Roger Chickering, Dennis Showalter, and Hans van de Ven, eds., *The Cambridge History of War*, Vol IV (Cambridge: Cambridge University Press, 2012). 296

836 David French, "The Strategy of Unlimted Warfare? Kitchener, Robertson and Haig," in *Great War, Total War: Combat and Mobilisation on the Western Front, 1914-1918*, ed. Roger Chickering and Stig Forster (Washington D.C.: Cambridge University Press, 2000), 281–95.

macro level. The sheer size of military forces limited the opponent's ability to manouevre, as would have been feasible in Napoleonic times.[837] This in conjunction with a military culture pre-disposed to the offence ensured that when massed German forces were on the offensive it would become an inevitability that British forces would meet them head on. Both forces were like in nature and therefore the environment at a micro level was leveraged due to the inherent motivation for survival.[838] The forces went underground. Key here is how the limitations imposed by the wider operational environment impacted operations at the tactical level forcing change. This impact of the macro operational environment shaping actions at the micro is a trend to be repeated regarding the operations of the United States within the Pacific during World War II.

However, without addressing in detail the evolution of tactics and technology during World War I, a revolution in military execution occurred. In addition to the limitations associated with technological developments, change was in large part also delayed through a cultural environment lacking a bias toward innovation and a disdain for the civil authority. The campaigns of 1915 and 1916, although bloody, had seen the inclusion of technological advancements into military actions, specifically the use of massed artillery to enable small victories within the tactical domain.[839] This action, employed successfully by General Rawlinson, had proven successful in securing terrain at the micro environmental level and became known as the 'bite and hold' action. Prior to execution of operations at the Somme and Flanders, the intent for this modified form of warfare was conveyed to Haig by Kitchener. However, due to an arguably toxic Civil-Military cultural environment, this advice was discounted.[840] The outcome was dire. Ultimately the results of these campaigns became the trigger to initiate change toward a more harmonious working environment within senior leadership.

---

837 Stephen Biddle, "Land Warfare: Theory and Practice," in *Strategy in the Contemporary World: An Introduction to Strategic Studies2*, ed. John Baylis et al., 1st ed. (Oxford: Oxford University Press, 2002), 91–112.

838 Abraham Maslow, *A Theory on Human Motivation*, 1943rd ed. (Mansfield Centre: Martino Publishing, 2014).

839 French, "The Strategy of Unlimted Warfare? Kitchener, Robertson and Haig." 285

840 Ibid.

The French Commander Foch, was appointed *Generalissimo* of Entente forces in July of 1918, and in effect Haig was now under his command.[841] There was an element of chance in his timing enabling him to excel operationally through the execution of the newly evolved method of warfare. Technological advancements, driven in part by the limitations imposed by the operating environment, had resulted in significant improvement in the execution of warfare. Massed artillery would now support infantry movements by suppressing enemy forces, with movement of dismounted forces then being conducted with support from armoured assets. Combined arms execution was now the norm within the operational environment, increasingly becoming joint with the inclusion of air assets for reconnaissance. However, Foch's selection was not simply based on military ability; he was also selected due to his deft leadership skills with his ability to engender support for his strategies identified as a strength.[842] The Supreme War Council had finally become harmonious in nature, Haig for the most part supported Foch's initiatives and all were united in the approach to defeating the Central Powers. In short, Foch had created an effective cultural environment were technological advancements and innovative approaches to warfare, notably Combined Arms, were integrated to positive effect within both the macro and micro operational environment.

United States and the Pacific

During the interwar period the United States, rightly, began to view the Japanese as their primary adversarial risk with this in large part being driven by the macro operational environment. Although during the interwar period relations had seemed cordial, the Japanese imperialist expansionist desire could not be discounted. Genuine concern existed regarding the risk that an interwar Naval Arms race could have on global stability with many nations still suffering financially from World War 1. Consequently, in 1921 the Washington Treaty was endorsed by the world's leading Naval Powers being the US, Great Britain, France,

---

841 Tasker H Bliss, "The Evolution of Unified Command," *Foreign Affairs1* 1, no. 2 (1922): 1–30.

842 William Philpott, "Marshal Ferdinand Foch and Allied Victory," in *Leadership in Conflict 1914-1918*, ed. Matthew Hughes and Matthew Seligmann (South Yorkshire: Leo Cooper, 2000), 38–53.

Italy and Japan.[843] Although well intended, a logic flaw existed in the Washington Treaty, with a self- imposed restriction on behalf of the United States reshaping contemporary warfare as it was then known. Fortunately, due to an innovative cultural environment, solutions could be found to what would be limitations associated with the operational environment.

As mentioned there was a rapid advancement in military technology during World War I. This led to an increasing focus on combined arms development and aviation during the interwar period. Supported by the air theorist's concepts, the realisation of the potential for strategic air attacks appeared based on the operational environment and islands in proximity to Japan.[844] From a United States perspective this naturally became viewed as a potential course of action to be employed against the Japanese mainland. However, restrictions imposed by the Washington treaty limited US expansionism in the Pacific, in effect a self-imposed environmental impediment. This removed the ability for the US to pre-emptively seize or develop land that held the potential to accommodate aviation assets. This reality was thus a strategic risk identified by the United States, as the Japanese in the event of war would defend islands within an environmental proximity to mainland Japan. Therefore, the concept of unavoidable opposed landings became a reality and as such this environmental limitation, like the British on the Western Front, drove the necessity for contemporary thought.

Consequently, military strategists focused on the development of a war plan centered on defeating Japan through land force invasion. This drove the development of 'Plan Orange' and with it came the impost for naval capability development. Arguably without this self-imposed operational environment restriction, Plan Orange may never have eventuated and amphibious capability as we know it may not have evolved in the required timeframes. It was the geo-strategic limitation driven by the Washington treaty in 1921 that led to the US investing in the development of an amphibious force.

843 John T Kuehn, "The U.S. Navy General Board and Naval Arms Lmitation: 1022-1937," *The Journal of Military History* 74, no. 4 (2010): 1129–60.

844 John Mccarthy, "Douhet and the Decisiveness of Air Power," in *The Strategists*, ed. Hugh Smith (Australian Defence Studies Centre, 2001), 65–72.

The execution of amphibious landings within the Pacific theatre in the 1940s was the culmination of development and adaptation driven by this perceived need. However, why the US was successful in the execution of this tactical action is largely a result of the establishment of a cultural environment within pockets of the military that supported innovative ideas.[845] Major General John Lejeune, the Commandant of the Marine Corps, was but one Commander within four naval organisations focusing on amphibious development. Based on the environmental limitations of War Plan Orange however, he was the only one who identified the critical requirement for an amphibious capability that could execute the implied task of opposed landings. His mission analysis on limitations imposed by the operational environmental was sound. Then based on an adaptive cultural environment he directed the necessary staff work required in developing the concept for 'Advanced Base Force Operations'.[846]

This concept ultimately become the basis for interwar training. Here the first of what could be termed long-term learning loops enabled by a positive cultural environment begin to present, and it is difficult to look past the parallels to John Boyd's adaption theories.[847] General Lejeune had made an assessment on the limitations likely to be imposed by the future operating environment. He identified how the five powers' treaty would limit the size of modern battle fleet development and limit the scope to establish new bases in South-East Asia and the Western Pacific. Consequently, expansion and development within the Philippines, Guam and Hong Kong was limited, with seizing vital terrain becoming critical. Key here is how the Marine Corps commander was predisposed to adaptation and presided over the cultivation of a cultural environment within the United States Marine Corps that supported innovation and initiative. In short, this foresight enabled the United States to be well positioned for a campaign within

845 Allan R Millett, "Patterns of Military Innovation in the Interwar Period," in *Military Innovation in the Interwar Period*, ed. Williamson Murray and Allan R Millett (Cambridge: Cambridge University Press, 1996), 329–68.
846 Allan R Millett, "Assault from the Sea: The Development of Amphibious Warfare between the Wars - the American, British and Japanese Experiences," in *Military Innovation in the Interwar Period*, ed. Williamson Murray and Allan R Millett (Cambridge: Cambridge University Press, 1996), 50–95.
847 Frans P B Osinga, *Science, Strategy and War: The Strategic Theory of John Boyd* (New York: Routledge, 2007). 124-25

the Pacific and when the campaign commenced the United States Army was already practised in joint Naval Fleet operations and had adopted naval doctrine regarding amphibious operations.[848]

As the campaigns progressed across the Pacific similarities between the operations of the British present. First there was an unavoidable element of attrition associated with the campaigns due to limitations imposed by the operating environment. However, the United States benefited from this knowledge and, like the British, increasingly employed massed artillery fires in support of land action. Although limited by largely predictable amphibious landing sites the immediate effects of integrated Japanese Defensive networks could, to a degree, be mitigated through Naval Gunfire. When secure on the beach-head and transitioning to offensive operations, combined arms integration had evolved to the point where it was integral to the execution of the land battle; with inter-service effectiveness evolving to the point where mutual support was the norm. Similarities exist also with regards to the concept of 'bite and hold'. Although the British executed this at a micro level in the trench environment, the United States employed the 'concept' at a macro level as they transitioned from East to West. The relative safety of securing one island prior to progressing to follow on operations was apparent as indicated by the state operations from Tarawa to Saipan and ultimately Okinawa.

Conclusion

The campaigns discussed span a period when the execution of military operations evolved at an unprecedented rate. The operational environment in a physical sense shaped operations and in a large part drove technological innovations based on these influences at a micro level. For the British in World War I, the limitations for manoeuvre were limited at a macro level due to the scale of forces present within the Western Front. This in turn forced restrictions on movement at the macro level and trench warfare became the norm for a period. The United States some thirty years later were also forced into an attritional battle against a well dug in and defended opponent. However, although there were similarities there was a key difference attributable to the relative

---

848 Millett, "Assault from the Sea: The Development of Amphibious Warfare between the Wars - the American, British and Japanese Experiences."

success of these belligerents in each campaign. It ultimately relates to the respective cultural environment present in both organisations and how this impacted on success. From a British perspective elements of command, notably Haig, were reticent to adapt to the style of warfare with these delays attributable to significant loss of life. In contrast, the United States, notably the Navy, identified a strategic risk imposed by the operational environment and thanks to a cultural environment that supported initiative, drove the establishment of the amphibious capability. Thus, when forced to execute operations within the Pacific, tactics that enabled opposed amphibious landings based on environmental constraints had been practised by an integrated military with an existing environmental culture predisposed to adaption. Thus, their movement across the Pacific operating environment was comparatively swift to that of the British on the western front and largely viewed in a positive light from an operational perspective.

World War II

'To what extent was land-based airpower the main strike weapon of MacArthur's South-West Pacific Theatre (1942-1945)' (Written 2017)

Introduction

This paper will explore how General MacArthur, Commander of the South-West Pacific Area (SWPA), employed his land based airpower and the degree to which it served as his primary strike weapon during the period 1942 through 1945. In accurately assessing the extent to which land based airpower was MacArthur's main strike weapon the focus will remain on air power in a strike capacity, meaning 'the application of lethal force in the conduct of offensive air operations to destroy, damage or disrupt the adversary's centres of gravity at all levels of conflict'.[849] This definition of strike highlights its applicability across the strategic spectrum and as such discussion will consider the impact of strike effects from the tactical to grand strategic level.[850] Within the SWPA the geographical environment predicated the use of air power in a logistical role to enable land force capabilities.[851] Air mobility will, therefore, be viewed in a supporting context and referred to as such: in and of itself, it is not a strike asset rather an enabler of other strike capabilities. To be clear from the outset, land-based air power was employed to great extent during the SWPA from 1942-1945 and was MacArthur's main strike weapon enabling operational victory through the now recognised concepts of manoeuvre theory.

Although unaware of the terms and concepts as they are now known, MacArthur's operational strategy possessed many of the hallmarks

---

849 Sanu Kainikara, *Essays on Air Power* (Canberra: Air Power Development Centre, 2012). 23

850 Kainikara, *Essays on Air Power*. 38

851 Gavin Long, *MacArthur: As Military Commander* (Sydney: Angus and Robertson, 1969). 111

of a manoeuvre campaign.[852] Manoeuvre theory makes a useful conceptual lens with which to consider MacArthur's use of land based airpower in a strike capacity. Key actions or battles will be analysed to highlight how this strike capability enabled victory over the Japanese through the defeat mechanisms of pre-emption, dislocation and/ or disruption.[853] In a militaristic sense manoeuvre theory has been defined as:

> Defeating the enemy's will to fight by 'destroying' the enemy's plan rather than destroying his forces. In its most kinetic form, manoeuvre seeks to shatter the enemy's moral and physical cohesion through a series of actions across multiple lines of operation to a single purpose, creating a turbulent and rapidly deteriorating situation with which the enemy cannot cope.[854]

This highlights two critical components relating to manoeuvre theory and how they correlate to MacArthur's SWPA campaign. Firstly, there is the need to focus actions toward destroying the opponent's plan as opposed to simply their military forces. Secondly, the intent is to manufacture an environment that affects the adversary's ability to execute sound decisions across the strategic spectrum due to cognitive pressure. When reviewing this definition, there are clear linkages between manoeuvre theory and other military concepts emphasising the need for decision superiority.[855] The ultimate intent however is to fracture capability and hence degrade clarity of thought with both the manoeuvre and attrition of forces being approaches to war that enable this. When viewing MacArthur's actions within the SWPA, it is clear his operational plan and application of land based air strike did create an environment that achieved both these components of manoeuvre theory and, although land and amphibious strike capabilities were

---

852 Peter J. Dean, "MacArthurs War: Strategy, Command and Plans for the 1943 Offensives," in *Australian 1943: The Liberation of New Guinea*, ed. Peter J. Dean (Melbourne: CUP, 2104), 45–67. 52

853 Robert Leonhard, *The Art of Maneuver: Maneuver-Warfare Theory and the Airland Battle* (Novato: Presido Press, 1991). 61-77.

854 Australian Army, *Land Warfare Doctrine 1: The Fundamentals of Land Power*, Unclass (Canberra: Commonwealth of Australia, 2014), https://www.army.gov.au/sites/g/files/net1846/f/lwd_1_the_fundamentals_of_land_power_full.pdf. 41.

855 Frans P B Osinga, *Science, Strategy and War: The Strategic Theory of John Boyd* (New York: Routledge, 2007). 124-127

integral to the campaign, land based air strike capabilities retained primacy enabling operational success.[856]

Pre-emption and Posturing

To effectively analyse the use of land based air power employed by MacArthur in the SWPA, mid-1942 will be used as a start point, as this period provides context to the operational plans being developed. By mid-1942 the operational areas within the Pacific were formally established and initial forces allocated.[857] Importantly, two other critical incidents had occurred. Firstly, the Japanese had secured Rabaul and due to existing infrastructure had the ability to execute air and naval actions within MacArthur's area of operations.[858] They had achieved operational reach. Secondly, in a genuine pre-emptive strike, the Japanese (like the allies) recognised the strategic importance of Buna and had successfully secured this terrain before the allies.[859] At the mid-point of 1942 air superiority and the ability to control sea and air lines of communication could not be assured; thus, MacArthur's initial campaign was land-centric in a maritime environment.[860] There were a number of limitations associated with land-centric warfare in a maritime environment. Perhaps most notably the terrain and means of land to air communication were poor, hence air strike in support of operations was relatively inconsequential.[861] At this stage, the Japanese held the operational advantage. MacArthur was yet to secure key airfields within New Guinea that would enable subsequent operations using land based air strike capabilities. The ability to execute land based air strike was recognised as integral to achieving the Joint Chiefs Direction as issued on 2nd July 1942.[862] On receiving this direction MacArthur, through an appreciation of Japanese success,

---

856 Dean, "MacArthurs War: Strategy, Command and Plans for the 1943 Offensives." 52-53

857 David Horner, *High Command: Australia and Allied Strategy 1939-1945* (Sydney: George Allen and Unwin Australia Pty Ltd, 1982). 178-215

858 Dean, "MacArthurs War: Strategy, Command and Plans for the 1943 Offensives." 46

859 Anthony Beevor, *The Second World War* (London: Phoenix, 2013). 345

860 Peter J. Dean, "Anzacs and Yanks: US and Australian Operations at the Beachhead Battles," in *Australia 1942: In the Shadow of War*, ed. Peter J. Dean (Melbourne: CUP, 2013), 223–27.

861 Dean, "Anzacs and Yanks: US and Australian Operations at the Beachhead Battles." 227

862 E. G. Keogh, Colonel (retd), *The South West Pacific 1941-45* (Melbourne: Grayflower Productions Pty Ltd, 1965). 121

began to recognise the importance of land basing strike aircraft and the capability it affords.[863]

Land based air strike success against the Japanese at Milne Bay is an example of how effectiveness at a tactical level can have wider operational and strategic impacts. Control of South East New Guinea was still being contested in mid-1942 and when Japanese forces learnt of an allied presence at Milne Bay, Major-General Tomitaro made the ill-advised decision to attack.[864] What was critical to this Allied success was how land-based airpower was employed in a manoeuvreist context to achieve success.[865] Firstly, a pre-emptive strike defined as 'seizing an opportunity before the enemy, to deny them a course of action or an objective and achieve your own' played a critical part.[866] One example relates to the destruction of sea-based mobility assets by Royal Australian Airforce (RAAF) land-based air elements on a 350-man Japanese detachment from Buna.[867] It would be disingenuous to suggest the success of Milne Bay rested solely with land based air assets as the reality was weather impacted on the timely and efficient support being provided from assets deployed from Port Moresby, Townsville and Cape York.[868] However, the ability of land forces to retain Milne Bay was enabled in large part by the effectiveness of land based air strike assets and their ability to pre-emptively destroy landing craft and target disembarked enemy forces.[869] This was achieved without the use of sea-based air strike assets as these had not been allocated to MacArthur.[870]

When viewing these actions against the definition of strike, it is clear land based air power was integral to the destruction of materiel, but additionally, it delivered a disruptive effect on the Japanese freedom of movement on the sea. Consequently, when viewing these strikes with regards to manoeuvre theory, it becomes apparent the Japanese

---

863 Long, *MacArthur: As Military Commander*. 130-131

864 Keogh, Colonel (retd), *The South West Pacific 1941-45*. 191-193

865 Note: 'Manoeuvreist' refers to a campaign or tactical action executed as per the concepts inherent to manoeuvre theory, though not recognised by the Macquarie Concise Dictionary the term is recognised within the military profession.

866 Australian Army, "Operations," *Land Warfare Doctrine 3-0*, 2015, https://www.army. gov.au/sites/g/files/net1846/f/lwd_3-0_operations.pdf. 4-2

867 Keogh, Colonel (retd), *The South West Pacific 1941-45*. 191-195

868 Keogh, Colonel (retd), *The South West Pacific 1941-45*. 192

869 Long, *MacArthur: As Military Commander*. 103-104

870 Horner, *High Command: Australia and Allied Strategy 1939-1945*. 205

operational plan is under pressure and the situation is in fact deteriorating. Therefore, the application of land-based airpower during the defence of Milne Bay was critical on two fronts. Firstly, it was clearly a successful strike weapon pre-emptively destroying forces and hence enabling tactical success. Secondly (and arguably of more importance), by supporting tactical success, air power had created a command dilemma at an operational level for the Japanese while simultaneously enabling operational flexibility for allied command. Thus, the allied forces within the SWPA had gained the operational initiative, however Buna was yet to be taken. The tactical actions needed to achieve this resulted in significant loss of life for ground based strike assets, however as highlighted by Malkasian, this tactical success was largely enabled by ground forces employing manoeuvre concepts.[871] Importantly for MacArthur the seizure of Buna represented a key moment regarding the execution of operational plans. MacArthur, having secured the South-Eastern tip of New Guinea and the airfields therein, was now positioned to execute operations in support of his wider plan, soon to be known as 'Operation Cartwheel'.[872] Before this condition was met he did not have the required operational reach as the lines of communication were not secure. Hence security to seaborne troop movement could not be guaranteed and thus the ability to employ amphibious and sea based forces in a strike capacity did not yet exist. Success at Milne Bay and Buna however had tipped the balance of initiative toward MacArthur and in large part is attributable to the effectiveness of land-based air strike weapons.

Pressure and Opportunity

For success to occur through manoeuvre theory military strategies must focus on the destruction of the enemy's centre of gravity, and as highlighted, the previous definition of air strike emphasises this imperative.[873] With regards to Japanese force structure throughout the SWPA, it is difficult to dispute Rabaul being the location from which they derived their freedom of action. Hence Rabaul could (and

---

871 Carter Malkasian, *A History of Modern Wars of Attrition* (Wesport: Praeger, 2002). 78-82
872 Keogh, Colonel (retd), *The South West Pacific 1941-45*. 290
873 Leonhard, *The Art of Maneuver: Maneuver-Warfare Theory and the Airland Battle*. 20-24; Kainikara, *Essays on Air Power*. 18

has) been defined as their operational centre of gravity.[874] Rabaul was the Japanese command headquarters for the SWPA housing General Imamura's Eight Area Army:[875] if Rabaul fell then the freedom of movement this terrain afforded the Japanese would be negated. Ultimately it would reduce Japanese command opportunities to the extent that clarity of thought would be negatively impacted. This is the very premise of success achieved through manoeuvre theory concepts.[876] It is not surprising the JCS Directive issued on 2nd July 1942 recognised the need to seize Rabaul.[877] MacArthur's initial direction stipulated the following:

> The general scheme of manoeuvre is to advance our bomber line towards Rabaul: first by improvement of existing forward bases; secondly, by the occupation of air bases which can be secured without committing large forces; and then by the seizure of successive hostile aerodromes.[878]

Two aspects are evident in MacArthur's command intent. First, he appreciates the operational restriction imposed on him through the absence of a carrier element (hence sea-based air strike); and secondly he recognises the need to generate tempo, which joint amphibious operations can enable. At this stage, MacArthur's operational focus still very much hinges on the necessity to seize, secure or develop land based airfields to support an advance toward the Philippines.[879] Ultimately MacArthur's intent was to 'leap frog' enemy strengths when possible to generate tempo (being a tenet of manoeuvre theory) and to achieve this land based air strike would be integral to his plan:

> By destructive air attack soften up and gain air superiority over each objective along the two axes of advance. Neutralise with appropriate aviation hostile supporting air bases and destroy naval forces and shipping within range. Prevent reinforcement or supply

---

874 Chris Field, "Testing the Tenets of Manoeuvre: Australia's First Amphibious Assualt since Gallipoli, The 9th Australian Division at Lae, 4-16 September 1943" (Canberra, 2012). 16

875 George Odgers, *Air War Against Japan 1943-1945* (Adelaide: The Advertiser Printing Office, 1957). 88

876 Army, "Operations." 41

877 Keogh, Colonel (retd), *The South West Pacific 1941-45*. 151

878 Keogh, Colonel (retd), *The South West Pacific 1941-45*. 287

879 Dean, "MacArthurs War: Strategy, Command and Plans for the 1943 Offensives." 51-54

of objectives under attack. Move Aviation forward onto captured aerodromes. Repeat this process to successive objectives...[880]

It's difficult to deny the primacy of land based air strike over other strike capabilities when reviewing MacArthur's concept of operations against these directives. However, to fully appraise this statement, it is important once again to re-orientate thought toward strike in the context of airpower being 'the application of lethal force in the conduct of offensive air operations to destroy, damage or disrupt the adversary's centres of gravity at all levels of conflict'.[881] MacArthur and his planners recognised that success in the SWPA was to be achieved through joint amphibious action with training based in Australia focused on enhancing this capability.[882] Although integral, amphibious strike operations could not commence until air cover was assured, allowing interdiction and pre-emptive strikes to be made against Japanese offensive capabilities.

The wider Allied focus during 1943 remained European-centric, with Europe being confirmed as the priority theatre for resource allocation during the Casablanca Conference.[883] Therefore the assets assessed as needed to secure Rabaul as recommended by MacArthur were unavailable.[884] The strategic direction for Rabaul was amended simply to focus on a future task that may require its "ultimate seizure".[885] MacArthur subsequently adhered to this shift in strategic direction, developing an operational plan that would allow his direct command forces and the supporting forces from the South Pacific Area (SOPAC) to advance simultaneously toward Rabaul.[886] The simultaneous advance along two avenues of approach was effectively a double envelopment executed at the operational level.[887] His plan centred on the necessity

880 Dean, "MacArthurs War: Strategy, Command and Plans for the 1943 Offensives." 52-53; William S. Lind, *Maneuver Warfare Handbook* (Boulder: Westview Press Inc, 1985). 6; Army, "Operations." 4-3; Keogh, Colonel (retd), *The South West Pacific 1941-45.* 289.
881 Kainikara, *Essays on Air Power.* 23
882 George Odgers, *100 Years of Australians at War* (Sydney: New Holland, 2001). 171
883 Desmond Flower and James Reeves, *The War 1939-1945* (London: Cassell and Company LTD, 1960). 622-23
884 Long, *MacArthur: As Military Commander.* 125
885 Odgers, *100 Years of Australians at War.* 170
886 Odgers, *100 Years of Australians at War.* 170
887 Australian Army, "Formation Tactics," *Land Warfare Doctrine 3-0-3,* 2016, https://www.army.gov.au/sites/g/files/net1846/f/lwd_3-0-3_formation_tactics_interim_0.pdf. 68

to secure airfields in three locations, all of which could threaten the security of Rabaul and exert pressure on Japanese command.[888] 'Operation Cartwheel' was in effect. The Cartwheel series was centred on land based air assets; however, this could not be achieved without the ground forces to either seize or secure these airfields from attack.[889] The reality when viewing this complementary support relationship is that land-based forces were employed at an operational level only to enable land-based air operations through their ability to either seize, secure or develop airfields.[890] They were acting primarily in a shaping or shielding function at an operational level and perhaps strike at a tactical.[891] MacArthur's primary strike weapon remained land-based air power as his wider operational plan centred on this capability.

MacArthur's concurrent drive toward Rabaul could achieve success through several defeat mechanisms. Firstly, the intent of the Cartwheel series was to position land based air assets in proximity to Rabaul, with this enabling a 'disruption' effect on the Japanese, meaning 'defeating the enemy by attacking his centre of gravity'.[892] As indicated, MacArthur's force allocation would not allow an opposed amphibious lodgement, thus the ability to employ an amphibious strike action was not achievable. Hence this disruption effect could only be achieved through air strike assets within proximity to Rabaul of which both land and sea based capabilities now existed.[893] The second defeat mechanism that Cartwheel could enable was one of 'functional dislocation', meaning 'setting the conditions for an enemy strength to be effectively neutralised for the circumstances'.[894] The establishment of airfields within proximity of Rabaul provided MacArthur with the ability to interdict Japanese air assets and additionally provided his amphibious forces secure sea lines of communication. This was the higher command intent, being to isolate Rabaul so as to neutralise the Japanese forces. Again, land based air assets were pivotal to this success

---

888 Keogh, Colonel (retd), *The South West Pacific 1941-45*. 288-290

889 Horner, *High Command: Australia and Allied Strategy 1939-1945*. 268-274

890 Odgers, *100 Years of Australians at War*. 176

891 Army, "Operations." 4-13

892 Leonhard, *The Art of Maneuver: Maneuver-Warfare Theory and the Airland Battle*. 73:; Keogh, Colonel (retd), *The South West Pacific 1941-45*. 290

893 Dean, "MacArthurs War: Strategy, Command and Plans for the 1943 Offensives." 52

894 Army, "Operations." 4-2

as they had created a turbulent and deteriorating environment in which enemy command would struggle to cope.

Cognitive Impacts

Land force strike operations in support of these simultaneous advances were integral to the larger air based concept of operations. Throughout 1943 land based elements would advance inland toward the Huon Peninsula, progressively securing terrain centred on locations with airfields or suitable for expeditious development.[895] Manoeuvre theory rests on the ability to generate not only physical tempo but also superior decision-making tempo so that ultimately the enemy command cannot cope or simply makes poor decisions.[896] It is here where the supporting actions of dismounted strike elements contribute to the wider campaign plan. The joint focus of the operational design would ultimately contribute to poor command decisions being made by the Japanese.

Because of land force success at Wau, the Japanese headquarters located within Rabaul directed reinforcement actions for Lae, with this troop movement requiring a sea based move.[897] On the 28th Feb 1943 the Japanese command stationed at Rabaul deployed close to 7,000 troops in eight transports to transit the Bismarck Sea toward Lae.[898] General Kenney, Commander Allied Air Forces under MacArthur, had however planned for and anticipated General Imamura's response.[899] Due to the established airfields at Milne Bay and Port Moresby ground-based air elements were able to neutralise the convoys close air protection (CAP) stationed in Lae and interdict the seaborne force.[900] The battle of the Bismarck Sea resulted in significant casualties being inflicted on the Japanese, perhaps most effectively articulated through the words of one survivor:

---

895 Keogh, Colonel (retd), *The South West Pacific 1941-45*. 297
896 Field, "Testing the Tenets of Manoeuvre: Australia's First Amphibious Assualt since Gallipoli, The 9th Australian Division at Lae, 4-16 September 1943."
897 Keogh, Colonel (retd), *The South West Pacific 1941-45*. 293
898 Keogh, Colonel (retd), *The South West Pacific 1941-45*. 293
899 George C. Kenney, "General Kenney Reports: A Personal History of the Pacific War" (New York, 1949). 197-206
900 Odgers, *100 Years of Australians at War*. 165-167

Then a second air attack came in. We were hit by thirty shells from port to starboard. The ship shook violently. Bullet fragments and shrapnel made it look like a beehive. All the steam pipes burst. The ship became boiling hot. We tried to abandon ship, but planes flying almost as low as the masts sprayed us with machine-guns. Hands were shot off, stomachs blow open.[901]

When considering the operational and strategic impacts of the Bismarck Sea action, the importance of land-based airpower acting as MacArthur's main strike weapon is clear. The ability to employ both fighters and medium bombers to interdict forces delivered not only pre-emptive strikes but also a disruptive effect through the direct targeting and attrition of enemy forces.[902] The course of actions available to the adversary had been reduced, with these disruptive effects impacting on the cognitive clarity and planning options available to Japanese command.[903] The ability for Allied land-based airpower to target sea-based troop movement removed the ability for Japanese command to execute massed sea-based troop and logistic movements.[904] Their freedom of manoeuvre had been negated and with that the initiative was firmly with the allies. This tactical success supported MacArthur's wider operational plan, additionally however through the removal of critical assets, Japanese effectiveness within the SWPA was adversely impacted with this arguably contributing to grand strategic success. This was not lost on MacArthur who relished the shifting dynamic, stating that 'Control of the air and sea had passed to the Allies, marking the end of the Japanese offensive in the Southwest Pacific'.[905]

The remainder of 1943 saw significant actions within the Huon Peninsula, all however focused on the need to seize or secure terrain suitable for airfields in Lae, Finschafen, Madang, Salamaua and Nadzab.[906] The reality was that the higher command intent for the SWPA had been achieved by the end of 1943. Rabaul was isolated and the enemy

901 Masuda Reiji, "Sunken Fleet: Transport War," in *Japan at War: An Oral History*, ed. Haruko Taya Cook and Theodore F. Cook (Sydney: HarperCollins Publishers, 1992), 300–304; Long, *MacArthur: As Military Commander*. 117

902 Wayne P. Rothgeb, *New Guinea Skies: A Fighter Pilots View of World War II* (Ames: Iowa State University Press, 1992). 156-163

903 Odgers, *Air War Against Japan 1943-1945*. 161

904 Odgers, *100 Years of Australians at War*. 166

905 Long, *MacArthur: As Military Commander*. 117-118

906 Keogh, Colonel (retd), *The South West Pacific 1941-45*. 297-343

strength neutralised due to the mobility restrictions being imposed by land based airpower. Any land force actions to secure future airfields were consistently supported by Kenney's forces with the focus clearly centred on establishing land-based air strike capabilities to increase the pressure being generated on Rabaul.[907] When viewing this in the context of the strategic spectrum, ground-based tactical strike actions, although costly, were a necessity in 1942-43. Arguably at the tactical level ground based forces were the main strike weapon, however only to the extent that their tactical actions secured airfields, enabling Allied freedom of movement through air supremacy. When seen in the joint context the dismounted and amphibious actions were only essential to the extent that they secured a requirement needed for operational success. In the case of the SWPA this requirement was clearly land-based airfields.[908] At the operational level land based airpower remains MacArthur's main strike weapon; it was his central capability and the very capability needed to generate tempo and momentum. Having established these requirements MacArthur was now positioned to capitalise fully on the shifting dynamics within the operational environment.

Bypass and Tempo

The importance of Rabaul's collapse and how this links to wider operational plans for both the Japanese and Allies is central to the justification that land based airpower was MacArthur's main strike weapon. The original plan had been to seize Rabaul, however, MacArthur acquiesced to a shift in strategic guidance toward the Admiralty Islands; which ultimately afforded similar logistical and airfield capabilities to that of Rabaul.[909] The Japanese were unaware of this shift and due to the pressure being applied by the advancing SWPA-SOPAC forces, the devastating effects of Kenney's air strikes and the collapse of Truk, the remaining Japanese aircraft ultimately withdrew from Rabaul in February 1944.[910] This achieved several critical actions. First, due to Allied air superiority, the Japanese fighting force of approximately 100,000 personnel located at Rabaul

---

907 Odgers, *100 Years of Australians at War*. 170-179
908 Australian Defence Force, *Plans Series: Joint Military Appreciation Process*, UNCLASS (Canberra: Defence Publishing Service, 2016). 2
909 Odgers, *100 Years of Australians at War*. 177
910 Odgers, *Air War Against Japan 1943-1945*. 133

were isolated through a lack of air mobility and by the fact that their sea lines of communication were compromised. This was achieved through the application of defeat mechanisms inherent to manoeuvre theory as the Japanese forces at Rabaul had simply become functionally dislocated.[911] More importantly the deteriorating situation confronting Japanese command provided MacArthur operational flexibility of which he could capitalise. As previously mentioned manoeuvre theory seeks to defeat the enemy's plans through decision superiority rather than simply the destruction of forces.[912] Clearly, the operational plan being executed within the SWPA was effecting the intended Japanese course of action and the integrity of their decision cycle had been compromised.[913] To employ the defeat mechanisms integral to manoeuvre theory (pre-emption, dislocation and disruption) a number of central tenets must be leveraged by command.[914] Three, however, are critical for MacArthur's actions throughout 1944 with these being reconnaissance pull, tempo and surprise. Land based air power will again prove integral to this, ultimately enabling a rapid transition toward Morotai by September 1944.

To capitalise on the success achieved through the isolation of Rabaul, MacArthur (on advice from Kenney) sought to exploit the initiative by directing a 'reconnaissance in force' on the Admiralty Islands to secure Los Negros.[915] His plan was now being 'pulled' through the provision of intelligence from reconnaissance forces. The land based air assets established within New Guinea and the Admiralty Islands had placed MacArthur in the advantageous position that afforded command flexibility. He now possessed decision superiority to the point that plans being developed by the Japanese Imperial General Headquarters were often superseded by the time they were ready for issue.[916] This situation again highlights how the application of land-based airpower was contributing to operational victory through a rapidly deteriorating situation with which the enemy could not cope. Although perhaps not

911 Leonhard, *The Art of Maneuver: Maneuver-Warfare Theory and the Airland Battle*. 68-69

912 Lind, *Maneuver Warfare Handbook*. 6

913 Lind, *Maneuver Warfare Handbook*. 6

914 Field, "Testing the Tenets of Manoeuvre: Australia's First Amphibious Assualt since Gallipoli, The 9th Australian Division at Lae, 4-16 September 1943." 4

915 Stephen R. Taaffe, *MacArthur's Jungle War: The 1944 New Guinea Campaign* (Lawrence: University of Kansas Press, 1988). 56-65

916 Keogh, Colonel (retd), *The South West Pacific 1941-45*. 392

recognising the actions by their now established terms; MacArthur's campaign plan was clearly achieving operational success through the principles inherent to manoeuvre theory. He was synchronising and orchestrating the application of strike effects, principally land based air, to defeat the enemy's plans through both operational and decision tempo.

Importantly this cognitive space afforded command clarity. MacArthur had identified the opportunity to generate force projection tempo through the bypass of Wewak, instead to focus actions toward the weaker location of Hollandia.[917] This proposed action typifies manoeuvre theory in seeking to avoid strengths (surfaces) and exploit weakness (gaps).[918] History demonstrates that the tactic worked. Although the lodgement at Hollandia was a joint amphibious assault, the ability for Japanese aircraft to strike the amphibious assault was negated through pre-emptive land base air strikes on critical nodes, including Hansa Bay, Aitape and Noemfoor.[919] Thus, when the lodgement occurred not only were the forces at Hollandia caught by surprise, but like Rabaul, the 40,000 man bastion of Wewak became functionally dislocated.[920] The principles and success associated with this bypass and complementary amphibious assault policy continued with success throughout 1944. Ultimately by mid-September 1944 forces were postured within Morotai and MacArthur had finally set the conditions for a triumphant return to the Philippines.[921]

Leyte and beyond

The focus of this paper is to assess the extent of land-based air power being MacArthur's main strike weapon in the SWPA. In doing so, discussion has centred on how this capability enabled victory as conceptualised within manoeuvre theory, notably the theories primary defeat mechanisms. Additionally, the success of land based air strike actions have been viewed based on their impacts across the strategic spectrum. The support to actions at Buna and Milne Bay enabled tactical success,

---

917 Odgers, *100 Years of Australians at War*. 180-181
918 Lind, *Maneuver Warfare Handbook*. 18
919 Odgers, *Air War Against Japan 1943-1945*. 208
920 Odgers, *Air War Against Japan 1943-1945*. 178
921 Keogh, Colonel (retd), *The South West Pacific 1941-45*. 391

which then established the conditions for wider operational actions through 1943-44. Actions executed during this period were successful with adversarial forces and materiel being either pre-emptively destroyed or in the case of Rabaul and Wewak, functionally dislocated. Their strength was rendered irrelevant, representing operational success in terms of manoeuvre theory.[922] However, when viewing the South-West Pacific campaign holistically, these actions were ultimately preliminary in nature so as to enable force projection into the Philippines. Although often viewed as merely a result of MacArthur's need to re-establish his self-esteem following its fall to the Japanese, this understanding belies the importance of the Philippines when considered in a grand strategic context. MacArthur assessed that if the Philippines were secured then the ability for resources from the SWPA to flow into Japan (and consequently materiel and reinforcements out) would be eliminated.[923] The Japanese ability to engage in and support a total war effort would be impacted and thus the effectiveness of forces deployed to the Pacific would be severely hampered. What this would achieve is the dislocation of the Japanese state in a grand strategic sense, removing their ability to wage successful military operations at any level. This is important to appreciate, as although the force structure for the subsequent seizures of Leyte Gulf, Luzon and Manila shifted to include a sizeable carrier based strike element, it was only enabled through the successful land based air strike actions executed in 1943-44.[924] Therefore, regardless of the force structure during these campaigns, the success achieved by land based air strike throughout the period 1942-1944 demonstrates its primacy as MacArthur's primary strike weapon as it enabled 'all' actions attributable to operational success.

The operational environment on approach to and around the Philippines continued to work in MacArthur's favour, as although the Japanese could anticipate that action would be taken to retake the Philippines, their ability to predict the initial lodgement location was problematic at best.[925] Again, like the seizure of Hollandia, capacity to exploit the

---

922 Leonhard, *The Art of Maneuver: Maneuver-Warfare Theory and the Airland Battle*. 66
923 Peter J. Dean and Kevin Holzimmer, "The Southwest Pacific Area: Military Strategy and Operations 1944-45," in *Australia 1944-45: Victory in the Pacific*, ed. Peter J. Dean (Melbourne: Cambridge University Press, 2014), 28–50.
924 Thomas J. Cutler, *The Battle for Leyte Gulf: 23-26 October 1944* (New York: HarperCollins Publishers, 1994). 53-61
925 Odgers, *Air War Against Japan 1943-1945*. 301

initiative so as to generate tempo and surprise for the seizure of Leyte was essential. Fortuitous observations made by carrier based aircraft indicated that Leyte was poorly defended and Kenney commenced planning for a rapid lodgement. Although this was done in MacArthur's absence, once appraised of the situation and intended course of action, MacArthur supported the concept of operations.[926] This is significant as it further highlights MacArthur's intuitive grasp of manoeuvre theory concepts and in this case his appreciation of mission command.[927] At this stage of the campaign, Kenney had clearly garnered MacArthur's trust and understood the commander's intent. Subordinate elements were thus empowered to exploit opportunity when it presented. These are the inherent elements of what is now referred to as mission command.[928] Consequently an operational plan was struck with a view to seize Leyte Gulf rapidly during October 1944.[929] The end-state was ultimately a successful joint amphibious lodgement. However, this amphibious lodgement was supported by significant preparatory actions from both carrier based and land based air assets from within the SWPA and wider commands.[930] As such, targeting sought to disrupt Japanese bases at Formosa, the Ryukus, and the Southern Philippines.[931] The fact that the action on Leyte had received such levels of support indicates the importance of its seizure with regards to supporting grand strategic objects and once again this was enabled to a large extent by land-based air power.

The final legitimate operational push for MacArthur within the SWPA was the seizure of the island of Luzon and its capital Manila. This would be the culmination of MacArthur's advance, resulting in the positioning of forces within the Philippines for a potential invasion of the Japanese mainland, an eventuality that never transpired. Luzon however did, following a now predictable and successful concept of operations. Reconnaissance would identify Japanese 'gaps' and thus pull operational planning toward these areas. Therefore, to support Luzon, preliminary actions focused on establishing airfields at Legaspi and Mindoro.[932] The

926 Odgers, *Air War Against Japan 1943-1945*. 301
927 Lind, *Maneuver Warfare Handbook*. 13
928 Lind, *Maneuver Warfare Handbook*. 13
929 Odgers, *100 Years of Australians at War*. 198
930 Odgers, *Air War Against Japan 1943-1945*. 301
931 Odgers, *Air War Against Japan 1943-1945*. 383
932 Long, *MacArthur: As Military Commander*. 159-163

establishment of these locations would subsequently afford land-based air support to future actions. When this land (and increasingly sea) cover was established, amphibious lodgements would follow supported by naval gunfire and airpower strike on multiple locations across the island.[933] By the first week of March 1945 all the primary objectives within Luzon had been secured, including vital air bases and Manilla.[934] The ability to seize terrain is, however, a facet of war reserved for the land based soldier and it would be a false representation of history to suggest Luzon fell through land-based air strike alone. However, the freedom of manoeuvre afforded to these elements was enabled by the effectiveness of the previous land-based air operations. There would be significant actions required yet within the SWPA to 'mop up' abandoned Japanese forces including the questionable and prolonged actions within Borneo.[935] However, from an operational perspective, MacArthur was victorious within the SWPA. The Japanese had been reduced to a disparate and dislocated force with no ability to wage any form of effective offensive or defensive action. The impost for further protracted actions to neutralise the remaining elements within the South-West Pacific Area was of course removed through the unconditional surrender of the Japanese on the 14th of August 1945.[936] Also, it might be noted, surrender driven through strike capabilities delivered via land base air assets.[937]

Conclusion

The South-West Pacific campaign, like many others throughout World War II, typifies the effects that can be generated through a joint approach to warfare. For General MacArthur, commander of the South-West Pacific Area, both the operational environment and his force allocation shaped him toward a campaign centred on amphibious strike action. However, to execute amphibious operations the sea lines of communication needed to be secured so that adversarial strike assets could be neutralised. Initially for MacArthur this capability could only be generated via land based air strike assets due to the absence of a carrier element within his command.

---

933 Kenney, "General Kenney Reports: A Personal History of the Pacific War." 493
934 Long, *MacArthur: As Military Commander*. 170
935 Horner, *High Command: Australia and Allied Strategy 1939-1945*. 399-404
936 Paul Ham, *Hiroshima and Nagasaki* (Sydney: HarperCollins Publishers, 2011). 404
937 Ham, *Hiroshima and Nagasaki*. 404

As shown, this capability could not be introduced until airfields were either seized or developed and subsequently secured. This was demonstrated through the actions taken to secure Buna, a significant tactical action involving land force strike assets focused on securing critical air fields. When achieved this enabled land based air strike actions to be executed in support of the wider operational plan, typified through the success in the Bismarck Sea. Having achieved this and dislocating Rabaul, MacArthur had the freedom of movement needed to execute his intended strategy of projecting forces into the Philippines. In achieving this MacArthur instinctively applied an operational strategy that would today be known as manoeuvreist in approach. Tactical level land based strike actions were only executed to secure airfields that would subsequently enable the wider operational plan centred on land based air strike capabilities. When, established this land based air strike capability afforded protection to MacArthur's amphibious elements allowing amphibious strike forces the ability to bypass known enemy strengths and hence achieve tempo and surprise. Today, in terms of manoeuvre theory, this would be seen as the dislocation of enemy forces. Although the seizure of Luzon and Manila was a joint amphibious, activity it was enabled by the previous successful actions of land based air strike assets throughout 1943-44. As such, land based air assets were MacArthur's main strike weapon within the South-West Pacific throughout 1942-45 as they ultimately enabled victory across the entirety of the strategic spectrum.

Other Wars

Essay 19

'What does the conduct of attrition and manoeuvre in the South-West Pacific theatre and the Korean War reveal about the nature and character of war?'
(Written 2017 - exam in 4 hours)

The aim, or nature of war, has remained constant throughout time and can be seen through Clausewitz's concept of engaging in an act of violence to compel an opponent to succumb to your will.[938] When reviewing military conflicts, including total war, this remains. To achieve this intent in a militaristic context those members of the profession of arms have several methods or approaches that can be employed for the execution of war. Attrition, being 'a gradual and piecemeal process of destroying an enemy's military capability' and manoeuvre being 'warfare that seeks to defeat enemy forces decisively through placing the enemy in a disadvantageous position on the battlefield' are but two approaches to warfare.[939] This paper will compare the actions of two campaigns being the South-West Pacific Area (SWPA) during World War Two and the Korean War in its entirety. The intent will be to identify how the conduct of attrition and manoeuvre impacts on the nature and character of war. The argument being that the nature does not change, it remains the intent to impose ones will on another. Rather the method of execution, being the character, will change based on the shifting dynamics of both the time and environment in which the campaign is executed as this has an impact on the overall political objective.

Military actions from the tactical through to the grand strategic do not occur in isolation, rather they occur within a competing and dynamic

---

938 Carl Von Clausewitz, *Carl von Clausewitz: On War*, ed. Michael Howard and Peter Paret, *On War* (New Yotk, 1976). 32

939 Carter Malkasian, *A History of Modern Wars of Attrition* (Wesport: Praeger, 2002). 1-5

system that experiences both internal and external influences.[940] This is important to appreciate prior to reviewing the SWPA and the Korean War. Although the time-period between the conflicts is small, a significant change had occurred that ultimately impacted the character of war for these conflicts. This relates to the advent of nuclear capabilities, not only for the United States, but also for the USSR as of 1949.[941] This advance in military technology contributed to a shift in perspective on the outcomes of war due to the prospect of mutually assured destruction. This must be considered when viewing both these campaigns as the technological advancements relating to nuclear capability impacted on the strategic culture of the belligerents.

For General MacArthur, commander of the SWPA, the higher command intent for his campaign was clear. His focus was to advance North West through New Guinea, into the Philippines to posture forces for a potential assault into the mainland of Japan. This ran complementary to Admiral Nimitz's drive through the Central Pacific, however the political objective was clear, being the unconditional surrender of Japanese forces. This concept however ran secondary to the defeat of Germany and the allies within the Pacific were thus initially directed toward a period of 'defensive attrition'.[942] The actions throughout New Guinea in 1941 were typified by the high levels of attrition executed in highly complex terrain. The Kokoda Track is notorious for its intensity and loss of life for both Australian and Japanese forces.[943] This attrition, however, was simply a necessary component of warfare based on the terrain and higher command intent. Attrition lacks a focus on the decisive defeat of the enemy, as opposed to manoeuvre, and is central to wearing down an enemy.[944] Additionally complex terrain is a recognised dilemma forcing an opponent toward an attrition campaign. Initially at least, the character of the SWPA was very much attrition focused due to higher command direction and the fact the operating environment forced this method of warfare. Perhaps more influential was the fact that sea lines of transit were not yet secure resulting in MacArthur being

---

940 Hal Brands, *What Good Is Grand Strategy? Power and Purpose in American Statecraft from Harry S. Truman to George W. Bush* (London: Cornell University Press, 2016). 14

941 Robert O'Neill, *Australia in the Korean War 1950-53* (Canberra: Australian Government Publishing Services, 1981). 39

942 Malkasian, *A History of Modern Wars of Attrition*. 52

943 George Odgers, *100 Years of Australians at War* (Sydney: New Holland, 2001). 161

944 Malkasian, *A History of Modern Wars of Attrition*. 6-9

forced to execute a land based campaign in a maritime environment.[945] Although attrition was necessary at this stage of the campaign, it needed to change so as to allow MacArthur the ability to manoeuvre toward the Philippines.

Due to an absence of a carrier element in his force structure MacArthur could not provide protection to his amphibious forces unless land based airstrips were secured. If this was achieved, then MacArthur would be afforded the freedom to manoeuvre amphibious and airmobile forces along the northern side of New Guinea allowing him to project forces into the Philippines. It is at this stage an interplay between attrition and manoeuvre begins to present. The Japanese had pre-emptively seized Buna prior to the allies as both recognised the operational advantage this held.[946] For MacArthur, Buna provides suitable air strips and hence provides operational reach into critical terrain, notably the Bismarck Sea and Rabaul. As a result of this, actions to seize Buna were directed and subsequently successful.[947] This placed MacArthur in the advantageous position of having land based air assets situated in several locations that had the ability to not only target the Japanese location of Rabaul but also interdict enemy airframes if they were to target his amphibious forces. This is a critical juncture of time as it signifies a shift in the character of the SWPA from one that was very much attrition focused, to one that could now employ manoeuvre. Rabaul was the Japanese headquarters within the SWPA and had been recognised as central to operational planning. Not surprisingly then the initial JCS Directive issued on 02 July 1942 identified the need to seize Rabaul.[948] Consequently, MacArthur's initial direction stipulated the following:

> The general scheme of manoeuvre is to advance our bomber line towards Rabaul: first by improvement of existing forward bases; secondly, by the occupation of air bases which can be secured

---

945 Peter J. Dean, "Anzacs and Yanks: US and Australian Operations at the Beachhead Battles," in *Australia 1942: In the Shadow of War*, ed. Peter J. Dean (Melbourne: CUP, 2013), 223.

946 Anthony Beevor, *The Second World War* (London: Phoenix, 2013). 345

947 Gavin Long, *MacArthur: As Military Commander* (Sydney: Angus and Robertson, 1969). 85-120

948 E. G. Keogh, Colonel (retd), *The South West Pacific 1941-45* (Melbourne: Grayflower Productions Pty Ltd, 1965). 151

without committing large forces; and then by the seizure of successive hostile aerodromes.[949]

Although actions within New Guinea had been attritional in focus they were ultimately centred toward establishing the conditions that would allow a shift in character to a more flowing and manoeuvre style of warfare. Once Buna was secured MacArthur could negate the influence of Rabaul, with this perhaps most notably typified through the success of the Battle of the Bismarck Sea. Tactical attrition had established the conditions that enabled operational manoeuvre because ground based forces had secured airfields which in turn afforded MacArthur the ability to secure his sea lines of communication. Consequently, MacArthur could generate significant tempo through amphibious manoeuvre along the north of New Guinea and ultimately into Luzon via Leyte gulf.

For MacArthur, the higher political objective remained constant throughout the SWPA campaign, being the defeat and unconditional surrender of the Japanese. As indicated the nature had not changed, however the character of war did fluctuate between an attrition focused or a manoeuvre focused action based on the operational environment and how this in turn impacted on operational planning. MacArthur employed attrition as necessary to achieve moderate goals as can be the intent of this characteristic of warfare.[950] In this case, however, these moderate victories at the tactical level enabled a significant shift at the operational level to a manoeuvre centric campaign, thus supporting the hypothesis that the character may change based on shifts in time and the operational environment.

As indicated the nature of war is effectively a constant, however based on shifts in time and the operational environment the character may change. This is particularly evident during the Korean War were by 1949 the world had transitioned to an environment that faced the reality of nuclear conflict.[951] Thus the character of the Korean War shifted significantly to a conflict that saw attrition being used as a tool for political leverage to attain a negotiated peace, as opposed to simply a means to destroy a military's capability.[952]

---

949 Keogh, Colonel (retd), *The South West Pacific 1941-45*. 287
950 Malkasian, *A History of Modern Wars of Attrition*. 9
951 O'Neill, *Australia in the Korean War 1950-53*. 39
952 Malkasian, *A History of Modern Wars of Attrition*. 120

Following the surprise attacks in 1950 by North Korea forces south of the 38th parallel and into Seoul, the under-equipped United States and ROKA forces were forced to withdraw to the relative safety of Pusan.[953] Like the SWPA, MacArthur was initially the commander of UNC forces and saw the need to regain the initiative. Based on his success in employing amphibious manoeuvre throughout the SWPA, he identified an opportunity to execute an opposed lodgement deep into the now North Korean held areas. The focus was an amphibious lodgement at Inchon with the intent being to place the enemy in a disadvantageous position on the battlefield.[954] Ultimately this amphibious lodgement was a success and allied forces advanced into North Korean held territory retaking Seoul and forcing North Korean elements back above the 38th Parallel.[955] However, at this stage focus on the political objective begins to drift. MacArthur sensed the opportunity to advance further north to achieve a total victory over communism. His perceived objective was a united anti-communist Korea.[956] MacArthur did have support for such an advance, however this shift in operational planning carried several potential underappreciated consequences. Perhaps the most obvious would be how the Chinese would react when UNC forces encroached toward their border, being the Yalu River. Mao Se Tung and the communist republic of China having only recently formed, viewed the UNC advance as an imperialist action that must be stopped. As such, in September 1950 the Chinese Peoples Volunteer Army (CPVA) was directed to advance into North Korea.[957] It is this action that signifies a significant shift in the character of war and how attrition would be employed in the Korean War.

Although the CPVA forces had the manning resource advantage, the UNC forces held the advantage with regards to technological advancements in war, notably artillery. The reality was, however, that the sheer volume of force available to CPVA forced the UNC forces to withdraw south. This advance and withdrawal of forces continued for

953 Odd Arne Westad, "The Wars after the War, 1945-1954," in *The Cambridge History of War: Volume IV*, ed. Roger Chickering, Dennis Showalter, and Hans van de Ven, ibook (Cambridge: Cambridge University Press, 2012). 701

954 Andrew Mulholland, *The Korean War*, iBook (William Cpllins, n.d.). 30-34

955 Saul David, *Military Blunders* (London: Robinson Publishing, 1997). 270-271

956 David, *Military Blunders*. 271

957 Jung Chang and Jon Halliday, *Mao: The Unkown Story* (London: Jonathan Cape, 2005). 381

a period until both the CPVA and UNC forces settled into a deadlock around the 38th parallel. It is at this stage of the Korean War were the need to align military intent to civilian objectives begins to appear. As indicated, by 1949 the USSR had a nuclear capability and were resourcing and supporting Chinese involvement in the Korean War. The options available to break this deadlock did in fact extend to the potentiality of nuclear actions; the character of war had shifted to the point that nuclear actions may be considered a viable option to break an operational deadlock.

Here the biggest divide becomes apparent forcing the political leadership to address the difference in objectives that existed between MacArthur and the civil authority. Ultimately President Truman was forced to remove General MacArthur from command as his views on the potential character or war contrasted with that of the US Government, specifically the use of nuclear weapons. In the end Truman removed MacArthur from command replacing him with General Ridgeway.[958] MacArthur was proposing actions not only on the Chinese within Korea but also strikes within China, whereas President Truman wished to reduce the potentiality for a Third Word War. It is important to appreciate at this stage that the world in general was attempting to recover financially from the demands of World War II and was effectively experiencing conflict fatigue. Additionally, the character of war had changed to include the reality of mutually assured destruction through nuclear effects with the strategic leadership adapting their approach to conflict to accommodate this shift. Consequently, a limited strategy that could avoid the prohibitive costs associated with total war and avoided the potential need for total annihilation of the threat became a palatable political objective.[959] The character of war had changed.

General Ridgeway engaged in a series of limited objective attacks the focus of which was to force the Chinese to the negotiating table due to high levels of attrition. In the static limited objectives attacks along the 38th parallel the UNC forces could achieve this due to superior firepower and an effective logistic system. As such, massed fires allowed limited objectives to be achieved without significant risk to

---

958 Malkasian, *A History of Modern Wars of Attrition*. 130
959 Malkasian, *A History of Modern Wars of Attrition*. 119

US forces whilst inflicting significant attrition on the CPVA forces.[960] The tactic worked, however was effectively reciprocated. The Chinese also engaged in limited offensives with both Mao and Peng being able to engage in this concept of attrition due to significant manpower advantages.[961] Like the UNC forces this was a tool to enable leverage during truce negotiations. Thus, the character of war had shifted to see attrition being employed as more than a method to simply destroy enemy forces, rather it became a tool of leverage to achieve a given political objective.

The South-West Pacific during World War II and the Korean War provide examples on the use of both Manoeuvre and Attrition as tools to achieve a political objective. Within the SWPA tactical attrition was necessary to the extent that it enabled operational manoeuvre, with this operational manoeuvre then contributing to a finite strategic objective. In this case the unconditional surrender of the Japanese. Both attrition and manoeuvre can simply be tools employed by military forces to compel an adversary to your will; with this being the inherent nature of war. However, the use of both attrition and manoeuvre can vary based on a shifting operational environment and based on time, be it duration of a campaign or holistically relating to technological advancements within society. In the case of the Korean War, the advent of nuclear capabilities had shifted the perspective on the character of war to the point that a negotiated settlement driven through the effects of attrition had become acceptable. Both manoeuvre and attrition will remain tools available to compel an adversary to adhere to your will and thus the nature of war remains. Today as shown through the significant change in their use in the SWPA and Korea, it seems the character of war has shifted to the point that limited objectives that avoid a total or nuclear war are now the inherent characteristics of war.

---

960 Malkasian, *A History of Modern Wars of Attrition*. 123
961 Carter Malkasian, *The Korean War 1950-1953* (Osprey Publishing, n.d.). 65

"The political leadership of a country cannot simply set objectives for a war, provide the requisite materiel, then stand back and await victory."

Evaluate this statement in relation to at least two cases; the Vietnam and Falklands War
(Written 2017 - exam in 4 hours)

Introduction

If the political leadership of a country has made the decision to engage in war, then other aspects of national power have failed be that diplomatic, informational or economic options. As such, the identification of a clear political objective is assessed as a key determinant with regard to the execution of successful military operations. The ability of political leadership to correctly identify the character of a potential conflict, and then align their resource allocation to this, is assessed as a fundamental tenet of success. This paper will demonstrate the importance of a correct political objective, employing the Falklands and Vietnam Wars as mediums which highlight how this contributes to strategic success. The premise of the argument being that when the political objective aligns with the character of the conflict the military can be resourced accordingly; which in turn enables operational planning and contributes to victory. By contrast if the potential character of the conflict is poorly identified and the military inappropriately resourced, the adversary holds advantage and defeat is likely. On reviewing both these conflicts the perspectives of opposing major belligerents will be reviewed, highlighting how this contributed to victory or defeat.

Political objectives and the drift toward limited objectives

In appreciating the political leadership's perception of warfare, two aspects relating to its evolving character must be considered; that being the impost of total war and the potential effects of nuclear war. This is an important aspect to appreciate as these developments have subsequently influenced the political leadership's approach to resourcing and executing war. The costs to a nation financially and through loss of life in total war has seen an increasing shift toward conflicts of a limited nature, meaning there is an increasing desire for a political resolution to conflict.[962] When overlaid with the threat of nuclear war and mutually assured destruction the desire for government to leverage the military to secure a political resolve is greatly increased prior to the escalation toward total war.[963]

The Vietnam War fought between the United States of America (US) and communist North Vietnam and the Falklands War between Britain and Argentina both occurred in the context of the Cold War; this however is where the similarities end. When reviewing these conflicts, it is important to appreciate this reality as both the major protagonists were nuclear powers with this capability being integral to their deterrence strategy. Thus, their action or inaction against an adversary may have had a wider impact other than simply the immediate conflict. In short, if seen to lack the political will to deter aggression through the application of military force, both the US and Britain may become vulnerable to attack by other larger states.[964] In conjunction to being conducted in the background of the Cold War both conflicts had vastly different characters. The Falklands was a traditional state based conflict with a small and largely British aligned host population on the islands. Thus, with regards to the operational spectrum, it would be defined as 'Major Combat' and was therefore effectively free from the ambiguities

---

962 Stephen Peter Rosen, "Vietnam and the American Theory of Limited War," *International Security* 7, no. 2 (1982): 83–113; Bruce Vandervort, "War and Imperial Expansion," in *Cambridge History of War: Volume IV*, ed. Roger Chickering, Dennis Showalter, and Hans van de Ven (Cambridge: Cambridge University Press, 2012), 108–47.

963 C Walton, Dale, "Weapons Technology in the Two Nuclear Ages," in *The Cambridge History of War: Volume IV*, ed. Roger Chickering, Dennis Shoalwater, and Hans van de Ven (New York: Cambridge University Press, 2012), 1277–1334.

964 Greg Cashman and Leonard C Robinson, *An Introduction to the Causes of War: Patterns of Interstate Conflict from World War 1 to Iraq* (Lanham: Rowman and Littlefield Publishers, Inc, 2007).

associated with irregular or insurgent conflicts.[965] The Vietnam War, by contrast, was to be waged in a complex operational environment with porous borders, a highly complex human terrain, and a diverse threat ranging from conventional forces through to insurgent forces.[966] In both cases the clarity (or otherwise) of the political objective was instrumental in the allocation of military resources.

For the British, the political objective for the Falklands campaign was very clear, being the expulsion of Argentine forces from the Falklands and the re-establishment of a British Administration.[967] It was, due to the concern for escalation, limited in nature with military action within Argentina discounted. For the Argentine political leadership, their objectives lacked this clarity. Although the intent was overtly displayed as the requirement to re-establish ownership on the contested Falkland Islands, there was a diversionary aspect due to the political pressures being experienced at the time within Argentina.[968] The military Junta's intent was that by invading and repossessing the Falklands, focus on the domestic situation within Argentina would be removed and their global stature enhanced due to their stance taken against a national power. However, the political leadership failed to appreciate the British response, which was being influenced in large part by the wider cold war deterrence pressures. Therefore, once political efforts failed, Britain executed the decision for war. In their attempt to achieve a decisive victory through the seizure of the Falklands the Argentine political leadership, although holding a clear political objective, failed to appreciate the potential military force that Britain may employ, and as such the Argentine military, in a joint sense, was poorly prepared and resourced.

Similarly the United States political objective regarding the Communist Vietnamese actions within South Vietnam was heavily influenced

---

965 Australian Army, "Operations," *Land Warfare Doctrine 3-0*, 2015, https://www.army. gov.au/sites/g/files/net1846/f/lwd_3-0_operations.pdf.

966 Dale Andradea, "Westmoreland Was Right: Learning the Wrong Lessons from the Vietnam War," *Small Wars & Insurgencies* 19, no. 2 (2008): 145–81, doi:10.1080/09592310802061349.

967 Stephen Prince, "British Command and Control in the Falklands Campaign," *Defense and Security Analysis* 18, no. May (2002): 333–49.

968 Cashman and Robinson, *An Introduction to the Causes of War: Patterns of Interstate Conflict from World War 1 to Iraq.* 10-15

by concern regarding escalation and the rise of communism within Asia.[969] And like the British, US credibility was in question regarding its ability to protect their interests based on their resolve to engage in military intervention.[970] However, in supporting their interest in South Vietnam the political leadership were nonetheless cautious about the risk of triggering a larger war through a form of conflict spiral if it was to spread wider or escalate.[971] The political objective was clear and limited in nature, being the expulsion of communist influence from South Vietnam and the establishment of a democratic government aligned to western influence.[972] To achieve this political objective, and based on the fear of escalation present within the political leadership, a number of restrictions were imposed on military command. Most notably was the direction to limit United States involvement of large scale military action to South Vietnam borders.[973] This in turn impacted operational planning and shaped the outcome of the war as the drift toward limited objectives had afforded the adversary the advantage of sanctuary; thus, limiting the utility of allocated US military resources. Not only did the imposition of this restriction imposed by the political leadership impact on the effectiveness of US military forces, it unfortunately enabled the effectiveness of the adversary as material and resources could be delivered to support communist objectives via the Ho Chi Minh trail within Laos and Cambodia.[974] Although the US had a clear political objective, the political leadership failed to appreciate the potential character of the war, ultimately across the full operational spectrum, and hence the allocation of military resourcing was fragmented. This in turn had a negative impact on operational planning. Conversely, the Communist North Vietnamese political leadership had an unambiguous political

969 Fredrick Logevall, "The Indo-China Wars and the Cold War, 1945-1975," in *Cambridge History of the Cold War Vol II* (Cambridge: Cambridge University Press, 2009), 281–302.

970 Gary R. Hess, *Vietnam: Explaining America's Lost War* (Malden: Wiley Blackwell, 2015). 28

971 Cashman and Robinson, *An Introduction to the Causes of War: Patterns of Interstate Conflict from World War 1 to Iraq.* 14

972 Paul H. Nitze, "The Evolution of National Security Policy and the Vietnam War," in *The Lessons of Vietnam*, ed. Scott W. Thompson and Donaldson D. Frizzell (St. Lucia: University of Queensland Press, 1977), 1–17.

973 Scott Thompson and Donaldson D. Frizzell, eds., *The Lessons of Vietnam* (St. Lucia: University of Queensland Press, 1977).

974 Neil Smith, *The Vietnam War* (London: HarperCollins Publishers, 2012). 44

objective being, the nationalist unification of Vietnam as a state and the removal of United States forces from South Vietnam.[975] The North Vietnamese, unlike the Argentine military, had, developed an approach to warfare that allowed them to shift their military resourcing priorities based on an assessment of the threat, whilst consistently retaining focus on their political object. This flexibility to adapt to the exigencies of the current battle is assessed as central to operational success and for this to occur the political leadership must equip the military with sufficiency redundancy.

Developing Flexibility

Due to financial limitations, the amphibious skills within the British military had degraded and the concept of an opposed landing remained an unpractised component of Royal Marines tactics. As had been the preferred British tactic amphibious concepts remained centred on the concept of an 'administrative' lodgement, meaning unopposed.[976] This failure to appreciate the reality of an opposed lodgement had permeated the political leaderships within the British government resulting in the drawdown of Naval and amphibious capability. This extended to a lack of integrated training activities between the Royal Marines and Naval forces which would have operational impacts, as forces had not practised together and failed to appreciate the needs and limitations of each service. The Argentine military, to a degree, were justified in their confidence regarding their ability to defend the Falklands once the seizure had taken place. The political leadership within Britain however, emboldened by the need to demonstrate a global deterrence strategy reacted swiftly including raising an amphibious capability that included more than 100 ships and merchant vessels as Ships Taken Up From Trade (STUFT). In short the British had the flexibility to adapt to the character of the conflict and although lacking contingency plans for operations within the Falklands or a detailed understanding of amphibious operations within this area, possessed two fundamental elements required for success:

975 Roger Chickering, Dennis Showalter, and Hans van de Ven, eds., *The Cambridge History of War*, Vol IV (Cambridge: Cambridge University Press, 2012). 795-810

976 Stephen Badsey, Rob Havers, and Mark Grove, *The Falklands Conflict: Twenty Lessons for the Future* (London: Frank Cass, 2004). 29

> Britain had two fundamentals of success, a clear and practicable aim and the resources, human and material to achieve it. The government quickly arrived at its political aim and stuck constantly to it: the removal of Argentine forces and the return of the islands to British administration.[977]

Therefore, having correctly identified the character of the conflict and resourcing their military appropriately, success, albeit problematic, was likely for the British. By contrast the actions of the adversary failed to appreciate the character of the conflict holding on to the belief that a political resolution was still the most viable course of action.[978] Thus although the Argentine political leadership had a clear political objective they were under resourced and failed to appreciate the resultant character of the conflict, being a traditional state on state war. Consequently, the Argentine military failed to allocate and employ the appropriate military capabilities at the right time and place.[979] This can be represented by their failure to allocate premier land forces to the conflict, rather assigning conscripts the tasks of defending against the highly trained British forces.[980] Perhaps more decisive was the removal of Naval forces from the operational area following the sinking of the Belgrano with this contributing to strategic failure as it afforded the British secure sea lines of communication.[981]

With regard to the US involvement within the Vietnam War perhaps the most effective way to further emphasis this point is from the position of the Communist North Vietnamese, whose political objective remained nationalist in focus being the unification of Vietnam.[982] The fact that this was through a communist approach ran secondary to the higher nationalist focus. The strength of this political objective had been developing for decades prior to the commitment of sizeable US ground formations. Both Ho Chi Minh and General Vo Nguyen Giap had been strategising on how to best structure and equip its military for the

---

977 Lord Haldane, "Naval Review" 70, no. 4 (1982). 248
978 Rene De La Pedraja, "The Argentine Air Force versus Britain in the Falklands Islands, 1982," in *Why Air Forces Fail: The Anatomy of Defeat*, ed. Robin Higham and Stephen J. Harris (Lexington: The University Press of Kentucky, 2006), 227–56.
979 Pedraja, "The Argentine Air Force versus Britain in the Falklands Islands, 1982." 227-56
980 Pedraja, "The Argentine Air Force versus Britain in the Falklands Islands, 1982." 227-56
981 Badsey, Havers, and Grove, *The Falklands Conflict: Twenty Lessons for the Future*.
982 Smith, *The Vietnam War*.

potentiality of another war centred on the unification of Vietnam.[983] As a result they developed a unique approach to warfare that saw them acknowledging the interrelatedness of the military and political aspects of warfare. The outcome was the synthesis of what had become known about the execution of warfare, with the *Dau Tranh* strategy leveraging aspects of military action from regular conventional force strategy through to Maoist and Guerrilla effects.[984] Perhaps more importantly any military action that was to be executed in support of the political objective would be complemented by a political aspect seeking to influence the outcome of war through influence on multiple population groups including those within mainland US.[985]

Thus, when the United States engaged in ground combat against the North Vietnamese they faced an adversary that appreciated the overmatch the US held militarily and had developed a strategy that enabled the political and military leadership to adjust their actions based on what the US was doing. Additionally, by developing a strategy that integrated both Viet Cong insurgent action within South Vietnam and conventional force build up, the objectives and subsequent force allocation from a US perspective were clouded from the outset 'Washington erred in asking the military to wage a counterinsurgency, since the insurgency was largely a sideshow'.[986] As a result of this ability to employ both a conventional and guerrilla style of warfare within South Vietnam, the increasing influence of the political leadership within the US limited not only the resources provided to the US military but how they were actually going to plan and executed military operations. This saw senior military commanders on the ground having to adjust operational strategy, as shown from the shift from search and destroy to clear and hold based on the involvement of the political leadership. It could be said that an over involvement from political leadership within the operational level of war once the decision to engage in war has been made, is counter-productive to the original political objectives.

---

983 Douglas Pike, *The People's Army of Vietnam* (Novato: Presido Press, 1986). 214
984 Pike, *The People's Army of Vietnam*. 215-217
985 Pike, *The People's Army of Vietnam*. 215-217
986 Andradea, "Westmoreland Was Right: Learning the Wrong Lessons from the Vietnam War." 146

Conclusion

In both the case studies highlighted, attempts were being made by the political leadership to achieve a political outcome that aligned with national interests. The statement that "The political leadership of a country cannot simply set objectives for a war, provide the requisite materiel, then stand back and await victory" is only accurate to a degree. If the political leadership clearly identifies the likely character of a conflict, which is ultimately a core function of the state, then equips a military effectively based on this, then they can in fact stand back and allow the military to delivery victory. The British victory against the Argentine Military during the Falklands War is a clear example of this. The British military having been provided the political objective and resources were effectively free from unnecessary political involvement at the operational level. This allowed them to execute a strategy that capitalised on the failure of Argentine forces to equip their forces appropriately for the actual conflict as they failed to appreciate the British response and subsequent character of the conflict.

Both however were ultimately conflicts of choice and for the United States, when facing an adversary who views the conflict as total in nature, as opposed to limited, the outcome can be dire. The Vietnam War in contrast to the Falklands War is an example were the political leadership was heavily involved in the conflict once the political objectives had been set. However, the utility of this is only of value if adjustment to the resourcing or approach to the campaign supports operational objectives. For the Communist North Vietnamese, the involvement of their political and military leadership and the use of the *Da Tranh* strategy enabled victory. Conversely, the United States ground forces within Vietnam would have benefited if in fact the political leadership had stood back and awaited victory, as it would seem their involvement had an adverse impact on operational planning contributing to strategic defeat.

Bibliography

Afrianty, Dina. "Islamic Education and Youth Extremism in Indonesia." *Journal of Policing, Intelligence and Counter Terrorism* 7, no. 2 (2012): 134–46.

Al-Khattar, Aref M. *Religion and Terrorism: An Interfaith Perspective*. Westport: Praeger, 2003.

Al-Tamimi, Aymenn Jawad. "The Dawn of the Islamic State of Iraq and Ash-Sham." *Current Trends in Islamist Ideology* 16 (2014): 5–15.

Alonso, Rogelio. "Why Do Terrorists Stop? Analyzing Why ETA Members Abandon or Continue with Terrorism." *Studies in Conflict and Terrorism* 34, no. 9 (2011): 696–716.

Aly, Anne. "Countering Violent Extremism Social Harmony, Community Resilience and the Potential Counter-Narratives in the Australian Context." In *Counter-Radicalisation: Critical Perspectives*, edited by Baker-Beall, 71–87. London: Routledge, 2014.

———. *Terrorism and Global Security: Historical and Contemporary Perspectives*. Melbourne: Palgrave Macmillan, 2011.

Andradea, Dale. "Westmoreland Was Right: Learning the Wrong Lessons from the Vietnam War." *Small Wars & Insurgencies* 19, no. 2 (2008): 145–81. doi:10.1080/09592310802061349.

Andre, Virginie. "Merah and Breivik: A Reflection of the European Identity Crisis." *Islam and Christian-Muslim Relations* 26, no. 2 (2015): 183–204.

Appleton, Catherine. "Lone Wolf Terrorism in Norway." *The International Journal of Human Rights* 18, no. 2 (2014): 127–42.

Argomanz, Javier, and Alberto Vidal-Diez. "Examining Deterence and Backlash Effects in Counter-Terrorism: The Case of ETA." *Terrorism and Political Violence2* 27, no. 1 (2015): 160–81.

Armistead, Leigh. *Information Operations Matters*. Viginia: Potomac Books, 2010.

Army, Australian. "Formation Tactics." *Land Warfare Doctrine 3-0-3*, 2016. https://www.army.gov.au/sites/g/files/net1846/f/lwd_3-0-3_formation_tactics_interim_0.pdf.

———. *Land Warfare Doctrine 1: The Fundamentals of Land Power*. Unclass. Canberra: Commonwealth of Australia, 2014. https://www.army.gov.au/sites/g/files/net1846/f/lwd_1_the_fundamentals_of_land_power_full.pdf.

———. "Operations." *Land Warfare Doctrine 3-0*, 2015. https://www.army.gov.au/sites/g/files/net1846/f/lwd_3-0_operations.pdf.

Army, United States. *Counterinsurgency*. Government, 2006.

Atwan, Abdel Bari. "Masters of the Digital Universe." In *Islamic State: The Digital Caliphate*, 15–32. Oakland: Saqi Books, 2015.

Australia, Commonwealth of. "Annual Report 2017-2018." Canberra, 2018.

———. "Australia's Counter-Terrorism Strategy: Strengthening Our Resilience." Canberra, 2015.

———. "Counter-Terrorism White Paper: Securing Australia - Protecting Our Community." Canberra, 2010.

———. *Land Warfare Doctrine: Employment of Infantry*. Canberra: Australian Government Publishing Services, 2008.

Australian Defence Force. *Plans Series: Joint Military Appreciation Process*. UNCLASS. Canberra: Defence Publishing Service, 2016.

Author, No. "Australia's Counter-Terrorism Strategy: Strengthening Our Resilience." Canberra, 2015.

———. *Defence White Paper*. Canberra, 2016.

———. *Defence White Paper: 2013*. Canberra: Defence Publishing Service, 2013.

———. *Defence White Paper: 2016*. Canberra: Defence Publishing Service, 2016.

———. *Defence White Paper: Australian Defence*. Canberra: Australian Government Publishing Services, 1976.

———. *Defence White Paper: Defence 2000 Our Future Defence Force*. Canberra: Defence Publishing Service, 2000.

———. *Defence White Paper: Defending Australia*. Canberra: Australian Government Publishing Services, 1994.

———. *Defence White Paper: Defending Australia in the Asia Pacific Century, Force 2030*. Canberra: Defence Publishing Service, 2009.

———. *Defence White Paper: The Defence of Australia*. Canberra: Australian Government Publishing Services, 1987.

———. "FM 3-13 Information Operations: Doctrine, Tactics, Techniques, and Procedures." Fort Leavenworth: Department of the Army (US), 2003.

———. "National Counter-Terrorism Plan." Canberra, 2017.

———. "Operation Series: Information Activities." *Australian Defence Doctrine Publication 3.13*, 2013. http://www.defence.gov.au/FOI/Docs/Disclosures/330_1314_Document.pdf.

———. *The Integrated Investment Program*. Canberra: Australian Government Publishing Services, 2016.

Badsey, Stephen, Rob Havers, and Mark Grove. *The Falklands Conflict: Twenty Lessons for the Future*. London: Frank Cass, 2004.

Barker, Cat, Helen Portillo-Castro, and Monica Biddington. "Telecommunications and Other Legislation Amendment (Assistance and Access) Bill 2018." *Bills Digest* 49, no. December (2018).

Barker, Kenneth, ed. *The New International Study Bible*. Michigan: Zondervan Publishing House, 1995.

Barnes, Russell. "Armistice." United Kingdom: Historical Documentaries, 2008.

Barnett, Correlli. *The Lords of War: From Lincoln to Churchill, Supreme Command 1861-1945*. South Yorkshire: The Praetorian Press, 2012.

Barr, Niall J A. "The Elusive Victory: The BEF and the Operational Level of War, September 1918." In *War in the Age of Technology: Myriad Faces of Modern Armed Conflict*, edited by Geoffrey Jensen and Andrew Wiest, 211–38. New York and London: New York University Press, 2001.

Bartol, Kathryn M, David C Martin, Margaret Tein, and Graham Matthews. *Management: A Pacific Rim Focus*. North Melbourne: McGraw-Hill Book Company Australia Pty Limited, 1995.

Bass, Bernard. "From Transactional to Transformational Leadership: Learning to Share the Vision." *Organizational Dynamics* 18, no. 3 (1990): 19–31.

Beevor, Anthony. *The Second World War*. London: Phoenix, 2013.

Behr, Ines Von, Anais Reding, Charlie Edwards, and Luke Gribbon. "Radicalisation in the Digital Era: The Use of the Internet in 15 Cases of Terrorism and Extremism." Brussels, 2013.

Berger, J. "The Dangerous Spread of Extremist Manifestos: By Sharing the Writings of Terrorists, Media Outlets Can Amplifyier Their Impact." *The Atlantic*, 2019. https://www.theatlantic.com/ideas/archive/2019/02/christopher-hasson-was-inspired-breivik-manifesto/583567/.

Bergin, Anthony, Michael Clifford, David Connery, Tobias Freakin, Ken Gleiman, Stephanie Huang, Grace Hutchinson, et al. "Gen Y Jihadists: Preventing Radicalisation in Australia." Canberra, 2015.

Berry, Phillip A. "From London to Lashkar Gah: British Counter Narcotics Policies in Afghanistan (2001-2003)." *The International History Review* 40, no. 4 (2018): 713–31.

Bew, John, Martyn Frampton, and Inigo Gurruchaga. *Talking to Terrorists: Making Peace in Northern Ireland and the Basque Country*. London: Hurst and Co., 2009.

Biddle, Stephen. "Land Warfare: Theory and Practice." In *Strategy in the Contemporary World: An Introduction to Strategic Studies2*, edited by John Baylis, James Wirtz, Eliot Cohen, and Colin s Gray, 1st ed., 91–112. Oxford: Oxford University Press, 2002.

Birmingham, John. "Appeasing Jakarta: Australia's Complicity in the East Timor Tragedy." *Quarterly Essay*, no. 2 (2001): 7–90.

Blake, Felice. "Global Mass Violence: Examining Racial and Gendered Violence in the Twilight of Multiculturalism." *To Contextualise This Ethnic and Racial Studies* 40, no. 14 (2017): 2615–33.

Bliss, Tasker H. "The Evolution of Unified Command." *Foreign Affairs1* 1, no. 2 (1922): 1–30.

Borum, Randy. "Radicalization into Violent Extremism II: A Review of Conceptual Models and Empirical Research." *Journal of Strategic Studies* 4, no. 4 (2011): 37–63.

Bou, Jean Dr. "The German Spring Offensives, and the Western Front." Canberra: Australian National University, 2017.

Bouchat, Cj. *Dangerous Ground: The Spratly Islands and US Interests and Approaches*. United States Army War College Oress, 2013. http://oai.

dtic.mil/oai/oai?verb=getRecord&metadataPrefix=html&identifier=A DA591530.

Brachman, Jarret. "Strategists." In *Global Jihadism: Theory and Practice*, 79–105. Routledge, 2009.

Brands, Hal. *What Good Is Grand Strategy? Power and Purpose in American Statecraft from Harry S. Truman to George W. Bush*. London: Cornell University Press, 2016.

Brose, Eric. *The Kaiser's Army: The Politics of Mlitary Technology in Germany during the Machine Age, 1870-1918*. New York: Oxford University Press, 2001.

Browne, Ryan. "Top US General in Middle East Says Fight against ISIS 'far from Over.'" *CNN Politics*, 2019. https://edition.cnn.com/2019/03/07/politics/votel-isis-fight/index.html.

Bulos, Nabih. "Iraq's New War against Islamic State: Halting the Groups Budding Rural Resurgance." *Los Angeles Times*. March 8, 2019. https://www.latimes.com/world/middleeast/la-fg-iraq-intel-20190308-story.html.

Burleigh, Michael. *Blood and Rage: A Cultural History of Terrorism*. London: Harper Press, 2008.

Byman, Daniel. *Al Qeada, the Islamic State and the Global Jihadist Movement*. London: Oxford University Press, 2015.

Carr, Mathew. *The Infernal Machine: A History of Terrorism from the Assassination of Tsar Alexander II to Al-Qaeda*. New York: The New Press, 2006.

———. *The Infernal Machine: An Alternative History of Terrorism*. London: Hurst and Co., 2011.

Cashman, Greg, and Leonard C Robinson. *An Introduction to the Causes of War: Patterns of Interstate Conflict from World War 1 to Iraq*. Lanham: Rowman and Littlefield Publishers, Inc, 2007.

Cawthorne, Nigel. *Vietnam: A War Lost and Won*. London: Arturus Publishing Limited, 2010.

CBS. "On 9/11, Al Qaeda Leader Calls for Attacks on U.S. and Slams Jihad 'backtrackers.'" *CBS News*, 2019. https://www.cbsnews.com/news/september-11-attacks-anniversary-al-qaeda-leader-ayman-al-zawahri-calls-for-attacks-on-us-today-2019-09-11/.

Chang, Jung, and Jon Halliday. *Mao: The Unkown Story*. London: Jonathan Cape, 2005.

Chickering, Roger, Dennis Showalter, and Hans van de Ven, eds. *The Cambridge History of War*. Vol IV. Cambridge: Cambridge University Press, 2012.

Citlioglu, Ercan. "Terrorism Today and Tomorrow: An Analysis and Projection Study." *Homeland Security Organization in Defence Against Terrorism* 5, no. 1 (2012): 1–14.

Clausewitz, Carl Von. *Carl von Clausewitz: On War*. Edited by Michael Howard and Peter Paret. *On War*. New Yotk, 1976.

———. *On War*. Edited by Michael Howard and Peter Paret. *English*. Indexed. Princeton: Princeton University Press, 1976.

Collins, Lance, and Warren Reed. *Plunging Point: Intelligence Failures, Cover-Ups and Consequences.* Sydney: HarperCollins Publishers, 2005.

Connell, Norreys. *How Soldiers Fight: An Attempt to Depict for the Popular Understanding the Waging of War and the Soldiers Share in It.* London: James Bowden, 1899.

Cox, Sebastian. "Sir Arthur Harris and the Air Ministry." In *Airpower Leadership and Practice*, edited by Peter W. Gray and Sebastian Cox, 210–26. Shrivenham: Joint Doctrine and Concepts Centre, 2002.

Coyne, Christopher J, Abigail R Blanco, and Scott Burns. "The War on Drugs in Afghanistan: Another Failed Experiment with Interdiction." *The Independent Review* 21, no. 1 (2016): 95–119.

Crenshaw-Hutchinson, Martha. "The Concept of Revolutionary Terrorism." *The Journal of Conflict Resolution* 16, no. 3 (1972): 383–96.

Crenshaw, Martha. "The Causes of Terrorism." In *Terrorism Studies: A Reader*, edited by John Horgan and Kurt Braddock, 99–114. New York: Taylor and Francis, 1981.

———. "The Logic of Terrorism." In *Explaining Terrorism: Causes, Processes, and Consequences*, 111–23. New York: Routledge, 2011.

Cronin, A K. "Chapter One: The Strategies of Terrorism." *The Adelphi Papers* 47, no. 394 (2007): 11–22.

Cutler, Thomas J. *The Battle for Leyte Gulf: 23-26 October 1944.* New York: HarperCollins Publishers, 1994.

D. Clayton, James. "American Japanese Strategies in the Pacific War." In *Makers of Modern Strategy from Machiavelli to the Nuclear Age*, edited by Peter Paret, 703–32. Princeton University Press, 1971.

Damon, Arwa, Ghazi Balkiz, Muwafaq Mohammed, and Brice Laine. "Iraq Defeated ISIS More than a Year Ago. The Group's Revival Is Already Underway." *CNN World*, March 5, 2019.

David, Saul. *Military Blunders.* London: Robinson Publishing, 1997.

Dean, Peter J. "Anzacs and Yanks: US and Australian Operations at the Beachhead Battles." In *Australia 1942: In the Shadow of War*, edited by Peter J. Dean, 217–39. Melbourne: CUP, 2013.

———. "MacArthurs War: Strategy, Command and Plans for the 1943 Offensives." In *Australian 1943: The Liberation of New Guinea*, edited by Peter J. Dean, 45–67. Melbourne: CUP, 2104.

Dean, Peter J., and Kevin Holzimmer. "The Southwest Pacific Area: Military Strategy and Operations 1944-45." In *Australia 1944-45: Victory in the Pacific*, edited by Peter J. Dean, 28–50. Melbourne: Cambridge University Press, 2014.

Dearden, Lizzie. "Islamophobic Incidents Rocket by 600% in UK during Week after New Zealand Terror Attack." *Independent*, 2019.

Deeb, Sarah El. "Hundreds Leave IS-Held Area in Syria as Fighting Slows down." *AP News*, 2019.

Delbridge, Arthur, and Bernard J, eds. *The Macquarie Concise Dictionary*. 2nd ed. Sydney: The Macquarie Library Pty Ltd, 1988.

Dibb, Paul. *Review of Australia's Defence Capabilities: Report to the Minister for Defence by Mr Paul Dibb*. Canberra: Australian Government Publishing Services, 1986.

Dick, Rolf Van, and Rudolf Kerschreiter. "The Social Identity Approach to Effective Leadership: An Overview and Some Ideas on Cross-Cultural Generalizability." *Front. Bus. Res. China* 10, no. 3 (2016): 363–84.

Diest, Wilhelm. "Strategy and Unlimited Warfare in Germany: Moltke, Falkenhayn and Ludendorff." In *Great War, Total War: Combat and Mobilisation on the Western Front, 1914-1918*, edited by Roger Chickering and Stig Forster, 265–79. Washington D.C.: Cambridge University Press, 2000.

Dishman, Chris. "The Leaderless Nexus: When Crime and Terror Converge." In *Terrorism Studies: A Reader*, edited by John Horgan and Kurt Braddock, 331–44. New York: Routledge, 2012.

Douhet, Giulio. "The Command of the Air." In *Roots of Strategy: Book 4*, edited by David Jablonsky, 263–408. Mechanicsburg: Stackpole Books, 1999.

Dupont, Alan. "The Australian-Indonesia Security Agreement." *The Australian Quarterly* 68, no. 2 (1996): 49–62.

Duzgun, Saban Ali. "Winning Back Religion: Countering the Misuse of Scripture." *Homeland Security Organization in Defence Against Terrorism* 5, no. 15 (2012): 15–33.

Echevarria II, Antulio J. "Clausewitz and the Nature of the War on Terror." In *Clausewitz in the Twenty-First Century*, edited by Hew Strachan and Andreas Herberg-Rothe, 197–218. London: Oxford University Press, 2007.

Elias, Salih. "Two Dead, 24 Wounded in Blast in Central Mosul." *Reuters World News*, March 1, 2019.

English, John. "The Operational Art: Development in the Theories of War." In *The Operational Art: Developments in the Theories of War*, edited by BJC McKercher and Michael A Hennessy, 8–29. Westport, 1996.

Falk, Richard. *The Great Terror War*. Gloucestershire: Arris Books, 2003.

Farrall, Leah. "Afghanistan." In *Counterterrorism Yearbook 2018*, edited by Isaac Kfir, Sofia Patel, and Micha Batt, 51–58. Barton: Australian Strategic Policy Institute, 2018.

Farwell, James P. "The Media Strategy of ISIS." *Survival: Global Politics and Startegy* 56, no. 6 (2014): 49–55.

Fealy, Greg. "Philippines." In *Counterterrorism Yearbook 2018*, edited by Isaac Kfir, Sofia Patel, and Micha Batt, 31–36. Canberra: Australian Strategic Policy Institute, 2018.

Fearon, James D, and David D Laitin Stanford. "Ethnicity, Insurgency, and Civil War." *The American Political Science Review* 97, no. 1 (2003): 75–90.

Field, Chris. "Testing the Tenets of Manoeuvre: Australia's First Amphibious Assualt since Gallipoli, The 9th Australian Division at Lae, 4-16 September 1943." Canberra, 2012.

Fishman, Brian H. *The Master Plan: ISIS, Al-Qaeda, and the Jihad Strategy for Final Victory*. Yale: Yale University Press Books, 2016.

Flower, Desmond, and James Reeves. *The War 1939-1945*. London: Cassell and Company LTD, 1960.

Forest, James J F. *The Terrorism Lectures*. Orange County: Nortia Press, 2012.

Forgas, Joseph P. *Interpersonal Behaviour: The Psychology of Social Interaction*. Sydney: Pergamon Press, 1989.

Freedman. "Grand Strategy and Levels." Canberra: Australian National University, 2017.

French, David. "The Strategy of Unlimted Warfare? Kitchener, Robertson and Haig." In *Great War, Total War: Combat and Mobilisation on the Western Front, 1914-1918*, edited by Roger Chickering and Stig Forster, 281–95. Washington D.C.: Cambridge University Press, 2000.

Fromkin, David. "The Strategy of Terrorism." *Foreign Affairs* 53, no. 4 (1975): 683–98.

Galbraith, Peter W. *The End of Iraq: How American Incompetence Created a War Without End*. London: Simon and Schuster, 2006.

Gerges, Fawaz. *Rise and Fall of Al-Qaeda*. New York: Oxford University Press, 2011.

Gerges, Fawaz A. *ISIS: A History*. Princeton: Princeton University Press, 2016.

Gill, Paul, Noemie Bouhana, and John Morrison. "Individual Disengagement from Terrorist Groups." In *Terrorism and Political Violence*, edited by Caroline Kenndey-Pipe, Gordon Clubb, and Simon Mabon, 243–67. London: SAGE Publications Ltd, 2015.

Gingell, John. "'Bomber' Harris - The Commander and The Man." *RUSI Journal* 130(2), no. June (1985): 65–66.

"Global Terrorism Database: ISIL." *Study of Terrorism and Responses to Terrorism*, 2019.

Goodwin, Jeff. "A Theory of Categorical Terrorism." *Special Forces* 84, no. 4 (2004): 2027–46.

Gray, Colin S. *Fighting Talk: Forty Maxims on War, Peace and Strategy*. Lincoln: Potomac Books, 2009.

Green, Michael J., Peter J. Dean, Brendan Taylor, and Zack Cooper. "The ANZUS Alliance in an Ascending Asia." *The Centre of Gravity Series2*, no. July (2015): 1–31.

Grossman, Dave Lt.Col. *On Killing: The Psychological Cost of Learning to Kill in War and Society*. Revised. New York: Hachette Book Group, 1995.

Guinn, Paul. *British Strategy and Politics 1914-1918*. Oxford: Oxford University Press, 1965.

Gyngell, Allan. "Ambition : The Emerging Foreign Policy of the Rudd Government." *Lowy Institute*, no. December (2008).

———. "Australia-Indonesia." In *Australia as an Asia-Pacific Regional Power: Fiendships in Flux?*, edited by Brendan Taylor, 97–115. London and New York: Routledge, 2007.

Haldane, Lord. "Naval Review" 70, no. 4 (1982).

Hall, Benjamin. *Inside ISIS: The Brutal Rise of a Terrorist Army.* New York: Hachette Book Group, 2015.

Hall, Richard. "ISIS Caliphate Defeated: How Did It Happen and Do They Still Pose a Threat?" *Independent,* 2019.

Ham, Paul. *Hiroshima and Nagasaki.* Sydney: HarperCollins Publishers, 2011.

Harris, Arthur. *Bomber Offensive.* London: Collins, 1947.

Hart, Liddell. *History of the First World War.* Revised. London: Redwood Burn Limited, 1973.

———. *Strategy.* Second Rev. London: First Meridian Printing, 1991.

Hartley, Dean S. "The DIME/PMESII Paradigm." In *Unconventional Conflict,* edited by Dean S Hartley, 99–106. New York: Springer International Publishing, 2017.

Haslam, Alexander S. *Psychology in Organisations: The Social Identity Approach.* London: SAGE Publications Ltd, 2004.

Haslam, Alexander S., Stephen D. Reicher, and Michael J. Platow. *The New Psychology of Leadership: Identity, Influence and Power,* 2009.

Helmus, Todd C. "Why and How Some People Become Terrorists." In *Social Science for Counter Terrorism: Putting the Pieces Together,* edited by Paul Davis and Kim Cragin, 71–112. New York: RAND Corporation, 2009.

Hennessy, Michael A, and BJC McKercher. "Introduction." In *The Operational Art: Developments in the Theories of War,* edited by BJC McKercher and Michael A Hennessy, 1–6. Wesport: Praeger, 1996.

Hennigan, W. "The U.S. Sent Its Most Advanced Fighter Jets to Blow Up Cheap Opium Labs. Now It's Canceling the Program." *Time,* 2019. https://time.com/5534783/iron-tempest-afghanistan-opium/.

Hersh, Seymour M. "Torture at Abu Ghraib." *The New Yorker* May (2004). https://www.newyorker.com/magazine/2004/05/10/torture-at-abu-ghraib.

Hess, Gary R. *Vietnam: Explaining America's Lost War.* Malden: Wiley Blackwell, 2015.

Hoffman, Bruce. *Inside Terrorism.* New York: Columbia University Press, 2006.

———. "The Changing Face of Al Qaeda and the Global War on Terrorism." In *Terrorism Studies: A Reader,* edited by John Horgan and Kurt Braddock, 392–402. New York: Routledge, 2012.

Hoffman, Bruce, and Fernando Reinares. "Conclusion." In *The Evolution of the Global Terrorist Threat: From 9/11 to Osama Bin Ladens Death.,* edited by Bruce Hoffman and Fernando Reinares, 618–39. New York: Columbia University Press, 2014.

Horgan, John. *The Psychology of Terrorism.* New York: Routledge, 2006.

———. *The Psychology of Terrorism.* Revised an. New York: Routledge, 2014.

Horner, David. *High Command: Australia and Allied Strategy 1939-1945.* Sydney: George Allen and Unwin Australia Pty Ltd, 1982.

"House of Representatives Official Hansard." *No Author* April, no. 15 (1967): 1139–1209.

Hughes, Matthew. "General Allenby and the Palestine Campaign, 1917–18." *Journal of Strategic Studies* 19, no. February 2013 (1996): 59–88.

Hughes, Matthew, and Matthew Seligmann. "People and the Tides of History: Does Personality Matter in the First World War?" In *Leadership in Conflict 1914-1918*, edited by Matthew Hughes and Matthew Seligmnn, 1–37. South Yorkshire: Leo Cooper, 2000.

"IS Is down but Not out." *The Canberra Times*. March 6, 2019.

"It Is Two and Half Minutes to Midnight." *Science and Security Board: Bulletin of the Atomic Scientists*, no. Jan (2017): 1–16.

Jenkins, Brian, and Bruce Butterworth. "An Anlaysis of Vehicle Ramming as a Terrorist Tactic." *Security Perspective*, 2018.

Jennings, Peter et al. "Chinese Investment in the Port of Darwin: A Strategic Risk for Australia?" *Strategic Insights* 101, no. Dec (2015): 1–20.

Jerad, Jolene. "Idelogical Rehabilitation: A Necessary Component of the Counter Terrorism Strategy in Singapore." *Homeland Security Organization in Defence Against Terrorism* 5 (2012): 201–11.

Jimenez, Fernando. "The Terrorist Challenge and the Governments Response." *Terrorism and Political Violence* 14, no. 4 (1992): 119–20.

Jomini, Antoine Henri de. *The Art of War*. E-Book. Rockville: Arc Manor, 2007.

Kaempf, Sebastian. "Violence and Victory: Guerrilla Warfare, 'Authentic Self-Affirmation' and the Overthrow of the Colonial State." *Third World Quarterly2* 30, no. 1 (2009): 129–46.

Kainikara, Sanu. *Essays on Air Power*. Canberra: Air Power Development Centre, 2012.

Kamil, Imam. "Core Values of Islam." *Islam Religion*, 2013.

Kenney, George C. "General Kenney Reports: A Personal History of the Pacific War." New York, 1949.

Keogh, Colonel (retd), E. G. *The South West Pacific 1941-45*. Melbourne: Grayflower Productions Pty Ltd, 1965.

Kiesling, Eugenia C. "Resting Comfortably on Its Laurels: The Army of Interwar France." In *The Challenge of Change: Military Institutions and New Realities 1918-1941*, edited by Harold R Winton and David R Mets, 1–28. Lincoln: University of Nebraska Press, 2000.

Kilcullen, David. *Counter Insurgency*. Carlton North: Scribe Publications, 2010.

———. *Out of the Mountains: The Coming Age of the Urban Guerrilla*. Melbourne: Scribe Publications, 2013.

Knippenberg, Daan, V., and Naomi Ellemers. "Social Identity and Group Performance: Identification as the Key to Group-Oriented Effort." In *Social Identity at Work: Developing Theory for Organizational Practice*, edited by Alexander S. Haslam, Daan Van Knippenberg, Michael J. Platow, and Naomi Ellemers, 29–42. New York: Psychology Press, 2003.

"Koran," n.d.

Kozak, Warren. *Curtis LeMay: Strategist and Tactician*. Washington D.C.: Regnery History, 2009.

Kramer, Franklin D., Larry Wentz, and Stuart Starr. "I-Power: The Information Revolution and Stability Operations." *Defence Horizon* 55, no. Feb (2007): 1–8.

Kruglanski, Arie E, and Edward Orehek. "The Role of the Quest for Personal Significance in Motivating Terrorism." In *The Psychology of Social Conflict and Aggression*, edited by Arie W Kruglanski and K Williams, 153–64. New York: Psychology Press, 2011.

Kuehn, John T. "The U.S. Navy General Board and Naval Arms Lmitation: 1022-1937." *The Journal of Military History* 74, no. 4 (2010): 1129–60.

Law, Randall D. *Terrorism a History*. 2nd ed. Cambridge: Polity Press, 2016.

Leonhard, Robert. *The Art of Maneuver: Maneuver-Warfare Theory and the Airland Battle*. Novato: Presido Press, 1991.

Lesperance, Wayne F Jnr. "The Rise of the Islamic State." In *The New Islamic State: Ideology, Religion and Violent Extremism in the 21st Century*, edited by Jack Covarrubias and Robert J Jnr Pauly, 15–28. Oxon: Ashgate, 2016.

Lind, William S. *Maneuver Warfare Handbook*. Boulder: Westview Press Inc, 1985.

Logevall, Fredrick. "The Indo-China Wars and the Cold War, 1945-1975." In *Cambridge History of the Cold War Vol II*, 281–302. Cambridge: Cambridge University Press, 2009.

Long, Gavin. *MacArthur: As Military Commander*. Sydney: Angus and Robertson, 1969.

Lupfer, Timothy T. "The Dynamics of Doctrine: The Changes in German Tactical Doctrine During the First World War." *Leavenworth Papers*. Vol. 4. Fort Leavenworth, 1981.

Lutz, James M, and Brenda J Lutz. "The Rise of the New Left and the Failure of Communism: Increasing Terrorism on a Global Scale." In *Terrorism: Origins and Evolution*, 99–128. Gordonsville: Palgrave Macmillan, 2005.

Mahnken, Thomas G. "Strategy Theory." In *Strategy in the Contemporary World: An Introduction to Strategic Studies*, edited by John Baylis, James Wirtz, Colin S. Gray, and Eliot Cohen, 66–81. Oxford University Press, 2007.

Makarenko, Tamara. "The Crime-Terror Continuum: Tracing the Interplay between Transnational Organised Crime and Terrorism." *Global Crime* 6, no. 1 (2004): 129–45.

Malkasian, Carter. *A History of Modern Wars of Attrition*. Wesport: Praeger, 2002.

———. *The Korean War 1950-1953*. Osprey Publishing, n.d.

Manne, Robert. *The Mind of Islamic State*. Carlton: Redback Quarterly, 2016.

Mao. "Slected Works of Mao Tse-Tung." *Foriegn Languages Press* II, no. May 1938 (1967): 1–26.

Marshall, PJ. "1783-1870: An Expanding Empire." In *British Empire*, edited by Marshall PJ, 24–51. Cambridge: Cambridge University Press, 1996.

Martin, Gus. *Essentials of Terrorism*. 3rd ed. London: SAGE Publications Ltd, 2014.

Maslow, Abraham. *A Theory on Human Motivation*. 1943rd ed. Mansfield Centre: Martino Publishing, 2014.

Massaro, Chris. "As Caliphate Crumbles, ISIS Fighters Rage over Absent Leader Al-Baghdadi." *Fox News*, 2019. https://www.foxnews.com/world/as-caliphate-crumbles-isis-fighters-rage-over-absent-leader-al-baghdadi.

McAllister, Bradley, and Alex P Schmid. "Theories of Terrorism: Social Identity Theory." In *The Routledge Hanbook of Terrorism Reserach*, 201–72. London: Routledge, 2011.

Mccarthy, John. "Douhet and the Decisiveness of Air Power." In *The Strategists*, edited by Hugh Smith, 65–72. Australian Defence Studies Centre, 2001.

McCauley, Clark, and Sophia Moskalenko. *Friction: How Radicalization Happens to Them and US*. New York: Oxford University Press, 2011.

McCulloch, Jude, and Sharon Pickering. "Counter-Terrorism: The Law and Policing of Pre-Emption." In *Counter-Terrorism and Beyond: The Culture of Law and Justice After 9/11*, edited by Nicola McGarrity, Andrew Lynch, and George Williams, 13–29. New York: Routledge, 2010.

Mendelsohn, Barak. "Formal Organizational Expansion." In *The Al-Qaeda Franchise: The Expansion of Al-Qaeda and Its Consequences*, 1–21. Oxford: Oxford University Press, 2009.

Merari, A. "Terrorism as a Strategy of Insurgency." In *The History of Terrorism: From Antiquity to Al Qaeda*, edited by G Chaliand and A Blin, 12–54. Berkeley: University of California Press, 2007.

Messenger, Charles. *"Bomber" Harris and the Strategic Bombing Offensive, 1939-1945*. London: Arms and Armour Press, 1984.

Michael, George. "Leaderless Resistance: The New Face of Terrorism." *Defence Studies* 12, no. 2 (2012): 257–82.

Middlebrook, Martin. "Marshal of the Royal Air Force: Sir Arthur Harris." In *The Warlords: Military Commanders of the Twentieth Century*, edited by Michael Carver, 317–33. London: Weidenfeld and Nicolson, 1976.

Miller, Richard B. *Terror, Religion and Liberal Thought*. New York: Columbia University Press, 2010.

Miller, Seumas. "Terrorism and Collective Responsibility." In *Terrorism and Counter-Terrorism: Ethics and Liberal Democracy*, edited by Seumas Miller, 60–82. Hokoken: John Wiley and Sons, Inc, 2008.

Millett, Allan R. "Assault from the Sea: The Development of Amphibious Warfare between the Wars - the American, British and Japanese Experiences." In *Military Innovation in the Interwar Period*, edited by Williamson Murray and Allan R Millett, 50–95. Cambridge: Cambridge University Press, 1996.

———. "Patterns of Military Innovation in the Interwar Period." In *Military Innovation in the Interwar Period*, edited by Williamson Murray and Allan R Millett, 329–68. Cambridge: Cambridge University Press, 1996.

Moghaddam, Fathali M. "The Staircase to Terrorism." In *Psychology of Terrorism*, edited by Bruce Bognar, Lisa M Brown, Larry E Beutler, James

N Breckenridge, and Philip G Zimbardo, 69–80. New York: Oxford University Press, 2007.

Monk, Paul M. "Secret Intelligence And Escape Clauses : Australia and the Indonesian Annexation of East Timor 1963-76." *Critical Asian Studies* 33:2 (2001): 181–208. doi:10.1080/14672710121652.

Moran, Mathew. "Terroris and the Banlieues: The Charlie Hebdo Attack in Context." *Modern and Contemporary France* 25, no. 3 (2017): 315–32.

Moxon-Brownw, Edward. *Spain and the ETA: The Bid for Basque Autonomy.* London: Centre of Security and Conflict Studies, 1987.

Mulholland, Andrew. *The Korean War.* IBook. William Cpllins, n.d.

Munoz, Arturo. *U.S. Military Information Operations in Afghanistan: Effectiveness of Psychological Operations 2001-2010.* Santa Monica: RAND Corporation, 2012.

Murray, Williamson. "Curtis E. Lemay: Airman Extraordinary." In *Air Commanders*, edited by John A Olsen, 132–43. Dulles: Potomac Books, 2013.

"NATO Mission Iraq (NMI)." *NATO Factsheet*, 2018.

Neame, Philip. *German Strategy in the Great War.* London: Edward Arnold and Co., n.d.

Neiberg, Michael S. "World War 1." In *The Cambridge History of War: Volume IV*, edited by Roger Chickering, Dennis Showalter, and Hans van de Ven, 315–43. Cambridge: Cambridge University Press, 2012.

Neillands, Robin. "Facts and Myths About Bomber Harris." *RUSI Journal* 146(2), no. April (2001): 69–73.

Newman, Edward. "Exploring the 'Root Causes' of Terrorism." *Studies in Conflict and Terrorism* 29, no. 8 (2006): 749–72.

Nitze, Paul H. "The Evolution of National Security Policy and the Vietnam War." In *The Lessons of Vietnam*, edited by Scott W. Thompson and Donaldson D. Frizzell, 1–17. St. Lucia: University of Queensland Press, 1977.

Noricks, Darcy. "The Root Causes of Terrorism." In *Social Science for Counter Terrorism: Putting the Pieces Together*, edited by P Davis and K Cragin, 11–70. New York and London: RAND Corporation, 2009.

Northhouse, Peter. *Leadership Theory and Practice.* London: SAGE Publications Ltd, 1997.

Nye, Joseph S Jnr. *Soft Power: The Means to Success in World Politics.* New York: PublicAffairs, 2009.

O'Malley, Padraig. "Migration and Conflict." *New England Journal of Public Policy* 30, no. 2 (2018): 1–15.

O'Neill, Robert. *Australia in the Korean War 1950-53.* Canberra: Australian Government Publishing Services, 1981.

Odgers, George. *100 Years of Australians at War.* Sydney: New Holland, 2001.

———. *Air War Against Japan 1943-1945.* Adelaide: The Advertiser Printing Office, 1957.

Oleksy, Walter. *Military Leaders of World War II.* New York: Facts On File Inc, 1994.

Olsen, Andreas John. "Operation Desert Storm 1991." In *A History of Air Warfare*, edited by John Andreas Olsen, 177–200. Washington D.C.: Potomac Books, 2010.

Osinga, Frans P B. *Science, Strategy and War: The Strategic Theory of John Boyd*. New York: Routledge, 2007.

Otto, Gustav A. "The End of Operational Phases At Last." *Interagency Journal* 8, no. 3 (2017): 78–86.

Pape, Robert A. *Dying to Win: The Strategic Logic of Suicide Terrorism*. New York: Random House, 2005.

Paret, Peter. "Clausewitz." In *Makers of Modern Strategy from Machiavelli to the Nuclear Age Edition*, edited by Peter Paret, 182–213. Princeton: Princeton University Press, 1986.

Parker, Robert, A, C. *Struggle for Survival: The History of the Second World War*. Oxford and New York: Oxford University Press, 1990.

Parker, Claire. "The Islamic State Is far from Defeated. Here's What You Need to Know about Its Affiliate in Afghanistan." *The Washington Post*. August 19, 2019.

Pedraja, Rene De La. "The Argentine Air Force versus Britain in the Falklands Islands, 1982." In *Why Air Forces Fail: The Anatomy of Defeat*, edited by Robin Higham and Stephen J. Harris, 227–56. Lexington: The University Press of Kentucky, 2006.

Pedrozo, Raul. "China versus Vietnam: An Analysis of the Competing Claims in the South China Sea." *CNA Analysis and Solutions* August (2014): 1–142.

Philpott, William. "Germany's Last Cards." In *Attrition: Fighting the First World War*, 301–22. New York: Overlook Press, 2014.

———. "Marshal Ferdinand Foch and Allied Victory." In *Leadership in Conflict 1914-1918*, edited by Matthew Hughes and Matthew Seligmann, 38–53. South Yorkshire: Leo Cooper, 2000.

Pike, Douglas. *The People's Army of Vietnam*. Novato: Presido Press, 1986.

Powell, Jonathan. "ETA's Weapons Surrender Brings to an End 50 Years of Killing." *Financial Times*, 2017.

Price, Edward H. "The Strategy and Tactics of Revolutionary Terrorism." *Comparative Studies in Society and History* 19, no. 1 (1977): 52–66.

Prince, Stephen. "British Command and Control in the Falklands Campaign." *Defense and Security Analysis* 18, no. May (2002): 333–49. doi:10.1080/14 75179022000024466.

Prior, Robin, and Trevor Wilson. *The Somme*. London: Yale University Press, 2005.

"Pro-ISIS Groups in Mandanao and Their Links to Indonesia and Malaysia," 2016.

Probert, Henry. *Bomber Harris: His Life and Times*. London: Greenhill Books., 2006.

———. *High Commanders of the Royal Air Force*. London: The Air Historical Branch, 1991.

Qassim, Adbul-Zahra. "Bombs in Iraq's Mosul Kill 1 Person, Injure 17." *AP News*, 2019. https://www.apnews.com/0256fd63080847c89885ae038b31f546.

Ranjan, Vinit, and Gaurav Agrawal. "FDI Inflow Determinants in BRIC Countries: A Panel Data Analysis." *International Business Research* 4, no. OCT (2011): 1–9.

Rapoport, David. "The Four Waves of Modern Terror: International Dimensions and Consequences." In *An International History of Terrorism: Western and Non-Western Experiences*, edited by Jussi Hanimaki and Bernhard Blumenau, 281–310. New York: Routledge, 2013.

Reicher, Stephen D., Alexander S. Haslam, and Michael J. Platow. "The New Psychology of Leadership." *Scientific American Mind*, no. August/ September (2007): 22–29.

Reiji, Masuda. "Sunken Fleet: Transport War." In *Japan at War: An Oral History*, edited by Haruko Taya Cook and Theodore F. Cook, 300–304. Sydney: HarperCollins Publishers, 1992.

Rice, Anthony J. "Command and Control: The Essence of Coalition Warfare." *Parameters* 27, 1, no. Spring (1997): 152–67.

Richards, Julian. "Intelligence and Counterterrorism." In *Routledge Hanbook of Terrorism and Counterterrorism*, edited by Andrew Silke, 395–404. New York: Routledge, 2019.

Ricks, Thomas E. *Fiasco. The American Military Adventure in Iraq*, 2006.

———. "Kilcullen Speaks: On COIN Going out of Style, His Recent Book, Syria and More." *Foreign Policy*, 2014. https://foreignpolicy.com/2014/02/12/kilcullen-speaks-on-coin-going-out-of-style-his-recent-book-syria-and-more/.

"Rights Group Urges Investigations in Murder of Journalist East of Baghdad." *The Baghdad Post*, 2019.

Roach, Kent. "The Eroding Disctinction between Intelligence and Evidence in Terrorism Investigations." In *Counter-Terrorism and Beyond: The Culture of Law and Justice After 9/11*, 48–68. London: Routledge, 2010.

Robbins, Stephen, T Waters-Marsh, R Cacioppe, and B Millett. *Organisation Behaviour: Concepts, Controversies and Applications*. Sydney: Prentice Hall, 1994.

Rogers, Katie, Rukmini Callimachi, and Helene Cooper. "Trump Declares ISIS '100%' Defeated in Syria. '100% Not True,' Ground Reports Say." *New York Times*. February 28, 2019.

Rothenberg, Gunther E. "Moltke, Schlieffen, and the Doctrine of Strategic Envelopment." In *Makers of Modern Strategy from Machiavelli to the Nuclear Age*, edited by Peter Paret, 296–325. Princeton: Princeton University Press, 1986.

Rothgeb, Wayne P. *New Guinea Skies: A Fighter Pilots View of World War II*. Ames: Iowa State University Press, 1992.

Scarlett, Craig. "Sir Arthur 'Bomber' Harris: An Effective Leader in Command?" *Geddes Papers*, 2004, 33–41.

Sedgwick, Mark. "IS in Syria." In *The New Islamic State: Ideology, Religion and Violent Extremism in the 21st Century*, edited by Jack Covarrubias and Robert J Jnr Pauly, 93–112. Oxon: Ashgate, 2016.

Seib, P, and D Janbek. "Terrorists' Online Strategies." In *Global Terrorism and the New Media*, 43–60. New York: Routledge, 2011.

Shamir, Boas, Eliav Zakay, Esther Brainin, and Micha Popper. "Leadership and Social Identification in Military Units: Direct and Indirect Relationships." *Journal of Applied Social Psychology* 20, no. 3 (2000): 612–40.

Sivagnanam, Maya, and J P I A G Charvat. "CONTEST II - The United Kingdom's Counter Terroris Strategy." *Homeland Security Organization in Defence Against Terrorism* 5 (2012): 63–72.

Slater, Matthew J., Andrew L. Evans, and Martin J. Turner. "Implementing a Social Identity Approach for Effective Change Management." *Journal of Change Management* 16, no. 1 (2016): 18–37.

Smith, Neil. *The Vietnam War*. London: HarperCollins Publishers, 2012.

Smith, Rupert. *The Utility of Force: The Art of War in the Modern World*. IBook: Penguin, 2008.

Smyth, Sir John. *Leadership in Battle*. London: David and Charles (Holdings) Limited, 1975.

Sookhdeo, Patrick. *Understanding Islamist Terrorism: The Islamic Doctrine of War*. McLean: Isaac Publishing, 2009.

Speckhard, Anne, Ardian Shajkovci, and Neima Izadi. "Using Counter-Narrative Campaigns to 'Break the ISIS Brand' in Iraq." *Government Technology and Services Coalitions: Homeland Security*, 2018.

Speckhard, Anne, and Ahmet Yayla. "The ISIS Emni: Origins and Inner Workings of ISIS's Intelligence Apparatus." *Perspectives on Terrorism* 11, no. 1 (2017): 1–15.

Spindlove, Jeremey R, and Clifford E Simonsen. *Terrorism Today: The Past, The Players and The Future*. 6th ed. New York: Pearson, 2018.

Stanford_University. "The Islamic State." *Mapping Militant Organisations: The Islamic State*, 2019. web.stanford.edu/group/mappingmilitants/cgi-bin/groups/view/1.

State, US Department of. "Foreign Terrorist Organisations." Accessed April 18, 1BC. https://www.state.gov/j/ct/rls/other/des/123085.htm.

Steffens, Niklas K, S Alexander Haslam, Stephen D Reicher, Michael J Platow, Katrien Fransen, Jie Yang, Michelle K Ryan, Jolanda Jetten, Kim Peters, and Filip Boen. "Leadership as Social Identity Management : Introducing the Identity Leadership Inventory (ILI) to Assess and Validate a Four-Dimensional Model ☆." *The Leadership Quarterly* 25, no. 5 (2014): 1001–24.

Sterman, John D. *Business Dynamics: Systems Thinking and Modeling for a Complex World. Management*. Boston: Irwin McGraw-Hill, 2000.

Stevens, Tim, and Peter R Neumann. "Countering Online Radicalisation: A Strategy for Action." London, 2009.

Stone, Norman. *World War One: A Short History*. Second. New York: Perseus Books Group, 2009.

Strachan, Hew. *Carl von Clausewitz's On War*. Vancouver: Douglas and McIntyre, 2008.

Strassler, Robert B. *Thucydides: A Comprehensive Guide to the Peloponnesian War*. New York: Schuster Inc, 1996.

Sutalan, Zeynep. "Major Ideologies Motivating Terrorism and Main Characteristics of Terrorism." In *Organizational and Psychological Aspects of Terrorism*, edited by Centre of Excellence Defence Against Terrorism, 13–21. Ankara: IOS Press, 2008.

———. "Major Ideologies Motivating Terrorism and Main Characteristics of Terrorism." In *Centre of Excellence Defence Against Terrorism. Organizational and Psychological Aspects of Terrorism*, 13–23. Ankara: IOS Press, 2008.

Taaffe, Stephen R. *MacArthur's Jungle War: The 1944 New Guinea Campaign*. Lawrence: University of Kansas Press, 1988.

Tanter, Richard. "Shared Roblems, Shared Interests: Reframing Australia-Indonesia Security Relations." In *Knowing Indonesia: Intersections of Self, Discipline and Nation*, edited by Jemma Purdey, 1–38. Melbourne: Monash University Press, 2012.

Taylor, Adam. "New Zealand Suspect Allegedly Claimed 'Brief Contact' with Norwegian Mass Murderer Anders Breivik." *The Washington Post*, 2019. https://www.washingtonpost.com/world/2019/03/15/new-zealand-suspect-allegedly-claimed-brief-contact-with-norwegian-mass-murderer-anders-breivik/.

Taylor, Brendan. "Introduction." In *Australia as an Asia-Pacific Regional Power: Fiendships in Flux?*, edited by Brendan Taylor, 25–32. New York and London: Routledge, 2007.

Tembo, Edgar. *US-UK Counter-Terrorism after 9/11: A Qualitative Approach*. New York: Routledge, 2014.

Terraine, John. *Ordeal of Victory*. Philadelphia: J.B. Lippincott Company, 1963.

"Terrorism Timeline." *Since 9/11*. Accessed September 19, 2019. https://since911.com/explore-911/terrorism-timeline#jump_time_item_391.

"The Hong Kong Protests Explained in 100 and 500 Words." *BBC News*, 2019. https://www.bbc.com/news/world-asia-china-49317695.

Thompson, Scott, and Donaldson D. Frizzell, eds. *The Lessons of Vietnam*. St. Lucia: University of Queensland Press, 1977.

Thomson, Mark. "Lecture: Trade, Investment and Strategy." Canberra, 2017.

Tillman, Barrett. *LeMay*. New York: Palgrave Macmillan, 2007.

Trevino, Jose A. "Spains Internal Security: The Basque Autonomous Police Force." In *Terrorism in Europe*, edited by Yohan Alexander and Kenneth A Myers, 142–53. London: Croom Helm, 1982.

Tucker, Spence T., ed. *500 Great Military Leaders*. Santa Barbara: ABC-CLIO, n.d.

"UN Assistance Mission for Iraq." *United Nations Iraq*, 2019.

Unknown. *Field Service Regulations: Part 1*. London: Harrison and Sons, 1901.

Vandervort, Bruce. "War and Imperial Expansion." In *Cambridge History of War: Volume IV*, edited by Roger Chickering, Dennis Showalter, and Hans van de Ven, 108–47. Cambridge: Cambridge University Press, 2012.

Wade, Norman. *The Military Engagement Security, Cooperation and Stability Smartbook: Foreign Train, Advise and Assist*. Lakeland: The Lightning Press, 2016.

Walker, Clive. "United Kingdom." In *Counterterrorism Yearbook 2018*, edited by Isaac Kfir, Sofia Patel, and Micha Batt, 141–49. Canberra: Australian Strategic Policy Institute, 2018.

Wallach, Jehuda L. *Uneasy Coalition: The Entente Experience in World War 1*. Westport: Greenwood Press, 1993.

Walsh, Johhny. "A Deal With the Taliban Is Only the First Step Toward Peace." *Foreign Affairs*, 2019. ttps://www.foreignaffairs.com/articles/afghanistan/2019-09-05/deal-taliban-only-first-step-toward-peace.

Walton, Dale, C. "Weapons Technology in the Two Nuclear Ages." In *The Cambridge History of War: Volume IV*, edited by Roger Chickering, Dennis Shoalwater, and Hans van de Ven, 1277–1334. New York: Cambridge University Press, 2012.

Webb, Brandon, Jack Murphy, and Peter Nealen. *The Isis Solution: How Unconventional Thinking and Special Operations Can Eliminate Radical Islam*. New York: St. Martins Press, 2016.

Weimann, G. "Emerging Trends." In *Terrorism in Cyberspace: The Next Generation*, 2–71. New York: Columbia University Press, 2015.

Wesley, Michael. "Australia's Grand Strategy and the 2016 Defence White Paper." *Security Challenges* 12, no. 1 (2016): 19–30.

Westad, Odd Arne. "The Wars after the War, 1945-1954." In *The Cambridge History of War: Volume IV*, edited by Roger Chickering, Dennis Showalter, and Hans van de Ven, Ibook. Cambridge: Cambridge University Press, 2012.

White, Jonathan R. *Terrorism and Homeland Security*. New York: Thomson Wadsworth, 2006.

Whittaker, David. *The Terrorism Reader*. London: Routledge, 2001.

Wiryono, Sastrohandoyo. "An Indonesian View: Indonesia, Australia and the Region." In *Different Societies, Shared Futures: Australia and the Region*, edited by John Monfries, 11–19. Singapore: Institute of Southeast Asian Studies, 2006.

Wood, Jack, Joseph Wallace, Rachid M. Zeffane, David J. Kennedy, John R. Schermerhorn, James G. Hunt, and Richard Osborn. *Organisational Behaviour: An Asia-Pacific Perspective*. Milton: John Wiley and Sons, Inc, 1998.

Woodworth, Paddy. "Why Do They Kill? The Basque Conflict in Spain." *World Policy Journal* 18 (2001): 1–12.

Woolcott, Richard. "Foreign Policy Priorities for the Howard Government'S Fourth Term : Australia, Asia and America in the Post-11th September World Fourth Term : Australia, Asia and America." *Australian Journal of International Affairs* 59, no. June (2005): 141–52. doi:10.1080/10357710500134491.

———. "Pathways of Modern Diplomacy." *Australian Journal of International Affairs* 51 (1997): 103–8.

———. "Reflections on Diplomacy: Australia's Role in an Ever-Changing World." *The Sydney Papers* Summer (2003): 108–20.

Yon, Rachael. "The Use of Propoganda and Social Media." In *The New Islamic State: Ideology, Religion and Violent Extremism in the 21st Century*, edited by Jack Covarrubias, Tom Lansford, and Robert J Jnr Pauley, 43–60. Oxon: Ashgate, 2016.

www.ingramcontent.com/pod-product-compliance
Lightning Source LLC
Chambersburg PA
CBHW062121020426
42335CB00013B/1054